Animals, Machines, and AI

Interdisciplinary German Cultural Studies

———

Edited by
Irene Kacandes

Volume 31

Animals, Machines, and AI

On Human and Non-Human Emotions
in Modern German Cultural History

Edited by
Erika Quinn and Holly Yanacek

DE GRUYTER

ISBN 978-3-11-127776-9
e-ISBN (PDF) 978-3-11-075367-7
e-ISBN (EPUB) 978-3-11-075373-8
ISSN 1861-8030

Library of Congress Control Number:2021944641

Bibliographic information published by the Deutsche Nationalbibliothek
The Deutsche Nationalbibliothek lists this publication in the Deutsche Nationalbibliografie;
detailed bibliographic data are available on the Internet at http://dnb.dnb.de.

Cover image: Chris Wille
Typesetting: Integra Software Services Pvt. Ltd.
Printing and binding: CPI books GmbH, Leck

www.degruyter.com

Acknowledgements

March 2020. The COVID-19 pandemic suddenly changed the lives of people around the world forever. We never could have imagined that we would start and finish writing the manuscript for a co-edited volume during a global pandemic. However, this work was incredibly stimulating and a welcome distraction during a time of many challenges and uncertainties. We loved collaborating on this volume, and we cannot express enough gratitude to the individuals who supported this project in different ways. First of all, we would like to thank James Madison University and Eureka College for funding that supported the volume's publication, as well as our colleagues and friends at these institutions for their encouragement. Funding from the JMU College of Arts and Letters and a Center for Global Engagement International Development Grant supported initial research for this project in Berlin. A faculty development grant from Eureka College and a JMU College of Arts and Letters Mini-Grant helped cover publication costs. Thank you to Irene Kacandes and Myrto Aspioti for the opportunity to publish this volume in De Gruyter's Interdisciplinary German Cultural Studies series. We are grateful for their insightful feedback and enthusiastic support at every stage of this project. It was a true pleasure to work with them, Stella Diedrich, and the entire editorial team at De Gruyter. Thanks to our colleagues in the German Studies Association, particularly other members of the GSA Emotion Studies Network, who engaged with our work and allowed us to test out some of these ideas at recent conferences. We are particularly grateful to Emotion Studies Network Co-Chair Derek Hillard for his interest in and support for this project. Thank you to historian Ute Frevert, Director of the Center for the History of Emotions at the Max Planck Institute for Human Development (MPIB) in Berlin. The opportunity to conduct preliminary research for this project as a Visiting Researcher at the MPIB in Summer 2019 was especially impactful. Special thanks to Mira Gruber and all of the former JMU students who participated in the Humanities 200 general education literature course on the topic "Humans, Animals, Machines" over the last few years. Their receptiveness to the course content encouraged the development of this project on emotions and human/non-human relationships. Many thanks to Sofia Samatar for reading an early draft of our introduction. We are also grateful to Thilini Prasadika for her enthusiasm for this project and the kind invitation to talk about our work on her humanities podcast. The Diversity, Decolonization, and the German Curriculum virtual writing groups organized by Carol Anne Costabile-Heming and Ervin Malakaj provided accountability and helped overcome the isolation of working on the volume manuscript during the pandemic. Thanks also to our contributors for their insightful essays and their interest in pushing the boundaries of emotion studies research to examine non-human emotions and human/non-human relationships, and to Chris Wille

https://doi.org/10.1515/9783110753677-202

for his striking cover art. Finally, we are filled with gratitude for our families, especially the human and non-human members of our quaranteams. We could not have written this volume without their love and support. This volume is dedicated to our families and our canine companions – Blaze; and Caspar and Luna – for the inspiration, companionship, and comfort they provided for the duration of this project.

Contents

Emotions and Human/Non-Human Boundaries

Emotional Functions of Non-Humans

Empathic Understanding between Humans and Non-Humans

List of Figures

Introduction: Feeling beyond the Human

Expressive Creatures

I Know What the Caged Cat Feels

https://doi.org/10.1515/9783110753677-204

Erika Quinn and Holly Yanacek

Introduction: Feeling beyond the Human

A human becomes emotionally attached to a machine – this basic plot is found in a number of recent books, films, and television series about humanoid robots and digital assistants;[1] however, depictions of the emotional attachment of humans to machines are not new. In German literary history, one of the most well-known examples is E. T. A. Hoffmann's novella "Der Sandmann" ("The Sandman," 1816), in which the young student and Romantic poet Nathanael projects his desires for a woman partner onto the automaton Olimpia. Not long after Nathanael calls his human fiancée Clara a "lifeless, damned automaton"[2] for rejecting his gruesome poetry, Nathanael becomes more and more attracted to Olimpia, who, unlike Clara, appears to listen to him with interest and only sighs "Oh, oh!" in response.[3] A critique of Nathanael's narcissistic projections and desire for a passive partner without her own thoughts or feelings is evident through Hoffmann's use of narrative irony, which also helps undermine the polarized early nineteenth-century gender roles in "The Sandman."

Olimpia is both an object of desire and danger for Nathanael, and the automaton changes human relationships in the town. When Olimpia is destroyed and Nathanael finally sees that she is a lifeless doll, the narrator notes that "madness seized him with its fiery claws and bored its way into his inner being, tearing his mind and thoughts apart."[4] His attraction to Olimpia consumes him and negatively impacts his thoughts and emotions as well as his relationship with Clara. Nathanael's spectacular destruction typifies early Romantic emotional styles and gender roles. The masculine antihero needed a female muse (Clara) to reflect back his genius to him; her refusal to do so ultimately leads to his passionate self-destruction.

The narrator reveals that the story of this automaton deeply affects the people of the town and their relationships with their human partners, not just Nathanael:

---

1 Examples include *Westworld* (1973; 2016–) and films such as *A.I. Artificial Intelligence* (2001), *Robot & Frank* (2012), *Her* (2013), and *Ex Machina* (2014). Another film, *Marjorie Prime* (2017) depicts a series of relationships between family members and the AIs programmed to stand in as their late loved ones.
2 E. T. A. Hoffmann, "Der Sandmann," in *Werke*, vol. 2 (Frankfurt a. M.: Insel, 1967), 7–40, here 25. Translations by Holly Yanacek.
3 Hoffmann, "Der Sandmann," 31.
4 Hoffmann, "Der Sandmann," 36.

> [. . .] [T]he story of the automaton had taken root deep in their souls, and indeed, a horrible distrust of human figures crept in. In order to be completely convinced that they were not in love with a wooden doll, a number of lovers wanted their beloved to sing and dance a little out of rhythm, to embroider, knit, play with their little dog, and so on, while being read to, but above all, to not merely listen, but also occasionally speak in such a way to demonstrate that their speech required actual thoughts and feelings.[5]

This passage suggests that imperfection (e.g., singing and dancing out of rhythm and being distracted) is desirable because imperfection, like having one's own thoughts and feelings, is authentically human. It also implies that a difference exists between real and simulated thoughts and emotions, something that is becoming more difficult to distinguish today with new artificial intelligence (AI) and emotion AI technologies like chatbots and virtual agents powered by conversational AI and natural language processing.

Non-human entities can affect communities by evoking not only fear and distrust, as seen in Hoffmann's tale, but also admiration and empathy. Franz Kafka's short story "In unserer Synagoge" (In our synagogue, 1922) presents such a dynamic. In the story, villagers encounter a mysterious animal that has been living in the synagogue for a long time. The narrator observes, "If only one could communicate with the animal, one could, of course, comfort it by telling it that the congregation in this mountain village of ours is becoming smaller every year."[6] He longs to connect with the mysterious animal living in the synagogue and imagines that the animal's emotional life is similar enough to his own that it can be understood. The narrator asserts that, in fact, the animal is more troubled than troubling; indeed, "if it were not for the women, one would hardly be aware of the animal's existence."[7] This puzzling story raises several questions about the emotions of non-human animals and humans' feelings about them. While humans may seek to understand and connect with animals, the animal's body itself is illegible. The narrator observes that the animal is the size of a marten, and it is thought to possess matted, bluish green fur, which could simply be the result of exposure to dust and mortar. The animal's body, and therefore its nature, remains inscrutable as it rarely shows itself, eludes categorization, and cannot speak. The pity and curiosity the animal evokes in the male narrator are belied by the other men's treatment of it. In the past, the men tried to drive the animal out as a nuisance, but because they don't come into physical proximity

---

5 Hoffmann, "Der Sandmann," 37.
6 Franz Kafka, "In unserer Synagoge . . .," in *Die Erzählungen und andere ausgewählte Prosa*, ed. Roger Hermes (Frankfurt a. M.: Fischer, 2010), 405–409, here 406. Translations by Erika Quinn.
7 Kafka, "In unserer Synagoge . . .," 406.

with it, they now, excepting the narrator, ignore it. The men exhibit emotional detachment or indifference to the animal, deeming it unthreatening. In this they adhere to normative gender roles as stoic protectors. They take no notice of the "pet" the animal has become.[8] Animals can present a threat to humans, as the men in the synagogue first imagined. However, animals can also be alluring or attractive to humans for a variety of reasons. We may use them for our own instrumental desires; at first glance the animal in the synagogue is "frightening,"[9] but the women in the story use their purported fear of the animal to garner the attention they crave (from men) while adhering to their town's and religion's emotional regimes around gender. They play the role of damsel in distress, using the animal as the threat, and engage (we assume) men's sympathy and protective stances.

What of the animal itself? It remains a mystery, a screen onto which human longing and fear is projected. The forms those projections take carry the cultural understanding of gender with them. Like Nathanael's relationship with the automaton Olimpia in Hoffmann's novella, the villagers' interest in the animal reflects their own agendas, to provide safety or to attract attention.

This interdisciplinary volume examines depictions of affective relationships between humans and non-humans in German cultural history from the Enlightenment to the present. Historically, dominant understandings of emotion have tended to limit the faculty of emotions to human beings, though some accounts have allowed that non-human animals, especially certain mammals, may also experience some emotions. By investigating claims that suggest the emotionality of machines or AI technologies, our volume questions established assumptions regarding emotions, such as distinctions between emotional experience and expression or real and simulated emotion as raised in Hoffmann's text. Yet rather than focusing on what or whether non-humans such as animals and robots feel, we ask what kind of emotional lives have been attributed to non-human animals and machines in German literary and cultural history and why? What do depictions of animals, robots, and machines in the modern era reveal about changing understandings of the human and the human/non-human boundary? Why are so many automata, robots, and virtual assistants, both real and imagined, gendered feminine? Which emotional functions have non-human animals and machines served in different historical periods? What are the implications of emotional attachments to and empathy for non-humans such as pets and humanlike social robots? Our volume seeks to use animals and machines as

---

8 Kafka, "In unserer Synagoge . . .," 406.
9 Kafka, "In unserer Synagoge . . .," 405.

heuristic lenses through which to investigate human emotions and more specifically, humans' affective relationships with non-human animals and machines. Following previous animal studies scholarship, we use the term "non-human animal" whenever possible in this volume.

In recent years, developments in robotics, fascination with machines, and the rapid growth of animal studies in the academy and beyond have given rise to questions about the nature of humanity. While older distinctions and definitions of what distinguishes humans from other organic animals, which rest on features such as tool use, use of language, and social structure, have been sidelined, questions persist about what, if anything, separates humans from other organic life forms. Neurologists' and psychologists' work on brain science also has deepened and complicated our understanding of brain functions, and studies of emotions, in particular, have been at the forefront of these scientific fields.

As cyberneticists currently work to create more and more sophisticated robots and AI algorithms, anthropologists, ethicists, and engineers ask questions about such developments and their potential hazards. Now that the old mind/body duality has been largely dismissed by brain scientists, the role of emotions in creating AI applications is all the more pressing. Thinking about human labor being replaced by robotic labor, and eventually, AI, has become a leading political and economic concern for some policy makers and corporate leaders. Creating AI forces programmers and engineers to investigate and confront the nature, function, operation, and expression of human emotions.

While anthropomorphism, the attribution of human characteristics, especially emotion, to non-human animals gained a bad reputation beginning in the Enlightenment era, the practice of imagining animal emotions, which emerged in the early nineteenth century, could well have served as a tool similar to empathy – one that aided in seeing animals as beings possessing minds, will, and pain. The development of biological and brain research has led to the growing recognition that humans are entangled with non-human animals. This has complicated the neat distinction of animal/human that has long reigned.

Scholarly interest in emotions can be traced back to the late nineteenth century with important developments in biology and the emergence of psychology as a field of study. Charles Darwin focused on one aspect of emotion – expression – in his pioneering study of the behavior of humans and non-human animals.[10] Psychologist William James began to investigate the causes and function of

---

10 Charles Darwin, *The Expression of the Emotions in Man and Animals* (Oxford: Oxford UP, 2009).

emotion, asserting they arose from physiological processes; similar work was undertaken by Danish physician Carl Lange. German philosophers Friedrich Theodor Vischer, Robert Vischer, and Wilhelm Dilthey developed principles of aesthetic empathy or *Einfühlungsästhetik*. The historians of the Annales school in France, such as Lucien Febvre and Georges Lefebvre, as well as Norbert Elias in Germany, also contributed to emotion studies in the 1930s with their conceptions of *mentalités*, which included examination of the values and assumptions that shape emotional expression and norms.[11] Critiquing the methodology of the Annalistes, psychohistory as a field emerged in the late 1960s. Its best known proponent, Peter Gay, focused attention on the emotional-cultural context in which individuals operate.[12] The 1980s and 1990s saw a resurgence of scholarly interest in emotions, for instance in the work on the emotional economy of the family by historians David Sabean and Hans Medick, the coining of "emotionology" in the research of Peter Stearns and Carol Stearns, and the development of the idea of "emotives" by William Reddy.[13] Groundbreaking research by Barbara Rosenwein on emotional communities, as well as theoretical interventions, individual case studies, and historical overviews have established the field of the "history of emotions."[14] Much of the historical work on emotions has been undertaken by specialists in medieval or early modern history, with the modern era, until recently at least, receiving relatively little attention.[15] One important exception to this in the German-speaking world is the Max Planck Institute for Human Development Research Center for the History of Emotions in Berlin, where Director Ute Frevert and her researchers focus on the modern period in Europe, North America,

---

11 Lucien Febvre, "La sensibilité et l'histoire: Comment reconstituer la vie affective d'autrefois?," *Annales d'histoires sociale*, 3 (Jan.–Jun. 1941): 5–20; Georges Lefebvre, *La Grande Peur de 1789* (Paris: Librairie Armand Colin, 1932); Norbert Elias, *Über den Prozess der Zivilisation* (Basel: Haus zum Falken, 1939).

12 See his *Freud for Historians* (Oxford: Oxford UP, 1986), and *The Cultivation of Hatred*: Vol. 3 of *The Bourgeois Experience: Victoria to Freud* (New York: W. W. Norton, 1993).

13 David Sabean and Hans Medick, eds., *Interest and Emotions: Essays on the Study of Family and Kinship* (Cambridge: Cambridge UP, 1986); Peter N. Stearns and Carol Z. Stearns, "Emotionology: Clarifying the History of Emotions and Emotional Standards," *American Historical Review* 90 (1985): 813–836; William Reddy, *The Navigation of Feeling: A Framework for the History of Emotions* (Cambridge: Cambridge UP, 2001).

14 Barbara Rosenwein, *Emotional Communities in the Early Middle Ages* (Ithaca, NY: Cornell UP, 2006).

15 A recent study does span the early modern and modern eras: Thomas J. Kehoe and Michael G. Pickering, eds., *Fear in the German-Speaking World, 1600-2000* (London: Bloomsbury Academic, 2020).

and South Asia. Inspired by their work, we hope to address the need for more scholarship on emotions in modern German cultural history in this volume.

The centrality of emotions to the human experience has recently been underlined in the sciences. Beginning around 2000 with fMRI and other brain imaging technology, cognitive psychology and neuroscience began "mapping" emotions onto the brain. Scientists Antonio Damasio and Lisa Feldman Barrett, and philosopher Martha Nussbaum, among others, demonstrated that thinking and feeling – cognition and emotion, rationality and hysteria – to sum up some of the binary pairs through which human experience has been understood in the past – are actually interconnected processes that cannot be disentangled from each other.[16] It is now widely maintained that emotions play an important role in moral reasoning, decision making, and communication.[17] Emotions scholars in the humanities have a varied response to the methodologies and findings of medical sciences. Indeed, cultural studies of emotions are adept at investigating this ongoing scientific curiosity with emotions as well as the public's fascination with scientific findings. "Today's experimental cognitive and neurosciences," according to Ute Frevert, "lack depth by comparison" with the extensive and rich discussions in the humanities regarding cultural meanings of emotions in recent decades.[18] Following Frevert, contributors to this volume observe that the range of emotions, their contexts and meanings is far greater than those investigated by psychology or neuroscience.

Explorations of emotions in literature, film, photography, painting, and other arts have been undertaken by scholars in recent decades, such that one can now speak of "emotion studies" as a field encompassing interdisciplinary critical cultural investigations of emotional phenomena in a cultural, material, and historical context. Emotion studies as such is a field also indebted to the decolonization of the academy beginning in the 1970s. With the establishment of women's studies, Chicano studies, and Black studies, the single hegemonic viewpoint – coded rational while supported by privilege – began to gain additions and attract challenges. Women's and ethnic studies scholars questioned how the key binary oppositions

---

16 Antonio Damasio, *The Strange Order of Things: Life, Feeling, and the Making of Cultures* (New York: Pantheon, 2018); Lisa Feldman Barrett, *How Emotions Are Made: The Secret Life of the Brain* (New York: Houghton Mifflin Harcourt, 2017); Martha Nussbaum, *Upheavals of Thought: The Intelligence of Emotions* (Cambridge: Cambridge UP, 2001).
17 On morality, see Rob Boddice, *The History of Emotions* (Manchester: Manchester UP, 2018), 192.
18 Ute Frevert, "Defining Emotions: Concepts and Debates over Three Centuries," in *Emotional Lexicons: Continuity and Change in the Vocabulary of Feeling 1700–2000*, eds. Ute Frevert et al. (Oxford: Oxford UP, 2014), 1–31, here 2.

shaped sex, gender, and race rather than describing them, and the long-held view of human superiority and distinction from other animals also started to erode.[19]

Donna Haraway's pioneering "Cyborg Manifesto" (1985) exemplified some of these trends. As Haraway sought to de-center power for women and other marginalized groups, she asserted that the old ideal – of one pure, unitary self or entity – was no longer imaginable nor desirable. In fact, by the late twentieth century, she asserted, humans were all cyborgs – "creatures simultaneously animal and machine."[20] Humans' hybrid and indeterminate nature provided a possibility to take responsibility for the construction (and therefore, destruction) of boundaries – political, social, or otherwise. Nature and culture could be reworked for the sake of liberation.

Perhaps inspired by Haraway's call to embrace hybridity, scholars of emotion often seek to problematize the heuristic value of such dichotomies as individual/social, mind/body, and emotion/rationality. In challenging such binary models, these scholars point to the liminality of emotions and their "location . . . at the thresholds" that connect such dichotomies.[21] This may include the binary most difficult for emotions scholars to take on: that is, the universalist, essentialist, transhistorical way of looking at emotions versus the social constructivist, culturally specific, historically grounded approach.[22] Thinking about liminality makes the interrogation of the relationship between humans and machines or animals particularly fruitful as recent decades have seen more and more challenges to a central dichotomy, that of the human/non-human. Examining the influence that robots, machines, and animals exert on human emotions helps to highlight how historical actors defined humanity in light of its adaptability and vulnerability.

A direction indicated by Haraway's work, along with that of many others, is the embodiedness of being human. Bodies are the site of sensory experience as well as of emotional experience. The embodied nature of existence is also heavily gendered, which holds true for non-human animals as well. Emotions are at the center of the "worlded body."[23] Feminist scholar Sara Ahmed's work, often associated with affect theory, engages with the embodiment of affect and emotion. Her most recent projects explore the intersectionality of race and gender as they

---

19 Kari Weil, *Thinking Animals: Why Animal Studies Now?* (New York: Columbia UP, 2012), 23.

20 Donna J. Haraway, "A Cyborg Manifesto," in *Simians, Cyborgs, and Women: The Reinvention of Nature* (New York: Routledge, 1991), 149–182, here 149.

21 Benno Gammerl, "Emotional Styles – Concepts and Challenges," *Rethinking History* 15, no. 2 (June 2012): 161–175, here 162.

22 Jan Plamper, *The History of Emotions: An Introduction* (Oxford: Oxford UP, 2017), 74.

23 Boddice, *The History of Emotions*, 2.

play out in emotional experiences and bodily sensations.[24] While gender, then, is central to emotional experiences and expressions, it has received relatively little treatment in emotion studies.[25]

Historically, and perhaps in more important ways in the bourgeois nineteenth century and the twentieth century, gender has been a key characteristic of humanness. For much of the period covered in this book, most specific emotions (fear, sadness, and hysteria, for example) and emotions generally were gendered feminine and believed to be unseemly, irrational, and embarrassingly exposing when expressed.[26] Emotions and rationality were thought to be polar opposites. As "rationality" had been used as a discourse of domination supported by property law, citizenship rights, and other structural means, so too had it been used as a benchmark of humanity, beginning with the Enlightenment.[27] The privileging of a linear, calculating thought process and the denigration of emotional expression coded women, people of color, and animals as Other. Ironically, this disavowal of emotions in elite males comes into direct conflict with the idea that the faculty of emotions defines all humans.

These binary models are also applied to non-human animals. Perhaps part of what makes the animal in the synagogue in Kafka's story so inscrutable is its lack of gender. Gender is a vital component of empathy and connection across species; often, it is part of anthropomorphizing animals or machines. Judith Butler observes that fields of discourse and the power articulated through them "orchestrate[], delimit[], and sustain[] that which qualifies as 'the human.'"[28] Abjected beings who are not properly gendered fall outside that qualification. A lot is at stake in gendering; the "human is . . . produced over and over against the inhuman; the construction of the human is a differential operation that produces the

24 Sara Ahmed, *The Cultural Politics of Emotion* (New York: Routledge, 2004); Sara Ahmed, *Living a Feminist Life* (Durham, NC: Duke UP, 2017).
25 Jan Plamper's important study of the field, *The History of Emotions*, for example, lacks any index entries under "gender." Another foundational book that does address gender and emotion in modern history is Ute Frevert's *Emotions in History – Lost and Found* (2011), which features a chapter on "gendering emotions."
26 Karin Hausen, "Family and Role-Division: The Polarisation of Sexual Stereotypes in the Nineteenth Century – an Aspect of the Dissociation of Work and Family Life," in *The German Family: Essays on the Social History of the Family in Nineteenth- and Twentieth-Century Germany*, eds. Richard J. Evans and W. R. Lee (London: Croom Helm, 1981), 51–83.
27 Isabel V. Hull, *Sexuality, State, and Civil Society in Germany, 1700–1815* (Ithaca, NY: Cornell UP, 1997).
28 Judith Butler, *Bodies that Matter: On the Discursive Limits of "Sex"* (New York: Routledge, 1993), 8.

more and the less 'human,' [and] the inhuman."[29] While the attribution of gender may not make animals or machines human per se, it does give them the quality of relatability, and therefore opens the door to other emotions such as empathy and love.

As we think about general currents in the study of non-human emotions, we can detect two distinct periods: the first, focusing largely on individuals, in which scholars and scientists investigated inner forms and mechanisms and developed concepts and vocabulary. In the field of robotics, for example, the internal features of robots were the central concerns; however, this narrow focus on questions of robot consciousness, rights, and personhood overlooks areas of concern in Human-Robot Interaction, as Alexis Elder notes.[30] The second period, beginning roughly in the early 2000s, showed much more interest in the relationality of emotions, in particular, their co-constitutiveness, as discussed in Haraway's *Companion Species Manifesto*.[31] Indeed, the co-creation of emotions could cross the human/non-human divide as Haraway notes with dogs.[32] This period also saw the development of academic fields in Human-Robot Interaction (HRI) and Canid-Human Relations.

This project is much more indebted to the second current of scholarship and seeks to extend interdisciplinary research in emotion studies by examining non-humans and the affective relationships between humans and non-humans in modern German cultural history. What constitutes emotion, or feeling, or affect, where it is to be found, and what it means has been explored in myriad ways throughout the history of Western modernity.[33] We are not, then, undertaking to answer questions about whether machines or non-human animals "actually" feel, nor will we seek to define emotions precisely. We understand that the capacity for emotions is hardwired into human (and many non-human) brains, while their expression, understanding, range, and meanings are socioculturally shaped. "Feeling beyond the human," this volume's central concept, concerns humans' feelings about entities outside their own lifeform. At the same time, emotions and how we attribute them to other beings compel humans to reassess the nature of the human.

---

29 Butler, *Bodies that Matter*, 8.
30 Alexis M. Elder, *Friendship, Robots, and Social Media: False Friends and Second Selves* (New York: Routledge, 2018), 75.
31 Donna Haraway, *The Companion Species Manifesto: Dogs, People, and Significant Otherness* (Chicago: Prickly Paradigm Press, 2003).
32 Haraway, *The Companion Species Manifesto*, 12.
33 Frevert, "Defining Emotions," 9–12.

Philosopher Martha Nussbaum, in her examination of political emotions, underlines the importance of conceptions of animals in defining humanness. Building on primatologist Frans de Waal's notion of "anthropodenial," she points out that humans have long viewed non-human animals as unwelcome reminders of human frailty and vulnerability. Humans have "disavowed their kinship" with other animals, who are seen as primitive or even atavistic.[34] On the other hand, robots or machines more generally have often been viewed as invulnerable, immortal beings onto whom humans can pin their hopes or fears. In times of rapid technological or social change, machines, robots, and AI have served as screens upon which to project anxieties. These relationships with the non-human are important expressions of humans' fears, longing, and self-conceptions. This is because the boundaries demarcating what is human and non-human are constantly in contention when regarding emotion. We suggest that such feelings indicate much about the human experience and can be instructive in formulating responses to difficult ethical issues; indeed, many of the essays in this volume put forward a possibility that intentional, mindful interactions with non-humans can enrich humans in developing a more inclusive ethics. Non-human animals and machines present experiential and imaginative possibilities.

This volume considers non-human animals, machines, and robots together in modern German cultural history. Thus, we aim to contribute to scholarship of the "non-human turn," which has emerged in the humanities and social sciences in academia over the past few decades. According to Richard Grusin, the non-human turn "is engaged in decentering the human in favor of a turn toward and concern for the nonhuman, understood variously in terms of animals, affectivity, bodies, organic and geophysical systems, materiality, or technologies."[35] One justification for this attention to the non-human is "that almost every problem of note that we face in the twenty-first century entails engagement with nonhumans – from climate change, drought, and famine; to biotechnology, intellectual property, and privacy; to genocide, terrorism, and war . . .."[36] While our volume participates in the non-human turn by decentering the human and considering animals, machines, and robots as worthy of study in their own right, our main intervention concerns filling a gap in emotion studies scholarship by exploring the emotional functions of non-humans and the affective relationships between humans and non-humans in modern German cultural history.

---

34 Martha Nussbaum, *Political Emotions: Why Love Matters for Justice* (Cambridge, MA: Harvard UP, 2013), 139, 159.
35 Richard Grusin, ed., *The Nonhuman Turn* (Minneapolis: U of Minnesota Press, 2015), vii.
36 Grusin, ed., *The Nonhuman Turn*, vii.

Examining representations of non-human animals, robots, and machines together also provides insight into the changing understandings of what it means to be human through history and across cultures. In literature and culture, non-humans, especially robots but also non-human animals, are often stand-ins for oppressed groups (e.g., women, people of color, or religious minorities). In addition, human psychology tends to anthropomorphize non-humans, especially certain animals and machines. While an anthropocentric view would deny the existence of emotional experience in non-humans, an example of anthropomorphism would be to attribute the full range of human emotions to non-humans, including complex emotions like guilt, jealousy, shame, and others.

Comparing animals with robots and machines has proved to be a useful way to develop and question assumptions about the nature of being, consciousness, rationality, emotions, and sensations. Least examined are both non-human animals and machines in the context of an attribute that has for centuries been limited to the human – emotions. Sentient robots can be found in recent cultural productions, and social robots with "artificial empathy" – "the ability to sense human feelings and anticipate affective reactions"[37] – are being developed today. Still, humans have persisted in believing that emotion is what distinguishes us from robots and machines. Emotions were long considered the primary distinction between humans and non-human animals, especially before the publication of Charles Darwin's *The Expression of the Emotions in Man and Animals* (1872), which asserted that humans and other animals "express the same state of mind by the same movements."[38] For example, René Descartes famously viewed animals as "natural automata," in other words, as complex machines without souls, experiences, or emotions.[39] This distinction has started to soften in recent decades with changes in ethology and brain science. *Animals, Machines, and AI* poses questions about the nature of the human through its investigation of emotions, non-humans, and relationships between humans, other animals, and machines. Why are accounts of animal or machine emotions so fascinating or threatening? How does the manifestation of animal or machine emotions unsettle our understandings of emotions, and thus humans? What are the stakes involved in projecting emotions onto animals or machines?

---

37 Paul Dumouchel and Luisa Damiano, *Living with Robots*, trans. Malcolm DeBevoise (Cambridge, MA: Harvard UP, 2017), ix.
38 Darwin, *The Expression of the Emotions in Man and Animals*, 348.
39 Michael Tye, *Tense Bees and Shell-Shocked Crabs: Are Animals Conscious?* (Oxford: Oxford UP, 2017), 35.

Unlike humans and non-human animals, machines do not possess bodies; they are built physical structures, frames, or mainframes.[40] Machines are constructed by humans to serve human purposes, whether utilitarian, aesthetic, or otherwise. An artificial person (e.g., robot, android, cyborg, or automaton) can be understood as "a being who is partly or fully anthropomorphic, mechanical, or constructed from a variety of technological or natural materials and considered autonomous, animated, or capable of being animated."[41] The chapters in this volume focus most heavily on representations of humanlike machines such as automata and robots, but we acknowledge that non-humanlike machines and new technologies can also alter human affective states and we aim to address such cases.

A long-held distinction between animate subjects and inanimate objects has been based on the ability to feel, in both the sensory and emotional meanings. Scholars have started to reexamine traditional assumptions about machines as human-made objects, emotions, and agency. "Object-Oriented Ontology" tries to question these definitions of objects as inert. Machines (which are a kind of object) possess the capacity to "act" on people's feelings, to alter human affective states. Objects can be understood as "actors that do not emote, that produce and transmit feeling [between human actors], but do not feel."[42]

Examining German language texts that feature machines can provide fruitful material to further explore non-humans' affective power. Beginning in the early nineteenth century, German writers focused on the abilities of automata to evoke love and dread in their human companions. E. T. A. Hoffmann, along with Achim von Arnim and Jean Paul wrote stories that reflected fears about political and epistemological instability.[43] These early texts influenced later thinkers, with Hoffmann's "The Sandman" (1816) especially notable for influencing explanations of the uncanny by psychiatrist Ernst Jentsch and psychoanalyst Sigmund Freud in the early twentieth century. Jentsch, who focused

---

40 Stewart Hampshire, "Biology, Machines, and Humanity," in *The Boundaries of Humanity: Humans, Animals, Machines*, eds. James J. Sheehan and Morton Sosna (Berkeley: UC Press, 1991), 253–258, here 253.
41 Despina Kakoudaki, *Anatomy of a Robot: Literature, Cinema, and the Cultural Work of Artificial People* (New Brunswick, NJ: Rutgers UP, 2014), 3.
42 Stephanie Downes, Sally Holloway, and Sarah Randles, "A Feeling for Things, Past and Present," in *Feeling Things: Objects and Emotions through History*, eds. Stephanie Downes, Sally Holloway, and Sarah Randles (Oxford: Oxford UP, 2018), 8–26, here 8–11.
43 Jean Paul Richter, *Jean Pauls Sämmtliche Werke* XVI Bd. 2, "Einfältige aber gut gemeinte Biographie einer neuen angenehmen Frau von bloßem Holz, die ich längst erfunden und geheirathet" (Berlin: G. Reimer, 1826): 187–224; Achim von Arnim, *Novellen von Ludwig Achim von Arnim*, Bd. 1, "Isabella von Ägypten" (Berlin: Veit & Comp, 1839), 1–188.

on the automaton Olimpia in Hoffmann's story, interpreted uncanniness as intellectual uncertainty about whether a figure is a human or an automaton. The figure of the uncanny automaton was so well known among educated Germans that by the 1930s, Walter Benjamin could use it as a figure representing "historical materialism" in his critique of Marxism, arguing that it, like the early-nineteenth century chess-playing automaton "The Turk," could "win" the game if it used the master – theology – hidden within it like the mechanism of the automaton. In this case, Benjamin's fears about the loss of agency in Marxism relied on a cultural reference from more than a century earlier.[44]

Machines grew to occupy a central place in conceptions of German national identity in the nineteenth century. The German lands were the first states to implement public education, beginning with Prussia in 1806. Seeking to modernize their economy and society, states saw an opportunity in founding engineering schools. Technical schools started to emerge in Central Europe in disproportionately large numbers beginning in the 1840s.[45] While the state may have seen value in such education, *Bildungsbürger* and the intelligentsia did not. Playing into Enlightenment ideas about French and English superficiality, materialism, and empiricism, Romantic writers like Heinrich Heine saw those national traits as tied to machines and mechanistic thinking and behavior. After traveling to England, Heine wrote in "Ludwig Börne, A Memorial" (1840):

> I shall never return to this despicable land, where machines behave like men and men like machines. The whirring and silence is [sic] so very annoying. When I was presented to the local governor and this thoroughly English Englishman stood motionless before me for several minutes without uttering a word, I inadvertently had the thought of looking at his back to determine whether one hadn't forgotten to wind up the machine.[46]

Heine saw a mechanical mindlessness worthy of scorn.

Yet, as industrialization began to take off in the German lands in the 1860s and was bolstered by the creation of the Second Empire in 1871, by the end of the 1800s, "made in Germany" was a mark of excellence in engineering and design. Outstripping British coal and steel production, the German industrial economy was a behemoth. The German "cult of technicism" (*Technik*), that is, "emphasis on scientism, efficiency, and management" and the commitment to excellence in

---

44 Walter Benjamin, "Theses on the Philosophy of History," in *Illuminations*, trans. Harry Zohn (New York: Harcourt Brace Jovanovich, Inc., 1968), 253.
45 Modris Eksteins, *Rites of Spring: The Great War and the Birth of the Modern Age* (New York: Anchor Books, 1990), 71.
46 Heinrich Heine, "Ludwig Börne: A Memorial," trans. Frederic Ewen and Robert C. Holub, in *The Romantic School and Other Essays*, eds. Jost Hermand and Robert C. Holub (New York: Continuum, 2002), 262.

building machines, had become a proud defining feature of German national identity, one that lasts into the twenty-first century.[47]

In late nineteenth-century Germany, writer Ernst Kapp was just one of many to emphasize the admiration given to machines. This admiration was based on a new conception of machines' power and function. Prior to the 1780s automata received their inspiration and analogies from mechanical clockworks without relying on an energy supply for movement. The newest machines around 1800, such as the steam engine, were routinely conceived as resembling and expressive of a vital life force shared with human and non-human animals.[48] The shift from mechanistic to vitalistic views made machines and non-human animals seem more similar. Kapp observed of the new steam-powered machines: "It isn't only technical details that determine the strong admiration for steam engines; . . . it is also the fueling of the machine, the setting of combustibles into warmth and movement, in short the peculiar demonic appearance of independent achievement."[49] In the eyes of writers, philosophers, and scientists such as Otto Liebmann, Hermann von Helmholtz, or Ernst Kapp, machines, like humans and other animals, not only had similar mechanical working parts, but, more importantly, required "nourishment" that had to be burned to produce heat so as to convert it to strength to continue to "live," and if deprived of their energy source, would meet their "death."[50] For Kapp, machines served as vehicles through which humans became conscious of themselves and their own inner workings and vitality.

German Realist artist Adolph von Menzel's oil painting *Das Eisenwalzwerk* (*The Iron Rolling Mill*, 1875) presents an example of a similar late nineteenth-century attitude toward machines in visual culture. The glowing flames, massive machinery, and workers' lack of sturdy footwear represent dangerous working conditions in the factory. Steam and smoke accumulate near the ceiling and occupy the upper third of the painting. The interplay of light and shadow created through Menzel's use of the chiaroscuro technique heightens the dramatic quality of the factory scene; the beholder can almost feel the warmth of the fire, which illuminates the workers' faces, tools, and muscular arms. Expressions of exhaustion are evident on the faces of a few of the men. However, the visual language of the painting seems to communicate neither outrage at the working conditions nor sympathy for the workers. Instead, Menzel's painting depicts the

---

47 Eksteins, *Rites of Spring*, 70, 72.

48 Kakoudaki, *Anatomy of a Robot*, 27.

49 Ernst Kapp, *Grundlinien einer Philosophie der Technik: Zur Entstehungsgeschichte der Cultur aus neuen Gesichtspunkten* (Braunschweig: Westermann, 1877), 137. Translation by Erika Quinn.

50 Kapp, *Philosophie der Technik*, 128–129.

Figure 1: Adolph von Menzel, *Das Eisenwalzwerk* (1872–1875), oil on canvas, Nationalgalerie, Staatliche Museen zu Berlin.

close interaction between the workers and the machines in the factory, and the powerful machines and the strength of the workers together inspire awe in the beholder. Yet while machines and the people trained to operate them could inspire admiration, machines could also evoke fear. In Gerhart Hauptmann's Naturalist novella "Bahnwärter Thiel" ("Flagman Thiel," 1888), the technologies of the railroad and the telegraph pose a threat to human life and nature. Interestingly, while the railroad cuts through natural landscapes and is responsible for the death of wildlife and Thiel's son Tobias, different parts of the inanimate railroad system are associated with animate non-humans. The telegraph cords are "like the webs spun by a huge spider" and the tracks are like "a monstrous iron net" that begins to glow and resemble "fiery snakes," while the narrator calls the train itself a "puffing monster."[51]

The terrifying experience of the First World War called into question the nature and limits of the human, in particular regarding humanity's perceived sovereignty over the machines they created. When battles like the Somme and Verdun took hundreds of thousands of lives, military planners and leaders sought new ways to break such stalemates. In the United Kingdom, that meant an emphasis

---

[51] Gerhart Hauptmann, "Bahnwärter Thiel," in *Erzählungen* (Gütersloh: C. Bertelsmann, 1957), 28–63, here 42–43. Translation by Holly Yanacek.

on and investment into technical knowledge, such as using better calculations to make artillery more precise and destructive. On the German side, however, that seems to have led to a blending of man and machine, not a distancing. Stormtroopers were equipped with flamethrowers, given much more autonomy to use them, and a cult of hardness and steel started to take shape, as soldiers and their commanders tried to contain the traumatic consequences and continue the war.[52] Indeed, German military medical programs sought to blend disabled soldiers with machines so that they could still "be of service"; amputated limbs were fitted with pieces to connect to machinery so soldiers could continue to contribute to the war effort, and regain their sense of pride and masculinity.[53] After the war, a range of artistic and political voices – from Dadaists and Marxists to proto-fascists – all became enamored with automata, cyborgs, and machines.[54] The aesthetic movement that came to be known as *Neue Sachlichkeit* (New Objectivity) is most associated with this fascination. Machines were depicted in the graphic arts, in fiction, and in essays, most notably by conservative writer Ernst Jünger, who called on soldiers to become machines – to objectify their bodies so that they felt no pain.[55]

Like the introduction of mechanized warfare had done early in the century, the use of robot technology in the workplace later in the twentieth century evoked disparate emotional responses. The 1970s in the German Democratic Republic (GDR) witnessed the growth of science fiction, due in part to Erich Honecker's proposed "socialist rationalization" of the economy, which aimed to increase production and efficiency through mechanization.[56] While the GDR only had 220 robots in 1980, the 1981–1985 Economic Plan called for the use of 40,000 to 45,000 industrial robots in the GDR by 1985.[57] However, uses of the word "robot" were misleading, as the term was applied to a range of different machines that fell short of the robotic standards in Western Europe, Japan, and

---

52 David Stevenson, *Cataclysm: The First World War as Political Tragedy* (New York: Basic Books, 2009), 156.

53 Heather R. Perry, *Recycling the Disabled: Army, Medicine, and Modernity in WWI Germany* (Manchester: Manchester UP, 2014).

54 Matthew Biro, *The Dada Cyborg: Visions of the New Human in Weimar Berlin* (Minneapolis: U of Minnesota Press, 2009).

55 Ernst Jünger, *On Pain* [*Über den Schmerz*, 1934], trans. David C. Durst (Candor, NY: Telos Press, 2008).

56 Sonja Fritzsche, *Science Fiction Literature in East Germany* (Oxford: Peter Lang, 2006), 163.

57 Arthur M. Hanhardt, Jr., "German Democratic Republic," in *Communism in Eastern Europe*, ed. Teresa Rakowska-Harmstone (Bloomington: Indiana UP, 1984), 154.

the United States.[58] GDR works of the 1960s and 1970s such as Erich Schmitt's *Kollege Blech* (Colleague tin) comics (1965), Klaus Beuchler's "Silvanus contra Silvanus" (1969), and Karl-Heinz Tuschel's *Die Insel der Roboter* (Robot island, 1973) feature robot characters. Interestingly, the robot character in "Silvanus contra Silvanus" gets out of control because, as an emotionless machine, it does not understand what love is. Beuchler's story has been interpreted as a "very naïve plea not to forget love and romantic tradition in the face of technological progress and the striving for rationalization under socialism."[59]

Robots and AI assistants are becoming increasingly visible in Germany today. In 2018 the Federal Government of Germany launched its Artificial Intelligence Strategy, which aims to achieve the following goals: "Increasing and consolidating Germany's future competitiveness by making Germany and Europe a leading center in AI; Guaranteeing a responsible development and deployment of AI which serves the good of society; Integrating AI in society in ethical, legal, cultural and institutional terms in the context of a broad societal dialogue and active political measures."[60] According to the German Federal Government's progress report published in 2019, Germany is currently ranked fifth in AI research publications (after China, the United States, Japan, and Great Britain) and is thus a player in the "Champions League" of AI.[61] While industrial robots are more widely used, AI voice assistants are being developed and integrated, such as the robot SEMMI tested at the Deutsche Bahn Travel Center at the Berlin Central Train Station in 2019. In April 2021 Deutsche Bahn's website stated that this AI-based voice assistant, described as the "Siri for train travelers," is set to be available on the website, DB Navigator app, and as a digital avatar at selected train stations.[62] Additionally, social robots are being designed with human needs for companionship in mind. Many social robots on the market respond to human facial expressions, tone of voice, and gaze. Unlike non-human animals, robots

---

58 Hanhardt, "German Democratic Republic," 154.

59 Karsten Greve, "Die Science-Fiction-Literatur der DDR," (PhD diss., Freie Universität Berlin, 2015), 137.

60 European Commission-Knowledge for Policy, "Germany AI Strategy Report," accessed 25 May 2020, https://ec.europa.eu/knowledge4policy/ai-watch/germany-ai-strategy-report_en.

61 Die Bundesregierung, "Zwischenbericht: Ein Jahr KI-Strategie," *Nationale Strategie für Künstliche Intelligenz*, November 2019, https://www.ki-strategie-deutschland.de/home.html.

62 Deutsche Bahn, "Smart Services: The 'Siri for Train Travelers,'" accessed 1 April 2021, https://www.deutschebahn.com/en/Digitalization/technology/innovations/Smart-services-the-Siri-for-train-travelers–4167438.

that exist today are not sentient, yet humans still anthropomorphize robots and interact with them as if they have emotions.[63]

Non-human animals are often associated with nature and the feminine, emotional, "natural" side of the binary – while animals themselves may not be gendered as individuals, they do serve as markers of Otherness, along with women, people of color, and other marginalized groups. They have bodies, which provide them with sensory information and experiences, and recent work has shown animals to construct complex social relationships which recognize individuals as such.[64] Although the capacity of non-human animals to think and have emotions remains contested in the sciences, today it is generally more acknowledged that at least certain mammals can feel in the sense of having emotions. The term *sentience* is commonly used in the field of animal studies to refer to this capacity to feel. Sentience can describe the ability to experience both pleasurable and aversive states, i.e., enjoyment and suffering, but scientific research concerning animal sentience tends to focus on animals' experiences of feelings of physical pain.[65] Our purpose in this volume is not to determine what non-human animals actually feel, but rather to build on previous scholarship and show how the ways that humans imagine and relate emotionally to other species have changed over time.[66]

Industrialization presented a significant shift in how humans related to non-human animals. It transformed humans' relationship to the natural world, and by extension, to non-human animals. As mechanization slowly altered the countryside and people moved to cities, interactions with farm animals – animals and humans performing work together – became less and less a part of everyday life.[67] With their new urban lifestyle, city-dwellers often sought domestic animal companions, especially to help cultivate empathy in their middle-class children.[68] The increasing emotional bonds between people and their pets in the nineteenth century set the stage for animal advocacy.

While a nascent animal-welfare movement emerged decades later in the German lands than it did in Britain, by the last half of the century an anti-vivisection movement called for the humane treatment of animals, based on their

63 Elder, *Friendship, Robots, and Social Media*, 77.
64 Carl Safina, *Beyond Words: What Animals Think and Feel* (New York: Henry Holt, 2015).
65 Gary Varner, "Sentience," in *Critical Terms for Animal Studies*, ed. Lori Gruen (Chicago: U of Chicago Press, 2018), 360.
66 Pascal Eitler, "Tierliebe und Menschenführung. Eine genealogische Perspektive auf das 19. und 20. Jahrhundert," in *Tierstudien 3: Tierliebe*, eds. Jessica Ullrich and Friedrich Weltzien (Berlin: Neofelis Verlag, 2013), 40–48.
67 Ulrich Raulff, *Farewell to the Horse: A Cultural History*, trans. Ruth Ahmedzai Kemp (New York: Liveright, 2018).
68 Eitler, "Tierliebe und Menschenführung," 41.

ability to feel pain and to suffer. Texts such as Anglo-German writer Elpis Melena's sentimental novel *Gemma; oder, Tugend und Laster* (*Gemma; or, Virtue and
Vice*, 1877) and Ernst von Weber's pamphlet *Die Folterkammern der Wissenschaft*
(*The Torture Chambers of Science*, 1879) spread anti-vivisectionist sentiment in
Germany. A number of gender-coded binaries, including male rationality vs. female emotion and morality and male vivisectors vs. female activists are evident
in discourses on animal rights and the anti-vivisection debate.[69] *Gemma*, for example, imagines the male vivisector as the personification of vice and the female
activist as the embodiment of virtue, thus depicting animal activism and compassion for non-human animals as a gendered issue. In animal rights discourses,
women were deemed responsible for the spread of animal advocacy and the moral
education of future generations based on the view that women are supposedly distinguished by greater capacity to feel.[70] However, anti-vivisectionist arguments
and publications were often dismissed as examples of "exaggerated sentimentalism" because of the centrality of feminine-coded compassion for animals.[71] Some
notable figures, including Richard Wagner, took the call for the humane
treatment of animals a step further and embraced vegetarianism, an important component of some *Lebensreform* (life reform) cultures that lasted well
into the twenty-first century. The relationship between the late nineteenth-
century anti-vivisection movement and antisemitism is well-documented,[72]
and it is both ironic and appalling that the compassion that Richard Wagner
and other anti-vivisectionists showed to animals was often denied to German
Jews.

This notion of animal suffering was articulated in fiction as well as scientific
texts that sought to cultivate empathy for animals. As a *Dinggedicht* (object poem),
a poem that typically centers the non-human animal or object in an attempt to
let it speak for itself, Rainer Maria Rilke's "Der Panther" ("The Panther," 1903)

---

69 Pascal Eitler, "Übertragungsgefahr: Zur Emotionalisierung und Verwissenschaftlichung
des Mensch-Tier-Verhältnisses im deutschen Kaiserreich," in *Rationalisierungen des Gefühls:
Zum Verhältnis von Wissenschaft und Emotionen 1880–1930*, eds. Uffa Jensen and Daniel Morat
(Munich: Wilhelm Fink, 2008), 180.
70 Elpis Melena, *Gemma; oder, Tugend und Laster* (Munich: G. Franz'sche Verlagshandlung,
1877), 148. For more on *Gemma*, see Holly A. Yanacek, "Mobilising Disgust and Compassion:
Elpis Melena's *Gemma; oder, Tugend und Laster* (1877) and the Anti-Vivisection Movement,"
German Life and Letters 73, no. 4 (October 2020): 564–580.
71 L. Goldstein, "Übersicht der neuern Verhandlungen über die Vivisektionsfrage. Nach den
Arbeiten von v. Weber, Iatros, Hermann, Ludwig, Heidenhain, usw," in *Schmidt's Jahrbücher
der in- und ausländischen gesammten Medicin* 182.3 (1879): 281–285, here 282.
72 Arnold Arluke and Clinton R. Sanders, *Regarding Animals* (Philadelphia: Temple UP, 1996),
143.

invites readers to adopt the perspective of a caged panther. Rilke wrote this poem after visiting the Jardin des Plantes in Paris, and the first stanza, which attributes agency and motion to the bars of the cage rather than the living being therein, evokes empathy for the powerful yet numbed panther: "His gaze, from the passing of the bars, has become / so weary that it can focus on nothing more. / For him it's as if there were a thousand bars / and behind those thousand bars no world."[73] In *Umwelt und Innenwelt der Tiere* (*Environment and the Inner World of Animals*, 1909), Estonian-German biologist Jakob von Uexküll issued a call to abandon anthropocentrism and instead adopt the viewpoint of the animal,[74] an idea that resonates with what Rilke achieved with "The Panther" and his other object poems. Uexküll's focus on the animal's environment or surrounding world (*Umwelt*) gave special attention to so-called lower animals and "resulted in striking portraits of an 'inner world' imagined from a nonhuman perspective, expressed in a lucid, dramatic prose style accessible to nonspecialists."[75]

Despite the rapid rate of industrialization and the mechanized nature of twentieth-century warfare, non-human animals – horses and dogs in particular – played very important roles in both World Wars. Millions of horses were employed in the First World War. And although the Second World War saw the introduction of trucks and tanks to battlefields in significant numbers, horses were still widely used by the Wehrmacht on the Eastern Front – as many as 70,000 horses were deployed in Operation Barbarossa.[76] These animals served vital support roles. One officer remembered, "Thank God for our horses! At times they are the last and only thing we can rely on. Thanks to them we made it through the winter, even if they died in their thousands from exhaustion, lack of fodder and their tremendous exertions."[77] In addition to animals' roles in transportation and communication in the World Wars, some animals also served as mascots and companions, providing comfort and improving morale.[78]

---

73 Rainer Maria Rilke, "Der Panther," in *Werke in drei Bänden*, vol. 1, *Gedicht-Zyklen* (Frankfurt a. M.: Insel, 1966), 261. Translation by Holly Yanacek.

74 Jakob von Uexküll, *Umwelt und Innenwelt der Tiere* (Berlin: Julius Springer, 1909), 6.

75 Mark M. Anderson, ed., "Jakob von Uexküll: From *The Environment and the Inner World of Animals*," in Franz Kafka *The Metamorphosis*, ed. Mark M. Anderson (New York: W. W. Norton, 2016), 95.

76 Richard Overy, *Why the Allies Won* (New York: W. W. Norton, 1995), 215.

77 Hans Meier-Welcker, *Aufzeichnungen eines Generalstabsoffiziers 1939–1942* (Freiburg im Breisgau, 1982), 168, qtd in Richard J. Evans, *The Third Reich at War: 1939–1945* (London: Penguin, 2010), 200.

78 Elizabeth D. Schafer, "Animals, use of" in *The European Powers in the First World War, an Encyclopedia*, ed. Spencer C. Tucker (London: Routledge, 1999), 52. Nastasja Klothmann notes that during the World Wars humans' emotional relationships with animals took on new

Non-human animals did not play solely benevolent roles in war; they could evoke feelings of dread and fear as well as comfort. Gerhard Richter's *Christa und Wolfi* (1964) captures this ambivalence toward animals. In the painting, Wolfi, a formidable German shepherd, sits on a chair in front of two women. Contemporaneous with the Auschwitz trials of the early 1960s, Richter had begun interrogating Germany's National Socialist past in conjunction with that of his own family. The painting, based on a family photo of his first wife's, places Wolfi as the center of the frame, and he is painted in a light metallic blue in contrast to the sepia tones of the rest of the work. It contrasts a simple family photo with a more painterly, formal work as it also contrasts a comforting domestic scene with the centrality of Wolfi's bright eyes and open mouth. In this image, one can detect a "resonance or trace of one of the brutal symbols of the SS and other Nazi perpetrators, that is, the German shepherd, or police dog."[79] While dogs employed at death camps appear in survivors' testimonies as terrifying figures of violence and brutality, many, if not most, of those dogs were also "friendly companion-dogs" to the families employed at the camps.[80]

The ambivalent status of such dogs and their ability to evoke oppositional emotions echoed in the former East Germany as the Berlin Wall fell. An estimated 5,000 dogs had been used to patrol the border and were rescued by families after their jobs became obsolete. Caught up in political debate, people on one hand argued that the dogs were vicious killers that should all be euthanized, while others claimed the dogs were "eager for affection" as the "last victims of Stalinism."[81]

Fondness for and connection to non-human animals persisted through the twentieth century: a recent book claims that Cold War Berliners were "animal-obsessed" – bestowing honors, awards, and mourning flowers upon their favorite zoo animals as they would on human friends and companions.[82] This kind of performative emotional demonstration highlights the relational and socio-cultural components of human emotions. Yoko Tawada's *Etüden im Schnee* (*Memoirs of a*

---

intensity and forms. *Gefühlswelten im Zoo: Eine Emotionsgeschichte 1900–1945* (Bielefeld: transcript, 2015), 29.

79 Paul B. Jaskot, "Gerhard Richter and Adolf Eichmann," *Oxford Art Journal* 28, no. 3 (2005): 457–478, here 474.

80 Robert Tindol, "The Best Friend of the Murderers: Guard Dogs and the Nazi Holocaust," in *Animals and War: Studies of Europe and North America*, ed. Ryan Hediger (Boston: Brill, 2013), 105–122, here 105.

81 Peter Schneider, *The German Comedy*, trans. Philip Boehm and Leigh Hafrey (New York: Farrar, Straus and Giroux, 1991), 210.

82 J. W. Mohnhaupt, *The Zookeepers' War: An Incredible True Story from the Cold War*, trans. Shelley Frisch (New York: Simon & Schuster, 2017), 5.

Polar Bear, 2014) explores anthropomorphism and human/non-human animal relationships through its narration of the lives of three generations of polar bears, from the division of postwar Germany into East and West to life in Berlin in the early twenty-first century. The novel invites readers to consider humans' entanglement with other species and the importance of decentering the human in approaches to solving contemporary issues such as climate change. *Memoirs of a Polar Bear* also exposes the possible dangers of becoming animal-obsessed, as we see in Knut's story in Part III. Based in part on the true story of Knut, a polar bear born in captivity in the Berlin Zoological Garden in 2006 and rejected by his mother, Tosca, at birth, Tawada's novel draws attention to the fine line between love for and exploitation of animals. For example, the novel comments on the "Knutmania" that swept the globe, as well as the polar bear's commercialization, death threats against him, and the use of his image to promote climate change action.[83]

Formal recognition of animal sentience and laws against animal suffering still vary around the world today, even among German-speaking countries. Animal sentience is not specifically mentioned in the German Animal Protection Act, but the concept of animal suffering is included, and the protection of animals has been listed as a state goal since an amendment to Article 20a of the Basic Law of the Federal Republic of Germany 2002.[84] Both Austria and Switzerland are ranked one position higher than Germany on the World Animal Protection Index. The Austrian Animal Welfare Act 2004 recognizes the responsibility of humans towards other animals as "fellow creatures," thereby implicitly but not explicitly recognizing the concept of animal sentience.[85] Similarly, the Swiss Animal Welfare Act 2005 recognizes but does not explicitly refer to the concept of animal sentience.[86] Since formal recognition of animal sentience varies within Europe and around the world, it is perhaps not surprising that views of animal emotions may be controversial and vary across space and time. Yet different understandings of what animals actually feel have not prevented writers, artists, and humans in general from anthropomorphizing non-human animals, imagining their inner lives, or relating to them emotionally.

---

83 Yoko Tawada, *Etüden im Schnee* (Tübingen: konkursbuch Verlag Claudia Gehrke, 2014), 261–267.
84 World Animal Protection, "Animal Protection Index: Germany," accessed 1 June 2020, https://api.worldanimalprotection.org/country/germany.
85 World Animal Protection, "Animal Protection Index: Austria," accessed 1 June 2020, https://api.worldanimalprotection.org/country/austria.
86 World Animal Protection, "Animal Protection Index: Switzerland," accessed 1 June 2020, https://api.worldanimalprotection.org/country/switzerland.

The following essays illuminate different aspects of the affective relationships between humans and non-human animals or machines through analyses of significant texts and moments in modern German cultural history. They are organized in three parts based on common themes: Part I: Emotions and Human/Non-Human Boundaries; Part II: Emotional Functions of Non-Humans; and Part III: Empathic Understanding between Humans and Non-Humans. Within each part, the essays are presented in chronological order of the cultural periods and sources discussed.

Part I illuminates concerns about emotions and the human/non-human boundary in modern German cultural history. These three contributions attest to the important role that emotions played in scientific, philosophical, literary, and aesthetic discourses that attempted to reinforce distinctions or blur the boundaries between humans, non-human animals, and machines. Madalina Meirosu draws on affect theory to explore the interaction of the personal and the impersonal and the boundary between human and non-human in E. T. A. Hoffmann's story "Die Automate" ("The Automata," 1814). Her essay considers the implications of the emotional reactions of the human characters to the Turk, the central automaton in the story, and shows that their encounter with the Turk blurs the boundary between the human and non-human by giving rise to a personal affective response best described in impersonal and mechanical terms. Meirosu demonstrates that the Turk, the human characters, and other automata in the story are all connected through webs of affect that control bodies, feelings, actions, and sanity. Her essay shows the need to posit, both in literature and psychosis, an impersonal "influencing machine" that dominates the personal psyche and speaks to the emotional turmoil experienced by human beings in a post-industrialized age, as they struggle to adapt to an increasingly regulated, technologized, and threatening world, one where bodies and machines have lost their solid boundaries and have begun to fluidly dissolve into each other.

Derek Hillard examines discourses on emotion and the human/non-human boundary in his essay on animals, empathy, and aesthetics in Germany around 1900. Does a shared substratum of feeling enable humans to identify with non-human animals? For humanists since the early modern period, one of the characteristics that distinguishes humans from non-human animals is an aesthetic sense – the ability to experience beauty, sublimity, ugliness, or feel disgust – in general, to appreciate aesthetic differences. Hillard's essay provides insight into different positions of German philosophers and zoologists, such as Adolf Göller, Johannes Volkelt, Karl Möbius, and Theodor Lipps. He shows that many of these thinkers contested the existence of an animal aesthetic, while others posited an unproblematic human identification with animals. Still other thinkers,

Hillard argues, imagined that animals have an aesthetic and even made feelings seem less human because they were infused with something animalistic, thereby granting animals a new kind of autonomy.

Jared Poley probes the interrelated history of biology and emotion studies. He argues that studies of the biological parameters of emotional experience provided a foundation upon which larger claims about the difference and sameness of the animal, the human, and the artificial were built. This chapter allows us to examine, through the history of science, how emotion was conceived as being an essential quality of being human, just as it was also found in other forms of life – both biological and artificial. By conceptualizing emotion in material ways, scientists before 1960 broadened the category in ways that allowed the inclusion of the non-human and the artificial as beings capable of experiencing emotion.

Part II explores different emotional functions of representations of non-human animals and machines in modern German cultural history. Taken together, these three chapters suggest that some possible emotional functions of non-human animals and machines include shaping what was considered human, signaling humans' capacity for sentiment and emotional attachment, establishing group identity and solidarity, critiquing Enlightenment discourses of rationality, and evoking unfamiliar dimensions of feeling. In doing so, non-human animals and machines gained gendered attributes and functions, particularly in regard to signaling humans' emotional capacities and establishing group identity and solidarity. Sarah L. Leonard examines the emotional functions that non-human animals served in early photography in the German States. Building upon John Berger's argument in his influential essay "Why Look at Animals?" (1980), Leonard points out that animals increasingly served emotional roles, as pets that encouraged particular kinds of affective learning and responses and as animals in the zoo that prompted carefully controlled fear and fascination. As the only animal to make regular appearances alongside their human counterparts in daguerreotype portraits from 1840–1860, dogs served important functions in the photographic studio and helped shape what was considered "human." Leonard argues that in the artificial spaces of the photographic studios, dogs, who helped relax the faces and the bodies of human sitters, and therefore, achieve an ideal expression in terms of emotional tone and gender performance, signaled the distinction between the animal and the human and suggested that the humans in the portrait were capable of sentiment and attachment.

Brett Martz focuses on how Robert Musil depicts human characters relating their dispositions to the inner lives of animals in order to explore the limits and alternatives to emotions structured by quotidian existence. His reading of Musil's short text "Kann ein Pferd lachen?" ("Can a Horse Laugh?" 1936) suggests that the application of anthropocentric concepts onto the behavior and inner life of a horse reveals not the shortcomings of the animal, but rather the arbitrary constraints of human frameworks. Musil's novella "Die Portugiesin" ("The Lady from Portugal," 1923) offers a potentially more optimistic assessment of human emotions and their relationship to vulnerability and structures of power. Focusing on an ailing cat, the novella suggests that ineffable emotions may not only deepen connections between humans and non-humans, but may also provide an alternative to gendered discourses and structures of oppression. Martz suggests that the protagonist Herr von Ketten is able to glimpse ways of relating outside of his own masculine acculturation through his confrontation with the Other, embodied not only by the Lady from Portugal, but also the cat.

Erika Quinn shows how Thea von Harbou's *Metropolis* (1925) uses machines and robots – human-made tools that lack emotions – to interrogate what it means to be authentically human in a modern world. While *Metropolis* has been analyzed through the lenses of Marxist theory and literary criticism, this highly melodramatic text has not yet been addressed in emotions scholarship. Quinn argues that Harbou's novel not only points out the dangers of machines replacing human labor, but through its interrogation of authenticity, also emphasizes human affective positions of aversion and attraction in regard to the Other as exhibited by various men's reactions to the robot Maria. By referencing contemporary thought about group dynamics and emotions, Quinn explores the realms of emotional styles and their function in creating group identity and solidarity, particularly by drawing contrasts with the ultimate Others, machines and robots.

Part III considers the capacity of humans to empathize with non-humans and vice versa as suggested in examples of literature, art, photography, and children's fiction in modern German cultural history. These three chapters analyze different kinds of affective understanding and influence between humans and non-human animals and machines, ranging from automata that can read human thoughts and feelings, to humans who empathize with caged animals, to children who nurture affective bonds of friendship with social robots. Claudia Mueller-Greene examines how E. T. A. Hoffmann's "Die Automate" ("The Automata," 1814) represents and reflects human-machine interactions, with a particular focus on emotion and the role of music. Her essay shows how Hoffmann's multi-layered text repeatedly undermines the human protagonists' low opinions of machines. Mueller-Greene argues that "The Automata" proves to be uncannily prescient by conjuring up technologies capable of reading human minds and feelings, predicting future developments, simulating human voices, and evoking strong emotional responses. Mueller-Greene ponders a number of questions that arise from Hoffmann's Romantic tale and brings concepts of other thinkers from the nineteenth century to the present into a diachronic and interdisciplinary dialogue on emotion, music, and machines.

Andrea Meyertholen interrogates the human/non-human divide by studying early twentieth-century artistic, literary, and photographic representations of animals displayed in cages in order to explore the limits of human empathy with and sympathy for them. She points out that the cage, a structure literally and figuratively framing our experience, creates meaning depending on standpoint (inside/outside), inhabitant (human/animal), and cultural connotation (prison/zoo). Meyertholen's literary and visual analyses reveal that the presence of bars affects how emotional depth is ascribed or denied to caged inhabitants, causing us to "humanize" animals in such a way that we believe to experience emotions in and with them. Meyertholen explores not only where we draw the line between animal and human, but where we are willing to draw it and why.

Holly Yanacek examines the depiction of social robots and child-robot friendship in recent German children's literature, including in the books *Schlupp vom grünen Stern* (Schlupp from the green star, 1974), *Orbis Abenteuer* (Orbi's adventures, 2011), *Roboter Sam* (Robot Sam, 2017), and *Roki: Mein Freund mit Herz und Schraube* (Roki: my friend with heart and bolt, 2018). Her essay focuses on the feelings of emotional attachment that the child protagonists develop for their robot friends and considers the extent to which these social robots serve as positive identification figures for child readers. Although the robots depicted in these books are non-threatening, toylike machines that bear little resemblance to the human characters, these stories blur the boundary between humans and machines by attributing emotions or a "soul" to the robot characters. Taken together, these books imagine a world in which humans and robots can peacefully coexist and even form meaningful friendships that do not threaten human relationships. Yanacek's analysis demonstrates that the greatest aim of these children's books is to teach respect and compassion for all life forms, both human and nonhuman, organic and artificial.

Animals, Machines, and AI ultimately sheds light on the centrality of non-human animals and machines within the context of the human emotional world. Much of this volume was written during the COVID-19 pandemic, which made us editors more keenly aware of the importance of non-human animals, machines, and technology in our daily emotional lives. Changing relationships between humans and non-human animals appear to be what "created" COVID-19. We can likely expect more such viruses in the future as a result of how we humans have altered our environment, specifically our relationship to non-human animal life. On a more personal note, those of us who live with domestic animal companions have turned to them even more than usual for comfort, affection, and distraction.

So, too, have our companion animals come to depend on us even more than before since they became accustomed to our continued presence at home during the months we spent working remotely. While quarantined in our homes, many of us became dependent on digital technology in much more significant ways. These digital technologies, which now play a central role in mediating human relationships, can provoke frustration, loneliness, or fatigue. Yet they can also facilitate human communication, emotional connection, and care when in-person contact is restricted or not available, for example, for remote learning, virtual dating, telemedicine, and online therapy and counseling.

Bibliography

Ahmed, Sara. *The Cultural Politics of Emotion* (New York: Routledge, 2004).

Ahmed, Sara. *Living a Feminist Life* (Durham, NC: Duke UP, 2017).

Anderson, Mark M., ed. "Jakob von Uexküll: From *The Environment and the Inner World of Animals*," in Franz Kafka *The Metamorphosis*. Ed. Mark M. Anderson (New York: W. W. Norton, 2016), 95–99.

Arluke, Arnold, and Clinton R. Sanders. *Regarding Animals* (Philadelphia: Temple UP, 1996).

Barrett, Lisa Feldman. *How Emotions Are Made: The Secret Life of the Brain* (New York: Houghton Mifflin Harcourt, 2017).

Benjamin, Walter. "Theses on the Philosophy of History," in *Illuminations*. Trans. Harry Zohn (New York: Harcourt Brace Jovanovich, Inc., 1968).

Biro, Matthew. *The Dada Cyborg: Visions of the New Human in Weimar Berlin* (Minneapolis: U of Minnesota Press, 2009).

Boddice, Rob. *The History of Emotions* (Manchester: Manchester UP, 2018).

Die Bundesregierung. "Zwischenbericht: Ein Jahr KI-Strategie." *Nationale Strategie für Künstliche Intelligenz*, November 2019. Accessed 28 May 2020. https://www.ki-strategie-deutschland.de/home.html.

Butler, Judith. *Bodies that Matter: On the Discursive Limits of "Sex"* (New York: Routledge, 1993).

Damasio, Antonio. *The Strange Order of Things: Life, Feeling, and the Making of Cultures* (New York: Pantheon, 2018).

Darwin, Charles. *The Expression of the Emotions in Man and Animals* (Oxford: Oxford UP, 2009).

Deutsche Bahn. "Smart Services: The 'Siri for Train Travelers.'" Accessed 1 April 2021. https://www.deutschebahn.com/en/Digitalization/technology/innovations/Smart-services-the-Siri-for-train-travelers–4167438.

Downes, Stephanie, Sally Holloway, and Sarah Randles. "A Feeling for Things, Past and Present," in *Feeling Things: Objects and Emotions through History*. Eds. Stephanie Downes, Sally Holloway, and Sarah Randles (Oxford: Oxford UP, 2018), 8–26.

Dumouchel, Paul, and Luisa Damiano. *Living with Robots*. Trans. Malcolm DeBevoise (Cambridge, MA: Harvard UP, 2017).

Eitler, Pascal. "Tierliebe und Menschenführung. Eine genealogische Perspektive auf das 19. und 20. Jahrhundert," in *Tierstudien 3: Tierliebe*. Eds. Jessica Ullrich and Friedrich Weltzien (Berlin: Neofelis Verlag, 2013), 40–48.

Eitler, Pascal. "Übertragungsgefahr: Zur Emotionalisierung und Verwissenschaftlichung des Mensch-Tier-Verhältnisses im deutschen Kaiserreich," in *Rationalisierungen des Gefühls: Zum Verhältnis von Wissenschaft und Emotionen 1880–1930*. Eds. Uffa Jensen and Daniel Morat (Munich: Wilhelm Fink, 2008), 171–187.

Eksteins, Modris. *Rites of Spring: The Great War and the Birth of the Modern Age* (New York: Anchor Books, 1990).

Elder, Alexis M. *Friendship, Robots, and Social Media: False Friends and Second Selves* (New York: Routledge, 2018).

Elias, Norbert. *Über den Prozess der Zivilisation* (Basel: Haus zum Falken, 1939).

European Union. "Germany AI Strategy Report." *European Commission – Knowledge for Policy*. Accessed 25 May 2020. https://ec.europa.eu/knowledge4policy/ai-watch/germany-ai-strategy-report_en.

Evans, Richard J. *The Third Reich at War: 1939–1945* (London: Penguin, 2010).

Febvre, Lucien. "La sensibilité et l'histoire: Comment reconstituer la vie affective d'autrefois?" *Annales d'histoires sociale* 3 (Jan.–Jun. 1941): 5–20.

Frevert, Ute. "Defining Emotions: Concepts and Debates over Three Centuries," in *Emotional Lexicons: Continuity and Change in the Vocabulary of Feeling 1700–2000*. Eds. Ute Frevert et al. (Oxford: Oxford UP, 2014), 1–31.

Frevert, Ute. *Emotions in History – Lost and Found* (Budapest: Central European UP, 2011).

Fritzsche, Sonja. *Science Fiction Literature in East Germany* (Oxford: Peter Lang, 2006).

Gammerl, Benno. "Emotional Styles – Concepts and Challenges," *Rethinking History* 15, no. 2 (June 2012): 161–175.

Gay, Peter. *The Cultivation of Hatred*: Vol. 3 of *The Bourgeois Experience: Victoria to Freud* (New York: W. W. Norton, 1993).

Gay, Peter. *Freud for Historians* (Oxford: Oxford UP, 1986).

Goldstein, L. "Übersicht der neuern Verhandlungen über die Vivisektionsfrage. Nach den Arbeiten von v. Weber, Iatros, Hermann, Ludwig, Heidenhain, usw," in *Schmidt's Jahrbücher der in- und ausländischen gesammten Medicin* 182, no. 3 (1879): 281–285.

Greve, Karsten. "Die Science-Fiction-Literatur der DDR." (PhD diss., Freie Universität Berlin, 2015).

Grusin, Richard, ed. *The Nonhuman Turn* (Minneapolis: U of Minnesota Press, 2015).

Hampshire, Stewart. "Biology, Machines, and Humanity," in *The Boundaries of Humanity: Humans, Animals, Machines*. Eds. James J. Sheehan and Morton Sosna (Berkeley: UC Press, 1991), 253–258.

Hanhardt, Arthur M, Jr. "German Democratic Republic," in *Communism in Eastern Europe*. Ed. Teresa Rakowska-Harmstone (Bloomington: Indiana UP, 1984), 137–161.

Haraway, Donna. *The Companion Species Manifesto: Dogs, People, and Significant Otherness* (Chicago: Prickly Paradigm Press, 2003).

Haraway, Donna J. "A Cyborg Manifesto," in *Simians, Cyborgs, and Women: The Reinvention of Nature* (New York: Routledge, 1991), 149–181.

Hauptmann, Gerhart. "Bahnwärter Thiel," in *Erzählungen* (Gütersloh: C. Bertelsmann, 1957), 28–63.

Hausen, Karin. "Family and Role-Division: The Polarisation of Sexual Stereotypes in the Nineteenth Century – an Aspect of the Dissociation of Work and Family Life," in *The*

German Family: Essays on the Social History of the Family in Nineteenth- and Twentieth-Century Germany. Eds. Richard J. Evans and W. R. Lee (London: Croom Helm, 1981), 51–83.

Heine, Heinrich. "Ludwig Börne: A Memorial," trans. Frederic Ewen and Robert C. Holub, in *The Romantic School and Other Essays*. Eds. Jost Hermand and Robert C. Holub (New York: Continuum, 2002), 261–284.

Hoffmann, E. T. A. "Der Sandmann," in *Werke*, vol. 2 (Frankfurt a. M.: Insel, 1967), 7–40.

Hull, Isabel V. *Sexuality, State, and Civil Society in Germany, 1700–1815* (Ithaca, NY: Cornell UP, 1997).

James, William. *The Principles of Psychology*, vol. 2 (London: Macmillan, 1890).

Jaskot, Paul B. "Gerhard Richter and Adolf Eichmann," *Oxford Art Journal* 28, no. 3 (2005): 457–478.

Jünger, Ernst. *On Pain*. Trans. David C. Durst (Candor, NY: Telos Press, 2008).

Kafka, Franz. "In unserer Synagoge . . . " in *Die Erzählungen und andere ausgewählte Prosa*. Ed. Roger Hermes (Frankfurt a. M.: Fischer, 2010), 405–409.

Kakoudaki, Despina. *Anatomy of a Robot: Literature, Cinema, and the Cultural Work of Artificial People* (New Brunswick, NJ: Rutgers UP, 2014).

Kapp, Ernst. *Grundlinien einer Philosophie der Technik. Zur Entstehungsgeschichte der Cultur aus neuen Gesichtspunkten* (Braunschweig: Westermann, 1877).

Klothmann, Nastasja. *Gefühlswelten im Zoo: Eine Emotionsgeschichte 1900–1945* (Bielefeld: transcript, 2015).

Lange, C. G. *Ueber Gemüthsbewegungen. Eine Psycho-Physiologische Studie* (Leipzig: Theodor Thomas, 1887).

Lefebvre, Georges. *La Grande Peur de 1789* (Paris: Librairie Armand Colin, 1932)

Meier-Welcker, Hans. *Aufzeichnungen eines Generalstabsoffiziers 1939–1942* (Freiburg im Breisgau: Rombach, 1982).

Melena, Elpis. *Gemma; oder, Tugend und Laster* (Munich: G. Franz'sche Verlagshandlung, 1877).

Mohnhaupt, J. W. *The Zookeepers' War: An Incredible True Story from the Cold War*. Trans. Shelley Frisch (New York: Simon & Schuster, 2017).

Nussbaum, Martha. *Political Emotions: Why Love Matters for Justice* (Cambridge, MA: Harvard UP, 2013).

Nussbaum, Martha. *Upheavals of Thought: The Intelligence of Emotions* (Cambridge: Cambridge UP, 2001).

Overy, Richard. *Why the Allies Won* (New York: W. W. Norton, 1995).

Perry, Heather R. *Recycling the Disabled: Army, Medicine, and Modernity in WWI Germany* (Manchester: Manchester UP, 2014).

Plamper, Jan. *The History of Emotions: An Introduction* (Oxford: Oxford UP, 2017).

Raulff, Ulrich. *Farewell to the Horse: A Cultural History*. Trans. Ruth Ahmedzai Kemp (New York: Liveright, 2018).

Reddy, William. *The Navigation of Feeling: A Framework for the History of Emotions* (Cambridge: Cambridge UP, 2001).

Rilke, Rainer Maria. "Der Panther," in *Werke in drei Bänden*, vol. 1, *Gedicht-Zyklen* (Frankfurt a. M.: Insel, 1966), 261.

Rosenwein, Barbara. *Emotional Communities in the Early Middle Ages* (Ithaca, NY: Cornell UP, 2006).

Sabean, David, and Hans Medick, eds. *Interest and Emotions: Essays on the Study of Family and Kinship* (Cambridge: Cambridge UP, 1986).

Safina, Carl. *Beyond Words: What Animals Think and Feel* (New York: Henry Holt, 2015).

Schafer, Elizabeth D. "Animals, use of," in *The European Powers in the First World War, an Encyclopedia*. Ed. Spencer C. Tucker (London: Routledge, 1999), 52–54.

Schneider, Peter. *The German Comedy*. Trans. Philip Boehm and Leigh Hafrey (New York: Farrar, Straus and Giroux, 1991).

Stearns, Peter N., and Carol Z. Stearns. "Emotionology: Clarifying the History of Emotions and Emotional Standards," *American Historical Review* 90 (1985): 813–836.

Stevenson, David. *Cataclysm: The First World War as Political Tragedy* (New York: Basic Books, 2009).

Tawada, Yoko. *Etüden im Schnee* (Tübingen: konkursbuch Verlag Claudia Gehrke, 2014).

Tindol, Robert. "The Best Friend of the Murderers: Guard Dogs and the Nazi Holocaust," in *Animals and War: Studies of Europe and North America*. Ed. Ryan Hediger (Boston: Brill, 2013), 105–122.

Tye, Michael. *Tense Bees and Shell-Shocked Crabs: Are Animals Conscious?* (Oxford: Oxford UP, 2017).

Uexküll, Jakob von. *Umwelt und Innenwelt der Tiere* (Berlin: Julius Springer, 1909).

Varner, Gary. "Sentience," in *Critical Terms for Animal Studies*. Ed. Lori Gruen (Chicago: U of Chicago Press, 2018), 356–369.

Weil, Kari. *Thinking Animals: Why Animal Studies Now?* (New York: Columbia UP, 2012).

World Animal Protection. "Animal Protection Index: Austria." Accessed 1 June 2020. https://api.worldanimalprotection.org/country/austria.

World Animal Protection. "Animal Protection Index: Germany." Accessed 1 June 2020. https://api.worldanimalprotection.org/country/germany.

World Animal Protection. "Animal Protection Index: Switzerland." Accessed 1 June 2020. https://api.worldanimalprotection.org/country/switzerland.

Yanacek, Holly A. "Mobilising Disgust and Compassion: Elpis Melena's *Gemma; oder, Tugend und Laster* (1877) and the Anti-Vivisection Movement." *German Life and Letters* 73, no. 4 (October 2020): 564–580.

Emotions and Human/Non-Human Boundaries

Madalina Meirosu
Mechanical Feelings

Artificial Bodies and Human Emotions in E. T. A. Hoffmann's "The Automata" (1814)

Ghosts, artificial humans, gruesome stories, and an eerie atmosphere are a commonplace in E. T. A. Hoffmann's work. The story at the heart of this essay is no exception, yet it did not garner as much critical interest as some other pieces by the same author. An abridged version of "Die Automate" ("The Automata") was published in February 1814 in the *Leipziger Allgemeine Musikalische Zeitung* (Leipzig general music newspaper) and again in April 1814 in the *Zeitung für die elegante Welt* (Newspaper for the elegant world). The entire story was later published in the second volume of the collection of stories *Die Serapions-Brüder* (*The Serapion Brothers*) in 1819. Critics were initially puzzled by the fragmentary and apparently incoherent plot; two hundred years later, critics still find the story baffling for the same reason. The plot of "The Automata" focuses on two young male characters, the well-to-do students Ferdinand and Ludwig, who undergo a number of strange experiences, including a traumatic encounter with an artificial humanoid that looks like an exoticized Turk. When the two friends discover that the artificial humanoid appears to have access to Ferdinand's innermost secrets, they set out to find the builder of such an uncanny machine. This quest overlaps with an attempt to understand the difference between artificial and natural music (hence the interest of the *Leipziger Allgemeine Musikalische Zeitung*), as well as the difference between artificial and natural beings. Throughout the various episodes, the text torments the reader with a question that is never answered: are the tumultuous feelings that lead to Ferdinand's psychosis somehow manufactured by the machine, or perhaps by some malevolent forces behind the machine? The elliptical and fragmentary plot leaves much to the reader's imagination.

And yet Hoffmann's narrative technique is not without purpose: it enacts the fragmentary state of mind of the human characters. Though the Turk only appears at the beginning of the story, he continues to exercise an influence throughout the plot. He is able to do this because he is the point of convergence for many of Ferdinand's frustrations: Ferdinand's troubled relationship with a secret beloved, his desire to understand the differences between the natural and the artificial, his problematic relationship with authority, and his final breakdown can all be traced back to the Turk. This essay examines Ferdinand's emotional response to

https://doi.org/10.1515/9783110753677-002

the automaton and locates his final psychic disintegration in a shifting world in which human identity is challenged and recast in the context of technology. The result is a blurring of personal boundaries that leaves Ferdinand dizzy and disturbed. I suggest that the idea of an "influencing machine" offers readers a way to conceptualize the Turk's pernicious influence on Ferdinand. For the mechanical Turk does not simply inspire the typical emotions of awe or repulsion experienced by an eager public when confronted with a life-like machine. More crucially, it elicits and controls human emotions in ways that deprive human beings of their autonomy and turn them into the playthings – the marionettes – of powerful and mysterious forces.

This last point is relevant to Sara Ahmed's political theory of emotion, and as I proceed I will refer when appropriate to her analysis of the political dimensions of emotions since it shines a light on some of the dynamics occurring in Hoffmann's story. Ahmed considers emotions through a critical lens that does not treat feelings as individual and private matters but rather perceives them as the effect of political forces.[1] These forces both construct the circumstances that give rise to certain emotions while also sanctioning what kinds of emotions are desirable in social contexts. Her work looks at the social mechanisms that induce and constrain human emotion, and E. T. A. Hoffmann provides an evocative sketch of just such a mechanism in his dramatization of the emotional effect that impersonal automatic characters have on the human characters in the story.

Ahmed contends that emotions alert us to the ways that power shapes our lives and the worlds we inhabit. For example, our feelings for family, for the nation, and for heterosexuality have been shaped by political forces, with the result that, no matter how satisfying, our emotional lives "can attach us to the very conditions of our subordination." The norms that govern our emotions "are effects of repetition [. . .] Such norms appear as forms of life only through the concealment of the work of this repetition."[2] Our emotions are thus constructed from the outside, as it were. In fact, emotions are never the private affair of an individual but are always implicated in a shared life – *Mitsein*, being-with others. Emotions are public not only by virtue of a political system that authorizes certain kinds of collective emotional responses, but they are also shared through an inevitable emotional contagion and sympathy. Nina Trcka points out that our collective emotions are generated by a range of interactions with others, "from the mere perception of other people, [to] the becoming aware of their feelings or moods and responding to them – all the way through to reflexively supported forms of

---

1 Sara Ahmed, *The Cultural Politics of Emotion* (Edinburgh: Edinburgh UP, 2014), 18–24; 229.
2 Ahmed, *Cultural Politics of Emotion*, 12.

empathy and sympathy [. . .] As embodied subjects we are always intertwined with others who are co-present."[3] Both aspects of collective emotions are on display in "The Automata," though my reading will focus on how Hoffmann dramatizes the way political conditions generate emotion.

The talking Turk

The historical figure of the original chess-playing Turk provides the source for Hoffmann's puzzling and oracular fictional Turk, and the mystery surrounding this historical figure sets the stage for the confusing atmosphere of Hoffmann's story. An object of fascination and controversy for mathematicians, engineers, and entertainers, as well as for members of every social stratum in the general public, the chess-playing Turk started his career in 1770 at the Viennese court of Maria Theresa, only to be dismembered at her death and then brought back to "life" at the behest of Emperor Joseph II. Among the highlights of the automaton's career were his presentation to Marie Antoinette in 1783, his encounter with Benjamin Franklin during the latter's visit to Paris, and, after his owner Wolfgang von Kempelen's death, his chess games against Napoleon in 1809 at Schönbrunn, along with meetings with other notable historical contemporaries. The automaton's adventures continued even after Hoffmann's story was published; taken to America by his new – and financially strapped – owner, Johann Nepomuk Maelzel, he fascinated members of the press and the general public. Following his travels in America, the career of the automaton continued under a succession of new owners, culminating with John Kearsley Mitchell who, after restoring the Turk yet again, revealed the nature of the hoax to his club of fellow Turk enthusiasts in 1840.[4] The machine had been designed to allow a small man to hide in the desk that supported the chessboard; concealed by a clever arrangement of mirrors, the operator was conveniently positioned to control the Turk's movements.

Throughout the public existence of this automaton, skeptics raised doubts about the possibility of inventing an intelligent machine: they suspected an elaborate hoax to be at the heart of its celebrity. Among these skeptics, the most familiar to the literary world is Edgar Allan Poe. In an article entitled "Maelzel's

---

3 Nina Trcka, "Collective Moods: A Contribution to the Phenomenology and Interpersonality of Shared Affectivity," *Philosophia* 45 (2017): 1653.
4 Gerald Levitt, *The Turk, Chess Automaton* (Jefferson, NC: McFarland and Company, 2006), 144.

Chess Player" (1836), he presents a brief history of automata and then debunks the Turk as an illusion, a mechanism manipulated by a man hidden inside it. Poe traces the history of published efforts to expose the automaton as a fraudulent illusion back to 1785 in Paris and quotes a 1789 book by a "Mr. Freyhere" as the popular source of the idea that a human being must be hidden in the machine, perhaps even a small boy or dwarf.[5] Poe appears to refer to Joseph Friedrich Freiherr von Racknitz's *Über den Schachspieler des Herrn von Kempelen, nebst einer Abbildung und Beschreibung seiner Sprachmaschine* (Regarding the chess player of Mr. Kempelen, along with a representation and description of his speaking machine), published first in the town of Leibnitz in 1784 and subsequently republished in 1789 in Leipzig and Dresden.

As such, the seeds of doubt about the genuineness of the machine had already been sown by the time Hoffmann wrote his text, though as yet there was no evidence to give the lie to the hoax. The mechanism managed to foil the close scrutiny of specialists and other skeptical investigators for decades. What is essential to Hoffmann's story, however, is the factual existence of the chess-playing Turk coupled with the elusive mystery surrounding his apparent ratiocination. The fact of this aura of mystery is much more important than the actual manner(s) of deception in making sense of Hoffmann's text. Of all the automata of his époque, the Turk is the only humanoid automaton to whom one could possibly attribute intelligent actions, which made it of central importance in the debate over artificial intelligence in the late eighteenth and early nineteenth centuries.[6] The mystery enveloping the machine and the confounded response of those who witnessed its performance first-hand are mirrored in the atmosphere created by Hoffmann in "The Automata."[7]

The Orientalized presentation of Hoffmann's Turk replicates the features of the original Turk of von Kempelen: he is dressed in "rich, tasteful Turkish dress"

---

5 Edgar Allen Poe, *Edgar Allan Poe: The Dover Reader* (Mineola, NY: Dover Publications, 2014), 844–845.

6 Hans-Günther Gassen and Sabine Minol, *Die Menschenmacher: Sehnsucht nach Unsterblichkeit* (Weinheim: Wiley-VCH, 2006), 220.

7 Other contemporary cultural concerns that have a bearing on "The Automata" are magnetism, mesmerism, galvanism, and spiritualism. For Hoffmann's involvement with these sciences, see Vanessa Nühnen, *Maschinenmenschen und künstliche Menschen in der Literatur zur Zeit der Industrialisierung: Vom Traum, Leben zu Erschaffen* (Munich: GRIN Verlag GmbH, 2010), 7; Marcus Krause, "Der zerstückelte Körper und die Sprachmaschine: Poes materialistische Experimente," in *Literarische Experimentalkulturen: Poetologien des Experiments im 19. Jahrhundert*, eds. Marcus Krause and Nicolas Pethes (Würzburg: Königshausen & Neumann, 2005), 17.

and because of his extraordinarily well-formed head he distinguishes himself from other wax figures by his "truly Oriental spiritual physiognomy," which gives him a life-like demeanor.[8] In the eyes of its public, the automaton is the site of a fusion of the Western world and the Orient; this is because Orientalist Western views relegated the paranormal to the East, while technology was associated with Western Europe. The main feature of the Turk, however, is his uncanny presence, and one reason for his uncanny presentation may be this very blending into one of what was usually kept separate. In his encounter with the uncanny Turk, Ludwig makes a silly joke presumably out of an instinctual need to defend himself against the dread invoked by the automaton. (Additionally, the automaton's comical effect on Ludwig may stem from finding oneself in front of a small and seemingly controllable machine in the shape of a Turk at the very moment when the Ottoman Empire still looms large and threatening in the European imagination at the beginning of the nineteenth century.) The laughter triggered by the joke spreads throughout the audience. Immediately the Turk's answers to the questions put to him begin to feel empty and hollow as the Turk struggles to understand Ludwig. At this point the narrative voice wonders whether the "hilarious mood" that convulsed the room may have influenced the functioning of the automaton. The narrator seems to suggest that the emotional environment in which the mechanism operates can render the machine ineffective. This is an unexpected development; the suggestion is that mechanisms are susceptible to human emotion, with automatic bodies somehow influenced by expressive human bodies. In an atmosphere of mocking laughter and distrust, everything turns momentarily sour: the machine ceases to function properly, the exhibitor is "out of temper," and the audience "ill-pleased and disappointed."[9] Nevertheless, after the first impression wears off, the encounter takes a serious turn, with the Oriental fortune teller startling Ferdinand with disturbing revelations about his secret beloved.

Along with Ludwig, the audience can see the shock of emotion on Ferdinand's face when the Turk returns to form and answers the question about the beloved that Ferdinand has uttered in a whisper. Ferdinand turns pale. The sudden and powerful emotional effect of the Turk on Ferdinand is the engine that drives the rest of the plot: "Though Ferdinand strove hard to hide what he felt, it was evident from his efforts to be at ease that he was very deeply moved, and the cleverest answer could not have produced in the spectators the strange sensation, amounting to a sort of awe, which his unmistakable emotion gave rise

---

8 E. T. A. Hoffmann, "Die Automate" in *Die Serapions-Brüder* (Munich: Winkler, 1963), 376–377. All translations of "Die Automate" are mine.
9 Hoffmann, "Die Automate," 379–380.

to in them."[10] Ferdinand finally stammers that "the Turk broke [his] heart" and the audience, having absorbed something of Ferdinand's disturbed feelings, leaves in "uneasy silence," a textbook example of affective contagion.[11]

Though the Orientalized features of the doll contribute to the emotional effect it has on its audience, the main source of the Turk's uncanny effect is to be found in its *lebendigtot* (literally "alivedead") status, a quality of the Turk that Ludwig fends off with forced laughter. Unlike a zombie ("livingdead"), which is first alive, then dead, then reanimated, the Turk is *alivedead* from the very beginning; it is inorganic matter, a mechanism that is both dead and alive at the same time through either technological miracles or magic. As such, the Turk is an ambivalent figure, both attractive and repulsive – attractive owing to its soulful, wise face and luxurious clothes; repulsive because of its *lebendigtot* presence.

The various and intricate parts of the machine, even when scrutinized by "the Argus-eyes of the most competent mechanics," cannot account for its holistic functioning, nor do they explain either the breath of air that whispers from it or its oracular sentences that unsettle its human audiences.[12] Still, the automaton appears to its onlookers to be the sum total of its mechanical parts, a shape empty of soul, but it is this very emptiness that allows the artificial creature, when confronted by the living, to serve as a "revealing agent for the fragmentation of the human being, and as such [bring] to light the human beings' duality, make visible its inanity."[13] Thus, Ferdinand is faced with his own duality, with his own alivedeadness, perhaps even with the futility of concerns in a world where death holds sway. When confronted by Ferdinand, the automaton demonstrates a knowledge that is utterly disturbing, something that cannot be explained as the result of the processes of its mechanical parts. Ferdinand's encounter with the Turk conjures up feelings of despair at his lack of control as he suffers the unwanted exposure of his innermost thoughts and feelings.

This question of whether an automaton is necessarily the sum of its parts, or is in fact something more, received its most famous treatment in section 17 of Gottfried Wilhelm Leibniz's *La Monadologie* (*Monadology*, 1714). There Leibniz considers the (remote) possibility of building an intelligent machine, one capable of thought, feeling, and perception. He performs a thought experiment whereby

---

10 Hoffmann, "Die Automate," 379.

11 Hoffmann, "Die Automate," 379.

12 Hoffmann, "Die Automate," 377.

13 Isabelle Krzywkowski, "Créature créaturée et créature créaturante: les jeux du dédublement et l'esthétique du morcellement" in *L'homme Artificiel: Hoffmann, Shelley, Villiers De L'isle-Adam* (Paris: Ellipses, 1999), 163.

the inner mechanism of the machine is magnified and enlarged so as to make its smallest aspect available to easy inspection. He argues that having full access to the intricacies of the thinking machine would only show us "pieces of the machine that push against one another, but never anything to explain a perception." According to Leibniz, perception or the intelligence of the machine should be sought "in the simple substance [monad] and not in the composite machine,"[14] that is, in immaterial substance and not in mere mechanization. This perspective offers a way to understand the mystery of the Turk's own functioning. According to this logic, the Turk is no mere sum of his parts, but rather at his most fundamental level he harbors a mysterious substance that cannot be reduced to mere matter or mechanics – in other words, he is composed of the same immaterial, spiritual substance found in all living things, though not available to observation. In this interpretation the Turk, though seemingly man-made, is also the sum of these invisible natural (as opposed to artificial) elements. These invisible natural elements are, at the same time, of a piece with the invisible natural elements that comprise each human being, that transform the matter of a human body (understood by Descartes and others as a kind of machine) into a *living* body, a *human* machine. It is in this affinity that the secret powers of the Turk may lie – he was built to access and connect with the elemental spiritual substance of everyone and everything around him.

Uncertainty and automatic doubles

The specter of the Turk and his catastrophic prediction haunts Ferdinand's imagination, though the automaton itself does not make another appearance in the text. It is my contention, however, that there are hints of other automatic beings in the story besides the obvious candidates of the Turk, the musical instruments, and the enchanted garden. The title of the story can also be understood to include in its referential sweep Professor X (the purported creator of the Turk) and Ferdinand's beloved singer, who, in my interpretation, are also automata. The automaton status of Professor X and the nameless beloved is crucial to bear in mind when seeking to understand the multiple valences of the metaphorical interpretations of the Turk. But first, their mechanical existence needs to be demonstrated.

The reader learns that the Turk is an automaton that was built in two different stages. The first creator of the Turk had merely assembled the metal frame;

---

14 Gottfried Wilhelm Leibniz, *The Monadology and Other Philosophical Writings*, trans. Robert Latta (New York: Oxford UP, 1971), 228.

Ferdinand and Ludwig soon discover that Professor X had actually brought it to life. Upon learning of Professor X's role in the bestowal of the automaton's uncanny, soul-penetrating powers, Ferdinand and Ludwig visit the Turk's second creator, the Professor. The two "found him to be an energetic-looking very old man, dressed in an old-fashioned outfit, whose grey eyes stared in an unpleasantly penetrating way, and around whose mouth fluttered a sarcastic smile that was not at all attractive."[15] This old-fashioned older man, who seems to be wearing a theatre costume, has a sardonic smile that reminds the reader of Faustian legends: is the Professor the devil himself or perhaps under the influence of the devil? His appearance deepens the dramatic suspense of the scene. In addition to his off-putting smile, the Professor's discordant voice foreshadows the failure of the two young men's enterprise: "the Professor's voice had something terribly repugnant about it, it was a high shrieking disorienting tenor that went well with the gimmicky manner in which he presented his artwork."[16]

More troubling still, before they can ask their questions the Professor plays the part of a showman, presenting his automata collection in a rehearsed, seemingly repetitive and thoughtless way. He then proceeds to perform with his orchestra of automata, taking his place in front of a piano in the middle of a row of various automatic musical instruments. Instead of offering answers or a thoughtful discussion, he offers music produced by automata and himself. These early signs – the Professor's performance as a member of the automatic orchestra, his repetitive speech, his restricted vocabulary, and his uncanny appearance – point to his status as an automaton. And yet the two friends can only think about the music, which Ferdinand finds to be "extremely artful and beautiful."[17] For his part, Ludwig finds the automatic music of the uncanny orchestra unnerving and disturbing: "For me, there is something oppressive, uncanny, indeed atrocious, already in the act of giving a human form to the dead look-alike figures that imitate human actions and activities."[18] Ludwig's lack of appreciation for artificial music is on par with his lack of appreciation for artificial beings such as the Turk and other automata, all of which disgust him. This is an example of what Ahmed calls an "economy of disgust."[19] In order to distance himself from the artificial humans and from the mechanical in general, and to insist upon the human/artificial distinction, Ludwig gives himself over to a reaction of disgust. As Ahmed explains, "the subject feels an object to be disgusting (a perception that relies on a

15 Hoffmann, "Die Automate," 395–396.
16 Hoffmann, "Die Automate," 396.
17 Hoffmann, "Die Automate," 397.
18 Hoffmann, "Die Automate," 397.
19 Ahmed, *Cultural Politics of Emotion*, 92.

history that comes before the encounter) and then expels the object and, through expelling the object, finds it to be disgusting. *The expulsion itself becomes the 'truth' of the reading of the object*."[20] Interestingly, after hearing Ludwig voice his disgust provoked by artificial music, Ferdinand changes his tune. He says that he has "always felt a repugnance to the stiffness and lifelessness of machine music; and, I can remember, when I was a child at home, how I detested a large, ordinary musical clock, which played its little tune every hour. It is a pity that those skillful mechanics do not try to apply their knowledge to the improvement of musical instruments, rather than to puerilities of this sort."[21] Ferdinand identifies with his friend's emotional response, which is one of the mechanisms by which community-life is consolidated. At the very moment when Ludwig distances himself through an expression of emotion, Ferdinand overcomes distance through a sharing of emotion.

This first encounter with the Professor, a disturbing experience for the two friends, neither offers any answers regarding the Turk's special abilities nor affords the reader an irrefutable clue regarding the question of whether the Professor is a person or an automaton. Later, a woman who appears to be the secret beloved reveals herself to the two young men in the form of a lovely singing voice when they happen upon the garden where they see Professor X walking silently, unaware of their presence. Singing out of sight, the young woman sings the same song that she sang when Ferdinand first saw her, the song that later resonates in the room where the Turk pronounces his unsettling sentence that the two shall be separated forever. A young child runs into a garden, telling the two friends that "Schwesterchen," her dear sister, sings even longer and more beautifully when given flowers.

Two clues point to the beloved's automatic nature here: first, when prompted by a certain signal, in this case flowers, she sings like any other musical machine triggered by the turn of a key. Second, her repertoire is confined to one song, which she repeats without change. Moreover, songs of disembodied female voices sung by off-stage mechanisms were, along with the chess-playing automaton and other speaking automata, one of the attractions of the age. The Italian song that Ferdinand hears, the lyrics of which were written by the eighteenth-century poet Pietro Metastasio, has for its theme love beyond death: "Remember my love, if I should die: / How much this faithful soul would love you. / And if cold ashes

---

20 Ahmed, *Cultural Politics of Emotion*, 87. Italics in the original.
21 Hoffmann, "Die Automate," 398.

could love: / Then in the urn I would still love you."[22] The Italian lyrics connect the singer to the country in which marionettes were invented, which supplies another reason for doubting her humanity, along with the repetitive song that is her only utterance. Additionally, the reference to eternal love described in this poem points to the possibility of love originating from death; the song speaks of the warmth of love originating from the "fredde ceneri" ("cold ashes"). It is not a stretch to hear this song as the anthem of an automaton, celebrating love's origin in an inorganic mechanism. In this song, love itself becomes as uncanny as the Turk; love can be *alivedead*.

If Professor X is an automaton, this is not the whole of the story, of course. For when considered comprehensively, Professor X proves to be an unsettling alternation of alive and dead, of kind and sardonic. The most likely reason for this duality is that he is a human being who has an *automatic double*. This is particularly evident during the two friends' second encounter with him from afar in the garden. Here he appears to be a completely different being from the one who met the two young men during their hopeful visit earlier in the story. Instead of the disturbing, ironic smile, the professor's face is human and deeply melancholic as he peers into the infinity of the sky. Everything comes to life around him as heavenly music pours out of blades of grass in the living artificial garden, presenting a stark contrast with the music that was forced upon the two young men in the Professor's house. This Professor X seems to be the human double of the threatening, sardonic, mechanical Professor X that met the two young men in the house. And yet, despite his humanity and apparently lofty aspirations, the Professor is unwilling to share his wisdom with others.

Thus, the man behind the preternatural automaton known as the Turk also remains a mystery. The Janus-faced duality of the Professor, evident in the contrast between the evil-looking, carnivalesque showman the two friends meet in the house and the human, wise, pensive scientist they glimpse in the garden, suggests to the reader the possibility of two professors. This possibility seems to be supported by the fact that later in the story, after Ludwig receives news of Ferdinand's encounter with the Professor in a distant town, he finds out "that Professor X had absolutely not left town."[23] It accounts for his ability to be in two places (at a considerable distance from each other) at once, and suggests that a mechanical double of Professor X is involved in a mysterious plot.

---

22 Translation courtesy of Jonathan Retzlaff and Cheri Montgomery, *Exploring Art Song Lyrics: Translation and Pronunciation of the Italian, German & French Repertoire* (New York: Oxford UP, 2012), 70.
23 Hoffmann, "Die Automate," 406.

The garden: A respite from anxiety

In addition to offering a reason for rethinking the status of the first Professor X, the garden scene also plays an important role in making sense of the general enigma of Hoffmann's plot. The concept of "the garden" is a double signifier in Western culture: on the one hand, it represents a space where nature flourishes, while on the other hand it connotes scientific and academic research through its implicit reference to the Athenian Academy. In the same vein, at the time Hoffmann was writing gardens had become a symbol of pioneering scientific progress in France with the creation and development of the Versailles gardens beginning in the seventeenth century. Furthermore, when Descartes described the human body in *L'Homme* (*Treatise of Man*, 1632), he compared its muscles with the artificial waterworks in the Versailles gardens.[24] Within this mechanistic context, Hoffmann's garden is the metaphoric representation of the secrets of the human body, which are no longer a mystery to Professor X. Just as the kind and serene Professor engenders vitality in each element of the artificial garden that he walks by, so he imbues with life the mechanical bodies in his care.

By the time E. T. A. Hoffmann was writing "The Automata," the mechanistic views of the Enlightenment had lost their charm. Recoiling from a world disenchanted by the mechanistic mentality, the *Naturphilosoph* (natural philosopher) sought to revive the binary of Spirit/Matter while maintaining that this and other dualisms ultimately resolve into an "original oneness." Importantly, this promise of resolution provided solace in the midst of the violent political and social upheavals at the beginning of the nineteenth century.[25] Writing with an eye to this rejection of the mechanical worldview, Dieter Müller contends that "the Professor, as a type, is in Hoffmann's work a permanent supporter of the mechanistic-automatic Enlightenment Weltanschauung, which is ultimately destructive."[26] Despite the Professor's serene demeanor in the garden, and despite the apparent harmony of the exquisite music resulting from his interaction with the machines he has created in the form of a garden, Müller suggests that the garden and its creator signify destruction, as all technology – all separation

---

24 Thomas Fuchs, "Being a Psycho-Machine: Zur Phänomenologie der Beeinflussungsmaschinen," in *Fremdkontrolle: Ängste – Mythen – Praktiken* (Wiesbaden: Springer Fachmedien Wiesbaden, 2015), 38.
25 Minsoo Kang, *Sublime Dreams of Living Machines: The Automaton in the European Imagination* (Cambridge, MA: Harvard UP, 2011), 191.
26 Dieter Müller, "Zeit der Automate: Zum Automatenproblem bei Hoffmann," in *Mitteilungen der E. T. A. Hoffmann-Gesellschaft-Bamberg* 12 (1966): 6.

from the natural – is dangerous. This hypothesis seems solid, considering that Ferdinand's life is derailed and his sanity threatened after his meeting with the mechanical Turk. And yet, Ludwig's cryptic words at the end of the text complicate this interpretation. In his view Ferdinand is, after all, much better despite his breakdown. An alternative reading, more attuned to the contemporary discourses of *Naturphilosophie*, might point out that though the Professor is a supporter of the Enlightenment in his persona as mechanical conductor of the automatic orchestra – a caricature of the view that a human being is nothing more than a machine – there is another kind of scientist (the Professor's garden persona) capable of understanding the world in more than merely mechanical terms, through communication with forces that lie beyond the physical, mechanical sphere.

The harmony between what appears to be artificial nature and its human creator alerts the reader to the possibility that there might be something more positive at work in the construction of this particular mechanical garden. This deeper interest refers to the primary goal of Professor X's work, which, as the narrator clarifies for the reader, is the deep investigation and understanding of nature.[27] Interestingly, Leibniz, in section 67 of his *Monadology*, imagines each portion of matter in terms of a garden or pond: "Each portion of matter may be conceived as a garden full of plants, and a pond full of fish. But each branch of the plant, each member of the animal, each drop of its humors is also such a garden or such a pond."[28] The vision of nature that emerges from this metaphor, where nature is conceived as a medium that replicates itself ad infinitum, a symmetrical fractal-like structure, sheds light on the reasoning behind the professor's choice to create a garden. Against the background of Leibniz's linking together of gardens and the extraordinary harmony of nature, the Professor's decision to create a harmonious, soulful, artificial-yet-alive garden, can be understood as his desire to divine the basic structure of nature, which replicates and repeats itself ad infinitum. In this he exemplifies Giambattista Vico's *verum-factum* principle, according to which we only understand what we make for ourselves. The professor's desire to understand nature through technology presents technology as a *way to nature*, rather than something that threatens nature. And so it may be that the way to nature appears under its technological opposite. In fact, the logic of Martin Luther's *sub contraria specie* (hidden beneath its opposite) may be operative in a number of ways in the story – for example, in the suggestion that losing a beloved may actually be the way to finding her in a deeper,

---

27 Hoffmann, "Die Automate," 405.
28 Leibniz, *The Monadology*, 297.

more permanent manner, or again in the suggestion that descending into madness can bring much needed clarity. With respect to the relationship between technology and nature, the suggestion is that artificial forms can contain their opposite, the very essence of spirit – what I earlier called the "immaterial, spiritual substance found in all living things" studied by mesmerism, magnetism, and spiritualism and present in the Turk.

The human – a feeling machine

And so the story presents an artificial Turk, an artificial orchestra, a potentially artificial beloved, an artificial garden, and a professor who may have an artificial double that can complete tasks his builder would prefer to avoid since they interfere with time spent thinking and meditating. Within a fictional world where mechanisms are both alive and able to love, and in which nature and its mechanical double are indistinguishable, it is not surprising to hear a human being described in mechanical terms, especially at a moment of intensely human emotion such as the painful loss of the beloved. As is evident in Ferdinand's breakdown, a human body, when exposed to a shock that empties it of its own emotion and agency, is a ready vessel for spiritual forces outside itself. Ferdinand describes the moment when he is emptied of his emotional vitality (which then leaves him vulnerable to being filled later by external mysterious forces): "Mechanically, I go into the church, I step in exactly at the moment when the priest finalizes the blessing ceremony. I look over, the bride is the singer, she sees me, she pales, she plummets, the man behind her catches her in his arms, it is Professor X."[29] The bride collapses, perhaps due to overwhelming emotion, or, if she is an automaton, perhaps owing to a malfunction of the mechanism. In light of the later revelation that the Professor had never left the town, the scene, if it is not a hallucination inspired by Ferdinand's obsessive thinking, accords with the earlier hypothesis that a mechanical double of Professor X is performing a role in some mysterious plot.

This anxiety-riddled scene is replete with ambiguous images, where the line between the human and the mechanical is blurred. Ferdinand, the Professor, and the bride feel and/or act like mechanisms. This blurring of boundaries between the human and the mechanical is a source of anxiety for human beings, most immediately in the form of the uncanny feeling a human has when they are unable to distinguish what is mechanical from what is natural. The whole scene boils with anxieties related to technology: it reflects readers' anxiety over the difficulty

---

29 Hoffmann, "Die Automate," 405.

of distinguishing between mechanical and natural, while also speaking to the anxiety they feel in a world made increasingly strange and foreign by the increased presence of artificial dolls that can replicate human actions and even produce music, which used to be proof of human creativity and emotion. The unnerving encounter with technology can lead, in its turn, to the mechanization of the human being: Ferdinand's mechanical movements are the embodied expression of the continuous pressure to which he has been subjected since his encounter with the Turk. In light of Ferdinand's subsequent psychic disintegration, it is evident that a human being cannot be reduced to a mechanism without breaking down. And because the Turk plays such a central role in this disintegration, he – and the technology for which he stands – functions as a door to madness.

Seen against the background of a period in which the proliferation of mechanisms began to affect human self-perception, I would like to suggest that the Turk acts as an *influencing machine* within the narrative frame. The first description of an influencing machine by English physician and apothecary John Haslam in his *Illustrations of Madness* (1810) presents the case of James Tilly Matthews who, after his imprisonment in France during the Reign of Terror, during which the continual threat of the guillotine loomed large, described upon his return to London an intricate mechanism that was used to wirelessly control his actions. He names this influencing machine the "air loom" and he depicts the "assailing gang" that controls the machine as

> assassins [who] are so superlatively skillful in every thing which relates to pneumatic chemistry, physiology, nervous influence, sympathy, human mind, and the higher metaphysic [that] whenever their persons shall be discovered, and their machine exhibited, the wisest professors will be astonished at their progress, and feel ashamed at their own ignorance.[30]

The way in which Matthews describes the "air loom's" transmission of its influencing waves, which can control the behavior of a human being, as well as that of a whole society, is similar to the wireless transmission at work in Franz Mesmer's animal magnetism, also known as mesmerism.[31]

Haslam's book on the "influencing machine" inaugurated a new era in which people began to describe their psychological disturbances, especially those cases of what would later be diagnosed as schizophrenia, in terms of evil influencing mechanisms, superseding "older delusions shaped by magic or religion."[32] This phenomenon of describing mental disturbances as a result

---

30 John Haslam, *Illustration of Madness* (London: G. Hayden, 1810), 57.
31 Fuchs, "Being a Psycho-Machine," 29.
32 Fuchs, "Being a Psycho-Machine," 26.

of influencing machines occurred more frequently as the nineteenth century proceeded. Impressed by the pervasiveness of notions about influencing machines among the mentally ill, the psychoanalyst Viktor Tausk addressed the phenomenon in 1919 with an analysis of the origins and functioning of such machines.

Tausk described the influencing machine as a mechanism of mysterious origins: though patients marshal all their technical knowledge to describe the complicated systems of wheels and mechanical contraptions that make up the machine, the present stage of mechanical development is never adequate to describe and explain how the mechanism functions and how it can follow and persecute the patient. The influencing machine presents the following characteristics:

> It makes the patients see pictures [. . .]; it produces, as well as removes, thoughts and feelings by means of waves and rays or mysterious forces which the patient's knowledge of physics is inadequate to explain [. . .]; it produces motor phenomena in the body, erections and seminal emissions [. . .]; it creates sensations that in part cannot be described, because they are strange to the patient himself, and that in part are sensed as electrical, magnetic, or due to air-currents [. . .].[33]

This modern manifestation of mental illness affords a new perspective on Hoffmann's Turk. The Turk functions as an influencing machine insofar as it elicits reactions and emotions from the public, and in particular from Ferdinand. It causes both Ferdinand and Ludwig to hear the mysterious song of Ferdinand's secret love;[34] it reads Ferdinand's secret thoughts about the very existence of this beloved; it causes bodily feelings in Ferdinand, who pales and suffers physical distress as a result of the encounter; it produces extreme emotional reactions in the public in general and in Ferdinand in particular; it plants the haunting thought of losing a secret beloved in Ferdinand's mind; it influences Ferdinand and Ludwig's actions on their journey to discover the automaton's secret. The actions described above parallel the effects of the influencing machine highlighted by Tausk.

These actions also accord with many aspects of the politics of emotions discussed by Ahmed, including the phenomenon of impersonal political forces generating compelling emotions in people. Hoffmann's Turk, an impersonal mechanism, puts *the fear of loss* into Ferdinand. It overwhelms Ferdinand with an emotion that has its provenance outside of him. Some might read this simply

---

33 Viktor Tausk, "On the Origin of the 'Influencing Machine' in Schizophrenia," trans. Dorian Feigenbaum, *The Journal of Psychotherapy Practice and Research* 1, no. 2 (1992): 186.

34 This shared experience is also an example of *Mitsein*, of an intense interpersonal emotional sympathy that allows Ludwig to join with Ferdinand as the latter relives an earlier experience of a song sung by his beloved.

as mesmeric influence. But in a text that features a level of complexity that rivals that of an intricate machine, very little is allowed to be what it "simply" seems to be. As I elaborate below, I read the Turk's injection of feeling into Ferdinand as Hoffmann's metaphoric imaging of the fact that political and social mechanisms generate emotion in their subjects. As Ahmed demonstrates, political forces create feelings in humans through repetitive actions (where feelings are "effects of repetition").[35] These repetitive actions reinforce acceptable feelings. The mechanical Turk, generating powerful feeling in Ferdinand, is a physical manifestation of this larger mechanistic production of emotion in the social sphere. This should not come as a surprise in a story that features mechanisms that produce repetitive music (in parallel with social mechanisms that produce repetitive emotions), and which troubles the ability to distinguish between mechanisms and human beings (which points to the fact that one cannot distinguish in one's own experience an emotion that has its origin in the human heart from emotion that is produced by external forces). Furthermore, the Turk represents political forces (both are impersonal mechanisms) that have the power, as Ahmed points out, not only to control feelings but to compel *action*, as can be seen by Ferdinand's subsequent obsessive need to get to the bottom of things.

Additionally, when the Turk injects the fear of loss into Ferdinand, this fear quickly mutates from a fear of loss of the beloved, to a fear of loss of the self to death, or to madness, or to a domineering father. By the story's end the fear is one of losing a secret, inviolable self, not just a secret beloved. All of Ferdinand's subsequent feelings are, in their origin, the work of the machine. This rapid-fire transference of fear to different objects is an instance of what Ahmed terms "stickiness": in Ferdinand's experience, objects of fear are substituted for each other, each one transferring the terror associated with it to the next object, just as one object communicates its stickiness to another.[36] The fact that the original emotion spreads its infection to other objects testifies to the reach and scope of the initially implanted emotion.

A further dimension of the influencing machine needs to be taken into account. A person is threatened, not only by the machine, but by the powers behind the machine. The person controlled by the machine – whether the machine is the Turk in the story or the "air loom" in James Tilly Matthews's account – is most fundamentally controlled by the powers that control the machine. Matthews names these powers behind the scene the "assailing gang."[37] In Hoffmann's own context,

---

35 Ahmed, *Cultural Politics of Emotion*, 12.
36 Ahmed, *Cultural Politics of Emotion*, 90–91.
37 Haslam, *Illustration of Madness*, 29.

the assailing gang can be understood in different ways: it can be construed in terms of a web of political powers whose connections were hard to pinpoint (especially after the Holy Roman Empire dissolved in 1806); or in terms of the societal structures that fixed each person's position in the social order; or in terms of the power relationships in the family. Interestingly, in Hoffmann's story the automaton qua influencing machine seems to be controlled by at least three people: the nameless peddler who presents the Turk to the townspeople; Professor X, who improved the automaton's mechanism; and a third man who appears to know some of the automaton's secrets. Taken together, the three appear as something like an "assailing gang," influencing Ferdinand and others in various ways. The fear of such a conspiratorial power leads to anxiety and loss of agency.

The placing of an "assailing gang" behind an influencing machine turns the machine itself into a front that masks the people or powers that control it. Hoffmann suggests as much when he wonders aloud if the Turk is not a mere distraction. The automaton has been constructed in such a way as to veil the secret behind it:

> With respect to our Turk, there was something quite peculiar about him. According to the description of all those who saw him, his face is very respectable and honorable. Yet this face is only of secondary importance, and the rolling of his eyes, as well as the turning of his head, are certainly only a ruse to turn the attention of the public entirely to *him*, for the key of its secret is most certainly *not* there.[38]

What interests Ferdinand is "the spiritual power of the unknown human being," the human spirit behind the machine who is the controlling power behind the smoke and mirrors.[39] With Ferdinand's suggestion that the automaton is a diversion, Hoffmann offers his readers a key to understanding the text. The Turk and his oracular sentences mask several things at once: they divert the readers' attention from other hidden automata in the story; they conceal the motives of the person or persons behind the Turk; and they distract both characters and readers from asking the question of what the Turk himself might represent (viz. an influencing machine).

The victims of influencing machines, as Haslam and Tausk make clear in their different ways, understand the machine itself to be a mere prop for the nefarious intentions of the human being(s) who control it. Hoffmann's Turk functions as such a prop; Ferdinand comes to believe that this machine is the apparatus through which both his future and his beloved are controlled by a maleficent Professor X. And, as if to underscore the machine's diabolical power, both Haslam

---

38 Hoffmann, "Die Automate," 331.
39 Hoffmann, "Die Automate," 332.

and Tausk claim that the influencing machine can exert its controlling power over both the individual and groups of people *without their knowledge*. For his part, Ferdinand is all too aware that he is at the mercy of a diabolical power. He pleads with Ludwig in a fit of despair:

> Be true to me! Do not abandon me! I feel, too clearly, some hostile foreign influence at work upon my whole existence, smiting upon all its hidden strings, and making them resound at its pleasure. I am helpless to resist it, though it should drive me to my destruction! Can that diabolical, sneering sarcasm, with which the Professor received us at his house, have been anything other than the expression of this hostile principle? Was it with any other intention than of getting rid of me forever, that he tricked us off with those automata of his?[40]

At the end of the story Ludwig considers the same idea in his own way: "Could all this, he thought, be merely the result of a clash of mysterious psychic connections that perhaps exist among several people, that manage to find their way into everyday life and which could influence in their circle events that are independent of them, but which the deluded inner self looks upon as phenomena resulting inextricably from oneself, and believes in them accordingly?"[41] These "several people" who are able to influence "events that are independent of them," could be seen, in Haslam's terms, as an "assailing gang."

The human as marionette in the hands of politics

Seeing the Turk as an influencing machine controlled by a malevolent power sets the stage for the revelation of the Turk's final function in the text: ultimately the influencing machine metaphorically dramatizes *the state's control* over the life of the individual. Both the mechanical Turk itself, and the nefarious force behind the machine – the powerful paternal figure Professor X – represent in different ways the power of the state. German cultural spaces were rife with political uncertainty at the time Hoffmann wrote his story, and the anxieties to which this situation contributed form an important context for Hoffmann's work.

The history of administrative power in German cultural spaces in the long nineteenth century was marked by the dissolution of the Holy Roman Empire of the German Nation and by various reactions to that dissolution. The Empire had been an intricate and decentralized political entity until its official dissolution

---

40 Hoffmann, "Die Automate," 404.
41 Hoffmann, "Die Automate," 406.

in 1806. It had provided political unity to what was, in fact, a fragmentary entity: under the giant tent of the Holy Roman Empire of the German Nation were united hundreds of various types of smaller or larger administrative units that were independent to the extent that the authority of the local princes (kings, abbots, counts, dukes, and so forth) superseded the imperial authority. This state of affairs was evident, for example, in the inconsistent reaction of the leadership of the various German cultural domains to the French Revolution in 1789, where the German response ranged from ardent support to condemnation.[42] In the wake of the official dissolution of the imperial entity, which had offered a semblance of unity to the many German states, conflicts and unrest began to flare up; these conflicts continued, in fact, even after the establishment of the German Confederation in 1815, which was a loose form of association without a head of state or superior court. As members of the new political entity, the independent states of the Confederation continued to go about their own business in a fragmentary manner.

Interestingly, this political state of affairs set the stage for literature to play an important role in bringing together the fragmented and politically diverse German states. As early as the eighteenth century, Gotthold Ephraim Lessing wrote about the importance of dramatic representation for crystallizing and maintaining a German cultural unity in the absence of political unity, proposing that cultural unity might ultimately lead to state unity. Georg Wilhelm Friedrich Hegel also emphasized the role played by dramatic theater in the cultivation of national awareness. It was in this fragmented German context that the German Romantics began to champion the idea of the *Volk* (people, nation) and its *Volksgeist* (spirit of a people). Johann Gottfried von Herder's interest in the *Volk* arose out of his experience of the fragmentary state of the German people.

The connection, then, between politics and literary automata can best be appreciated by acknowledging the constant feeling of threat associated with politics that hung, like a sword of Damocles, over the heads of Germans living in the early nineteenth century. A feeling of inescapable flux, brought on by the succession of revolutions in France, began to pervade German political life, generating considerable anxiety. The threat of revolution in Germany posed a continual danger, not only to one's livelihood, but to one's life. This new political flux and the insecurity it brought with it gave rise to vexing, anxious questions – who is in power? what shall become of us? The whole situation threatened acute psychological disturbance for people living in Central Europe. It is in this context that the Turk emerges as a compelling literary figure. The Turk stands in for the

---

42 David Blackbourn, *The Long Nineteenth Century: A History of Germany, 1770–1918* (New York: Oxford UP, 1998), 47–90.

political menace felt by many; the questions asked in the political sphere – who is in power? what shall become of us? – are questions directed to the Turk in Hoffmann's story.

The fact that the Turk is a *mechanism* is also relevant to the political discourse of the time, for the state had been described metaphorically with mechanistic terminology throughout the eighteenth and nineteenth centuries. Nathan Ross discusses Johann Gottfried Herder's displeasure with a modern state "guilty of overstepping its bounds and stifling the natural organic process of culture": Herder "often refers to the state as a machine, a mechanism. But in his usage of this figure, he is reversing the largely positive meaning that it had for the Enlightenment thinkers [. . .] Herder views these [. . .] machine-like aspects of the state as forces that threaten to undermine the organism of society."[43] Dietrich Kreplin condenses the various ways in which Hoffmann describes the state apparatus as machinery in his fiction:

> The life of the princedom, of the state apparatus of the ruler, is operated by the interaction of many interconnecting wheels. This interconnection of the various state functions is compared to the wheel mechanism of a machine, and the course of events inside the little princedom is compared to the image of an operating machine.[44]

This representation of the state or social organization in terms of a mechanism may have been inspired by Heinrich von Kleist's *Über das Marionettentheater* (*On the Marionette Theatre*, 1810), which is usually read as a satirical remark "on socially imposed mechanical movements."[45] For Timothy Mehigan, Kleist's marionette was a clear mirror to Kleist's own feelings in regard to being controlled, as the marionette "vividly expressed what had troubled Kleist throughout [the] early years of his life – namely a deep sense of a man's powerlessness in the face of overwhelming chaotic forces that usurp his freedom of action."[46]

Kleist spoke of the "puppet's soul, but praised in it its perfect mechanical accord with the law of gravity, whereas humans were always placing their souls, as it were, at odds with it."[47] Consequently, perfection is embodied only in the marionette and in God. In the case of "The Automata," Professor X and his automata are

---

43 Nathan Ross, *On Mechanism in Hegel's Social and Political Philosophy* (New York: Routledge, 2008), 17.

44 Dietrich Kreplin, *Das Automaten-Motiv bei E. T. A. Hoffmann* (PhD diss., Rheinische-Friedrich-Wilhelms-Universität Bonn, 1957), 22–23.

45 Katherine Hirt, *When Machines Play Chopin: Musical Spirit and Automation in Nineteenth-Century German Literature* (Berlin: De Gruyter, 2010), 2–3.

46 Timothy Mehigan, *Heinrich von Kleist: Writing after Kant* (New York: Boydell & Brewer, 2011), 87.

47 Barbara Johnson, *Persons and Things* (Cambridge, MA: Harvard UP, 2008), 87.

the "perfected" beings who are untouchable and incomprehensible to mere mortals. As such it comes as no surprise that the mechanical beings in Hoffmann's story enjoy a stability and serenity, as does their creator, in sharp contrast to the continual distress of the young men. Human beings in general, Hoffmann seems to say, are distressed creatures, equipped with little agency and at the mercy of implacable powers. Ironically, he suggests that if they only accepted their lack of agency and stopped bucking against it, if they only allowed themselves to become automata or marionettes so as to let the forces that control them act through them, then they would attain serenity. Madness comes from opposing the powerful forces of the state, society, and family.

Kleist describes the movements of the marionette in terms of a single impulse that can cause complicated dances:

> Every movement, he said, had a centre of gravity; it sufficed if this, inside the figure, were controlled; the limbs, which were nothing but pendula, followed without further interference, mechanically, of their own accord. He added that this movement was a very simple one; that whenever the centre of gravity was moved *in a straight line* the limbs described a *curve*; and that often, if shaken by accident, the whole thing was brought into a kind of rhythmical activity similar to dancing.[48]

In order to achieve the graceful movements of the dance, the manipulator of the doll has to project herself into the doll's center of gravity, and thus in a sense she herself is dancing or, better yet, she *is* the doll while the doll moves. The smallest movement originating with the manipulator produces complex and ongoing reactions in the puppet. In the same way, a small sentence uttered by the Turk affects Ferdinand in his very center of gravity; both he and Ludwig lose their own equilibrium as a result. The same dynamic was at work in the relation between a state and its citizens: the smallest legal stipulation generated predictable behavior on the part of the citizens as they followed the law's lead and danced to its tune. The route of escape from the ubiquitous influence of the Turk, as well as the controlling power of the state, is either to abscond to a region beyond the reach of these controlling forces – in Ferdinand's case he flees to the "North," presumably to the large unchartered area of the frozen Arctic – or to allow one's mind to wander into regions not governed by reason and so find refuge in madness.

---

48 Heinrich von Kleist, *Selected Writings*, ed. and trans. David Constantine (London: J. M. Dent, 1997), 411–412.

Conclusion

Gathering together all these various threads, we can see the multiple roles played by the Turk in Ferdinand's (d)evolution. Through his *alivedeadness*, the automaton is a mirror to the fact that Ferdinand's life harbors death at its core. It is the mysterious force that penetrates the victim's most intimate thoughts, foretelling disaster in the future. It is the mouthpiece of an inimical force that seeks to control Ferdinand's life. It is the metaphorical representation of controlling systems that elude the young man's understanding, including the family (representing the social system) and the state (representing the political system) that determine his existence.

Professor X, the paternal figure who controls both knowledge and access to the libidinal object (the mysterious singer in Ferdinand's case, the Turk in Ludwig's case), is also the manipulator of the Turk. Professor X and his double play the ultimate role in Ferdinand's breakdown: while Ferdinand is on his way to see his father upon the latter's request, he sees the professor (or his double), who is the father of the Turk, performing the role of the father of the mysterious singer as he is escorting her to the altar to give her away in marriage. As such, Professor X – the father of the automata, the father who gives away the beloved, the desired father-in-law – also melds with Ferdinand's own father. At the same time, he is the absolute ruler of his orchestra of automata and of an entire artificial garden.

Nonetheless, Ferdinand's father, the Professor, and the Professor's automata are only a small-scale representation of the larger mechanisms and manipulators that are controlling the young man's life. The father and the Professor are the equivalent of an absolutist ruler who controls the lives of his subjects. Within this framework, the Turk himself is the state's political mechanism that leaves little space for independent action: it gives an oracular sentence regarding a person's future which thereafter influences the person's every action, just as Kleist's marionettes needed a mere impulse in their center of gravity to start to dance.

Ferdinand's mechanical movements on his way to his father's home, most pointedly on display during the scene at the church that leads to his breakdown, cast him in the role of an automaton. In fact, members of society are all automata insofar as they seemingly act independently within an established framework, but they do so according to social conventions which, when internalized, are transmuted into the impulses that control their lives. Viewed within the context of the "air loom" and its invisible ways of controlling human beings, Hoffmann's story reconceives the nature of the Great Puppeteer that controls the trajectory of a human being's life. Challenging the traditional emphasis on fate or God, the story bestows the controlling power both to mechanical forces and that which drives them – both to the Turk and Professor X, both to the state and its ruler. The invisible influences exerted by these mechanical forces can transform human beings into marionettes, which is one step removed from madness.

Bibliography

Ahmed, Sara. *The Cultural Politics of Emotion* (Edinburgh: Edinburgh UP, 2014).

Boie, Bernhild. "Die Sprache der Automaten: Zur Autonomie der Kunst," in *German Quarterly* 54, no. 3 (1981): 284–297.

Fuchs, Thomas. "Being a Psycho-Machine: Zur Phänomenologie der Beeinflussungsmaschinen," in *Fremdkontrolle: Ängste – Mythen – Praktiken* (Wiesbaden: Springer Fachmedien Wiesbaden, 2015), 127–143.

Gassen, Hans-Günther, and Sabine Minol. *Die Menschenmacher: Sehnsucht nach Unsterblichkeit* (Weinheim: Wiley-VCH, 2006).

Haslam, John. *Illustration of Madness: Exhibiting a Singular Case of Insanity, and no Less Remarkable Difference in Medical Opinion: Developing the Nature of Assailment, and the Manner of Working Events; With a Description of the Tortures Experienced by Bomb-bursting, Lobster-cracking and Lengthening the Brain. Embellished with a Curious Plate* (London: G. Hayden, 1810).

Hirt, Katherine. *When Machines Play Chopin: Musical Spirit and Automation in Nineteenth-Century German Literature* (Berlin: De Gruyter, 2010).

Hoffmann, E. T. A. "Die Automate" in *Die Serapions-Brüder* (Munich: Winkler, 1963).

Johnson, Barbara. *Persons and Things* (Cambridge, MA: Harvard UP, 2008).

Kang, Minsoo. *Sublime Dreams of Living Machines: The Automaton in the European Imagination* (Cambridge, MA: Harvard UP, 2011).

Kleist, Heinrich von. *Selected Writings*. Ed. and trans. David Constantine (London: J. M. Dent, 1997).

Krause, Marcus. "Der zerstückelte Körper und die Sprachmaschine: Poes materialistische Experimente," in *Literarische Experimentalkulturen: Poetologien des Experiments im 19. Jahrhundert*. Eds. Marcus Krause and Nicolas Pethes (Würzburg: Königshausen & Neumann, 2005), 287–304.

Kreplin, Dietrich. *Das Automaten-Motiv bei E. T. A. Hoffmann* (PhD diss., Rheinische-Friedrich-Wilhelms-Universität Bonn, 1957).

Krzywkowski, Isabelle. "Créature créaturée et créature créaturante: les jeux du dédoublement et l'esthétique du morcellement," in *L'Homme artificiel: Hoffmann, Shelley, Villiers De L'isle-Adam* (Paris: Ellipses, 1999), 160–176.

Leibniz, Gottfried Willhelm. *The Monadology and Other Philosophical Writings*. Trans. Robert Latta (New York: Oxford UP, 1971).

Levitt, Gerald. *The Turk, Chess Automaton* (Jefferson, NC: McFarland and Company, 2006).

Mehigan, Timothy. *Heinrich von Kleist: Writing after Kant* (New York: Boydell & Brewer Group Ltd, 2011).

Müller, Dieter. "Zeit der Automate: Zum Automatenproblem bei Hoffmann," in *Mitteilungen der E. T. A. Hoffmann-Gesellschaft-Bamberg* 12 (1966): 1–10.

Nühnen, Vanessa. *Maschinenmenschen und künstliche Menschen in der Literatur zur Zeit der Industrialisierung: Vom Traum, Leben zu erschaffen* (Munich: GRIN Verlag GmbH, 2010).

Poe, Edgar A. *Edgar Allan Poe: The Dover Reader* (Mineola, NY: Dover Publications, 2014).

Retzlaff, Jonathan, and Cheri Montgomery. *Exploring Art Song Lyrics: Translation and Pronunciation of the Italian, German & French Repertoire* (New York: Oxford UP, 2012).

Ross, Nathan. *On Mechanism in Hegel's Social and Political Philosophy* (New York: Routledge, 2008).

Tausk, Viktor. "On the Origin of the 'Influencing Machine' in Schizophrenia." Trans. Dorian Feigenbaum. *The Journal of Psychotherapy Practice and Research* 1, no. 2 (1992): 184–206.

Derek Hillard
Animals and Aesthetic Empathy in Germany around 1900

Empathy has emerged as a key concept in discussions about relations between humans and non-human animals. Scholars of animal studies typically conceive of empathy as a phenomenon that is explicitly ethical, one that is often guided by specific norms with an eye to particular desired processes and outcomes. Lori Gruen, for instance, favors the concept of "entangled empathy," which "includes perception, reflection, and care" in a process that, while it "may not be linear," begins by noticing the "well-being of another," is followed by a reflective imagining of the Other, "making sure to more or less partition [one's] own perspective," with a subsequent step of forming a "judgment" of the other's state, and concludes by assessing and determining "what information is pertinent to effectively help" the empathetic object.[1] Informed by ethical norms, this model of empathy has become the most prominent in animal studies.

I would like to explore a German historical discourse that developed an *aesthetic* framework for empathy, and thereby expand the range of empathetic modes up for discussion in animal studies. This discourse devoted greater attention to the role that imagination plays in empathy, which we could also refer to as "make-believe" or illusion. The nineteenth-century German discourse of *Einfühlung* ("feeling-into"), which bears a family resemblance to empathy, emphasized these features of aesthetic perception and imagination. Whereas contemporary theory stresses Otherness and radical difference of non-human animals, the discussion about empathy can benefit from the exploration of meaningful relatedness based on shared features of human and non-human animal worlds, which was a key feature of *Einfühlung*. In particular, the possibility that emotion plays a role in the sensuous perception of non-human animals may point to new ways for imagining human/non-human animal relations. What would it mean for our understanding of empathy if the basic ways in which humans and animals perceive each other have similarities?

Scholars such as Elisa Aaltola and Ralph R. Acampora wonder what allows humans to be empathetic "not only towards human subjects but also towards

---

1 Lori Gruen, "Empathy," in *Critical Terms for Animal Studies*, ed. Lori Gruen (Chicago: U of Chicago Press, 2018), 147.

https://doi.org/10.1515/9783110753677-003

non-human beings?"[2] Linking the urgency of this question to a new validation of a moral relation to animals based not on rationality but on emotions, Aaltola stresses empathy's quality that "renders us into moral creatures" and enables mind reading.[3] Aaltola relies on the ethologist Frans de Waal's work on empathy derived from primate studies, which argues for a notion of evolutionarily hardwired empathy activated by "neural and bodily representations" through which one can attend to the states of another.[4] In turning to emotion, Aaltola emphasizes "affective empathy," which, she contends, is "immediate, the typical example being when we witness someone undergoing sorrow and begin to feel tearful."[5] Preferring the term "compassion" as a mediation for "interspecies morality," Acampora emphasizes the bodily condition of humans as a source for this emotion.[6]

It is intriguing that scholars such as Aaltola, Acampora, and Gruen turn to empathy for a productive mode of human-animal relations. However, this turn to empathy is hardly new. As Thomas A. Kohut has recently shown, in the nineteenth and early twentieth century, empathy was central to epistemological discussions regarding both the human and natural sciences.[7] While predecessors such as Maurice Merleau-Ponty, Max Scheler, or Edith Stein have been acknowledged in animal studies, the roots of empathy for animals in the nineteenth-century German discourse of *Einfühlungsästhetik* (empathy aesthetics) have not been mentioned in discussions.[8] Writers who engaged with aesthetics and empathy between 1860 and 1900 developed suggestive notions for explaining how humans rely on emotions and imagination to make sense of animals. By recalling this nineteenth-century German focus on aesthetics, contemporary discourses on empathy can benefit from a consideration of its emphasis on the emotional and aesthetic qualities involved in the sensuous perception of non-human animals.

---

2 Elisa Aaltola, *Varieties of Empathy: Moral Psychology and Animal Ethics* (London: Rowman & Littlefield, 2018), 11. See also Lori Gruen, *Entangled Empathy* (New York: Lantern Books, 2015), as well as Josephine Donovan, "Attention to Suffering: Sympathy as a Basis for Ethical Treatment of Animals," in *The Feminist Care Tradition in Animal Ethics*, eds. Josephine Donovan and Carol Adams (New York: Columbia UP, 2007), 58–86.
3 Aaltola, *Varieties of Empathy*, 17.
4 Frans de Waal, "Putting the Altruism Back into Altruism: The Evolution of Empathy," *Annual Review of Psychology* 59 (2008): 280.
5 Aaltola, *Varieties of Empathy*, 82–83.
6 Ralph R. Acampora, *Corporal Compassion: Animal Ethics and Philosophy of Body* (Pittsburgh: U of Pittsburgh Press, 2006), 23.
7 Thomas A. Kohut, *Empathy and the Historical Understanding of the Human Past* (London: Routledge, 2020), 18–21.
8 For an overview of Scheler and Stein, see Kohut, *Empathy*, 30–32.

The notion that emotions are central to empathetic interaction with animals was a key thesis in discourses of *Einfühlung*, where assumptions of corporal empathy or somatic compassion have roots. Far from wishing to dismiss empathy, I would like to build on contemporary discussions and their concerns with emotions and corporeality to explore aesthetic empathy, that is, the reliance on imaginative and sensuous processes to track human/non-human animal relations. For the purposes of the present study, aesthetics is understood not as synonymous with making something beautiful. Instead, my use here is guided by eighteenth-century meanings of aesthetics in terms of being affected by the sensuous qualities of what is perceived.

This sense of "aesthetic" was initiated by the German philosopher Alexander Gottlieb Baumgarten. Seeing the need for a "science of cognition by the senses," Baumgarten developed the idea that the sensuous perception of the world possesses its own unique clarity, which can be distinguished from that related to logical processing. In a return to ancient understandings, Baumgarten considered this science to be one that concerned both sensual cognition and its expression or representation.[9] This idea was clearly influential for Immanuel Kant's understanding of aesthetics as "a science of all principles of sensibility."[10] While it is not the purpose of this essay to explore extensively the history of aesthetics in Germany, it is interesting to note that Friedrich Theodor Vischer, whom we can consider the first to discuss *Einfühlung* psychologically, found it necessary in the 1860s to revise his otherwise Hegelian philosophy so as to give greater consideration to the question of sensuous perception. In other words, it is not by chance that the new philosophy of *Einfühlung* coincided with a return to or reevaluation of sensuous aesthetics.[11]

Before continuing with a discussion of *Einfühlung* and non-human animals, some comments regarding emotions are in order. For centuries, affective discourses have been largely indebted to assumptions about subjective interiority as the origin of emotions. According to this model, emotions are more or less contained within us where they rise to the surface and get expressed or released, often overwhelming the rational and restrained self in the process. Scholars have traced this emotional model to the early modern

---

9 Martin Fontius, "Ästhetik/ästhetisch," in *Ästhetische Grundbegriffe*, eds. Karlheinz Barck, Martin Fontius, Dieter Schelenstedt, Burkhart Steinwachs, and Friedrich Wolfzettel, vol. 1, *Absenz – Darstellung* (Stuttgart: Metzler, 2000), 324.
10 *Oxford English Dictionary Online*. June 2020. Oxford UP, s.v. "aesthetic."
11 Fontius, "Ästhetik/ästhetisch," 369.

period and Martin Luther's notion of the "inner man."[12] Pietist movements, the context of the court versus the intimate realm of the heart, eighteenth-century sentimentality, and German Romanticism remain touchstones in the development of emotional interiority. This model of emotions is also prevalent in many areas of ethology and cultural animal studies. Frans de Waal, for instance, views feelings as internal, known only to those who have them, while emotions are external expressions, observable from the outside.[13] While this has been the most dominant conception of emotions, it is not the only one. In developing a broader range of emotional models, scholars have recently investigated the role that materiality, things, and bodies take.[14] The way in which objects, such as works of art, tools, or things in nature, and bodies can be said to possess agency and place demands on us has led to new insights.

Animal emotions and human compassion

The question of animal emotions was widely contested in nineteenth-century Germany. Popular lexica, for instance, which Pascal Eitler has investigated, indicate how views regarding animal sentience diverged and developed.[15] In the first half of the 1800s, writers of such reference works considered it highly doubtful that animals experienced feelings beyond sensations. This assumption relied on a distinction dating back at least to the eighteenth century between sensations (*Empfindungen*), which were readily ascribed to both animals and humans, and emotions (*Gefühle* or *Affekte*), which had an ideational, intellectual (*geistig*) quality, and were limited to humans. Yet by the middle of the nineteenth century, debate in the pages of the same lexica became more spirited, as some thinkers and scientists began to assert that animals indeed were in possession of a "geistige[s] Gefühlsleben" ("mental-emotional life").[16] By 1875, *Brockhaus*,

12 Rüdiger Campe and Julia Weber, eds. *Rethinking Emotion: Interiority and Exteriority in Premodern, Modern, and Contemporary Thought* (Berlin: De Gruyter, 2014).
13 Frans de Waal, *Mama's Last Hug: Animal Emotions and What They Tell Us about* Ourselves (New York: W. W. Norton, 2019), 4.
14 Stephanie Downes, Sally Holloway, and Sarah Randles, eds., *Feeling Things. Objects and Emotions through History* (Oxford: Oxford UP, 2018); Hartmut Böhme, *Fetishism and Culture: A Different Theory of Modernity* (Boston: De Gruyter, 2014); Derek Hillard, Heikki Lempa, and Russell Spinney, eds., *Feelings Materialized: Emotions, Bodies, and Things in Germany, 1500–1950* (New York: Berghahn Books, 2020).
15 Pascal Eitler, "'Weil sie fühlen, was wir fühlen.' Menschen, Tiere und die Genealogie der Emotionen im 19. Jahrhundert," *Historische Anthropologie* 19, no. 2 (2011): 211.
16 Eitler, "'Weil sie fühlen, was wir fühlen,'" 216.

a leading lexicon, could simply state "the assertion that only humans are capable of emotions [*Affekte*] is baseless."[17]

Informing these changes in popular lexica concerning knowledge about animal emotions were the debates taking place in the works of philosophers and scientists. These creators of knowledge argued over the nature or objective existence of animal emotions as well as the extent to which humans are conditioned to feel empathy toward non-human animals. For instance, in the late 1800s, the promotion of experiencing "Mitgefühl" (compassion) for animals, both for the moralizing effect on humans and for the protection of animals, was widely discussed.[18] In the eyes of many, this widened the distance assumed to exist between animals and things while at the same time closing the distance placed between humans and animals. The Hegelian philosopher Max Schasler wrote in the 1880s:

> the animal is distinguished in particular not just because it has "life" but also a soul along with the organs and senses that are appropriate to its activity. It expresses itself in a form analogous to humans, particularly through the voice, in which higher animals are skilled. This state of ensoulment is primarily responsible for placing animals in a position that is sympathetic to humans.[19]

In a range of late nineteenth-century publications, *Mitgefühl* for animals was promoted as an essential part of moral pedagogy. At the same time, as the passage above shows, a different interest in aesthetic and symbolic processes of perceiving non-human life was growing.

German naturalists increasingly claimed not only that animals possessed a range of emotions, but that they also displayed empathy. Writing in 1865, the entomologist Maximilian Perty argued that "Animals will at times display empathy [*Mitgefühl*] for other sick, wounded, older animals, for young animals, also for humans."[20] Such contentions indicate that empathy was at times believed to be a condition of both animals and humans. Scholars such as the literary historian Richard Weltrich widened the discussion to assert a connection between moral empathy (*Mitgefühl*) and *Einfühlung*, which I will discuss presently. Writing in 1898, Weltrich saw Friedrich Theodor Vischer – considered the initiator of the new discourse on empathy – in a line of German thinkers, including Johann Gottfried Herder and Arthur Schopenhauer, who advocated for an improvement for the lot of animals:

---

17 Eitler, "'Weil sie fühlen, was wir fühlen,'" 216.
18 Eitler, "'Weil sie fühlen, was wir fühlen,'" 218.
19 Max Schasler, *Ästhetik. Grundzüge der Wissenschaft des Schönen und der Kunst, Erster Teil* (Leipzig: G. Freytag, 1886), 151. All translations are mine unless indicated otherwise.
20 Maximilian Perty, *Über das Seelenleben der Thiere* (Leipzig: C. F. Winter: 1865), 60.

Among the Hegelians, Friedrich Th. Vischer preached compassion [*Mitgefühl*] for animals as a requirement of a developed humanity: compassion with the suffering of animals, for him, derives from the notion that it makes present the inner state of another being, and whoever has not yet progressed this far, remains a brute.[21]

It is curious and significant that at least two of the thinkers that Weltrich mentioned, Herder and Vischer, were considered to form part of the discourse of *Einfühlung*. Slipping between the language of aesthetics and animal protection ethics (*Schonung der Tiere*), the author asserts that the pantheistic view (*der Pantheismus*) calls for "an affectionate and knowing empathy [*Einfühlung*]" for all fellow creatures.[22] In the 1890s, the psychiatrist Robert Sommer summarized the development in philosophical views regarding animals from René Descartes via Gottfried Wilhelm Leibniz to Johann Gottfried Herder as "progressive animation of nature" (*Naturbeseelung*). He asserted that "the preoccupation with animal life and the creation of animal psychology" was not a mere side effect of the transition to a Herderian *Pandynamismus*, but was instrumental for its rise.[23]

Einfühlung and aesthetics

The linkage of moral empathy to aesthetic empathy by scholars such as Weltrich notwithstanding, we would do well to recall that *Einfühlung* was an aesthetic discourse. While the aim of this essay is to discuss *Einfühlung* and non-human animals, rather than to give an account of the history of *Einfühlung*, a sketch of its conceptual emergence is useful. The place where *Einfühlung* first historically appears as a concept is a matter of some debate. Since the late nineteenth-century, most thinkers assumed that *Einfühlung* grew out of German Romanticism.[24]

More recently, scholars have sought to locate the emergence of the figure of identification with fictional characters and their emotions – if not the word *Einfühlung* itself – in the German Enlightenment, specifically, in letters of 1757 written by Gotthold Ephraim Lessing. Lessing discussed the way in which the viewers of tragedy experience an emotional (*Seele*) resonance with the tragic protagonist's experiences on the stage. Calling this a "secondary affect," Lessing was dismissive of its relevance for the development of theater, privileging

---

21 Richard Weltrich, *Christian Wagner, der Bauer und Dichter zu Warmbronn: eine ästhetisch-kritische und sozialethische Studie* (Stuttgart: Strecker & Moser, 1898), 224.
22 Weltrich, *Christian Wagner, der Bauer und Dichter zu Warmbronn*, 182.
23 Robert Sommer, *Grundzüge einer Geschichte der deutschen Psychologie und Aesthetik von Wolff-Baumgarten bis Kant-Schiller* (Stuttgart: Stahel, 1892), 89–90.
24 Fontius, "Ästhetik/ästhetisch," 126.

instead emotions that viewers experience more directly from the impact of dramatic events.[25] Herder is credited with the first known use of the term *sich einfühlen* in his *Auch eine Philosophie der Geschichte zur Bildung der Mensch-heit* (Yet *Another Philosophy of History of the Education of Humanity*, 1774), where he urges scholars wishing to grasp the language of different cultures of the past to "sympathize" with these cultures' history, expressions, and habits: "feel yourself into it all – only then are you on track to understand the word."[26] While Herder wrote of *sich einfühlen* with regard to the hermeneutical-aesthetic capability to step into different cultures of the past, it was Novalis in 1802 who first used the term in a fashion that resonates with its subsequent nineteenth-century usage. Fathoming nature, Novalis wrote, is impossible for one "who does not, almost effortlessly, [. . .] through sensation, commingle oneself with all natural beings and feel oneself into them."[27]

The psychological phase of *Einfühlung*, which is the focus of this study, was born in the 1860s. The most prominent discourse of psychological aesthetics, *Einfühlung* came to place bodies, things, and our emotions relative to them at the core of its project. Today, we might conceive of the project of *Einfühlung* as a dual attempt both to widen the range of specific emotions adhering in aesthetic events beyond the duality of pleasure/displeasure promulgated by formalists working in a Kantian framework, and at the same time to recognize the presence of the body and the particularities of material worlds.

Einfühlung was frequently discussed in theoretical terms with reference to natural phenomena, landscapes, abstract and architectural lines, and, less frequently, animals. Typically, thinkers of *Einfühlung* did not explore visual art, but instead natural and abstract forms.[28] They mused about what it entails for us when the shapes and lines of landscapes or inanimate objects seem to have the properties of life; how by relying on our emotions and moods we identify animals and what they mean to us as we recognize ourselves in animals. A primary reason for this focus on abstract or natural form, instead of content-based representations, was the opposition to formalist aesthetics in its effort to locate

25 Fontius, "Ästhetik/ästhetisch," 126.
26 Johann Gottfried Herder, *Werke*, vol. 4, *Schriften zu Philosophie, Literatur und Altertum: 1774–1787* (Frankfurt: Suhrkamp, 1994), 33: ("fühle dich in alles hinein – nun allein bist du auf dem Wege, das Wort zu verstehen").
27 Novalis, *Werke*, ed. Gerhard Schulz (Munich: Beck, 1969), 123: ("der nicht, wie von selbst, [. . .] durch das Medium der Empfindung, sich mit allen Naturwesen vermischt, sich gleichsam in sie hineinfühlt").
28 For further discussion, see Jutta Müller-Tamm, *Abstraktion als Einfühlung: Zur Denkfigur der Projektion in Psychophysiologie, Kulturtheorie, Ästhetik und Literatur der frühen Moderne* (Freiburg: Rombach, 2005), 214–248.

beauty and aesthetic pleasure in pure form. By positing the projection of the self into abstract form, *Einfühlung* was able to use the subjective, symbolic act of projection to attribute a content to otherwise meaningless natural and abstract forms. As I will discuss, one can read *Einfühlung* somewhat against the grain, insofar as it, especially as it took shape in the works of Theodor Lipps around 1900, postulated a radical subjectification of form.

Given a renewed interest in the history and contributions of *Einfühlung*, it is an interesting question what role animals had in this discourse.[29] Were the processes of *Einfühlung* regarding humans or objects different from those pertaining to animals? What was the nature of the *Einfühlung* that humans experienced concerning animals? To date there is no research on historical *Einfühlung* in relationship to non-human animals.

Friedrich Theodor Vischer's 1866 book *Kritische Gänge* (Critical paths) was recognized by successor scholars as the post-Romantic beginning of the new aesthetics of *Einfühlung*, which began to develop rapidly after its publication. His son, Robert Vischer, considered the first to use the word in its noun form, later developed his father's analysis in his 1873 dissertation *Über das optische Formgefühl: Ein Beitrag zur Ästhetik* (*On the Optical Sense of Form: A Contribution to Aesthetics*). While much scholarship from the 1890s until today has sought to locate the origins and the sense of *Einfühlung* in the pantheistic attitude of German Romanticism, no such origins or meanings were claimed by Vischer. On the contrary, Vischer's point of departure was not a purported pantheistic kinship with animals and nature, but rather a sense of a distance existing between the human and nature. Vischer makes it quite clear that the desire of humans to aesthetically encounter themselves in the things of the world is one of our basic qualities. What we experience aesthetically must have "an abundance of life, through which it can relate and speak to the human."[30] Vischer's intention – in his revised aesthetic of 1866 – is to address the material effect of things ("die stoffartige Wirkung"), to explore "the way in which the substance calls forth the movement of emotion."[31]

Discussion about the place of animals in *Einfühlung* was present from the beginnings of this discourse. In *Kritische Gänge*, Vischer discussed empathy for

---

29 See for instance, Robin Curtis and Gertrud Koch, eds., *Einfühlung: Zur Geschichte und Gegenwart eines ästhetischen Konzepts* (Munich: Fink Verlag, 2009). See also Müller-Tamm, *Abstraktion als Einfühlung* as well as Susan Lanzoni, *Empathy: A History* (New Haven: Yale UP, 2018).

30 Friedrich Theodor Vischer, *Kritische Gänge*, *Neue Folge*, vol. 5, Kritik meiner Ästhetik (Stuttgart: Cotta, 1866), 135–136: ("muß eine Lebensfülle haben, wodurch es zum Menschen in Beziehung tritt, ihn als verwandt anspricht").

31 Vischer, *Kritische Gänge*, 136: ("in welchem Sinne die Gefühlsbewegung, die durch den Inhalt hervorgerufen wird").

animals in the context of a symbolic personification of things and nature: "This humanizing of things can take place in a variety of ways [. . .] certainly, an animal can also, but need not be, perceived symbolically for it to be an aesthetic object. If animals were not related to human beings, we would not understand them, they would not matter to us or be an object of our perception in an aesthetic sense or in any other."[32] From the start of this discourse in Vischer's oeuvre, the bodily state shared by humans and animals was core to this line of thinking, as was the assertion that we pay attention to animals aesthetically because they mean something to us. The concern in contemporary animal studies with the corporeal and embodiment is in many ways a return to nineteenth-century discoveries.

For Vischer, the sensuous qualities of what we perceive lend to our sentience the contour of our emotions, emotions that are subsequently recognized in external natural phenomena: "We may assume that every mental act takes shape and is at the same time reflected in particular vibrations and indeterminate neural modifications in such a way that they express the image of these modifications. That is, a symbolic image takes shape in the organism's concealed interior."[33] To briefly restate Vischer's assumption: we experience entities in the world through our aesthetic-emotional receptors, so to speak, which have emotional effects for us, emotions that we then find transferred through our perception into the entity that, we believe, occasioned them.

Drawing on neural knowledge made available at the time through the fields of psychology and physics, Vischer continued:

> The external phenomena that affect us to the degree that we automatically underlay them with emotional atmospheres behave for this inner image like its objective depiction and unfolding. The corresponding natural phenomenon meets the given nerve's predisposition for the vibrations in question, stimulates it, boosts and confirms it, and with it, the emotion that reflects itself in the vibrations.[34]

---

32 Vischer, *Kritische Gänge*, 95–96.

33 Vischer, *Kritische Gänge*, 143: ("Wir werden annehmen dürfen, daß jeder geistige Akt in bestimmten Schwingungen und – wer weiß welchen – Modifikationen des Nervs sich in der Art vollzieht und zugleich reflectirt, daß diese sein Bild darstellen, daß also ein symbolisches Abbilden schon im verborgenen Innern des Organismus statt findet"). It is likely that Vischer is drawing on writings of Wilhelm Wundt in his discussions.

34 Vischer, *Kritische Gänge*, 143: ("Die äußeren Erscheinungen, welche so eigenthümlich auf uns wirken, daß wir ihnen unwillkürlich Seelenstimmungen unterliegen, müssen sich zu diesem innern Abbilde verhalten wie seine objective Darstellung und Auseinanderlegung; der vorausgesetzten Neigung des Nervs zu den betreffenden Schwingungen kommt das entsprechende Naturphänomen entgegen, weck sie zur Action, stärkt und bestätigt sie und hiemit die in ihr sich spiegelnde Seelenbewegung").

We underlay natural phenomena that emotionally impact us with emotions that accompany the scene of impact and the specific phenomena that seem to call us.

To paraphrase Vischer, certain features of perception, potentially explained by human psychology and physiology, possess sensitivities to different impressions of the natural world. In terms of animals, the specific animal contours and behaviors that reach our perception have consequences for the sort of emotions that we then perceive in our human-animal interactions. Vischer is very clear about how, regarding the essentials, animals behave in the same way as do humans, that *Einfühlung* concerns human and non-human animals. Animals respond to external expressions, such as sounds, by projecting their emotional images into those entities producing the expressions: "that a tone feels like a symbolic expression is something that an animal could convey [. . .], one that instantly distinguishes by a hair's breadth the intention behind a call, a warning, or a threat in a tone of one its kind."[35] Vischer describes this as perceiving the world in an aesthetic-symbolic mode. Emotionally making sense of nature is synonymous with symbolically perceiving the world, something that both humans and non-human animals do. The symbolic activity relates to the merging of the thing whose materiality impacts us with the emotions of the impact, which are then (re)routed back to the object, which we perceive through our emotions. That which impacts us winds up receiving the appearance of the impact. While a thinker under the influence of Darwin would explain such animal behavior with reference to sexual and natural selection, and hence, self-preservation, Vischer dwells on expressive emotions.

To give an example – consider a hawk. In the moment that I perceive the hawk, be it through a single sense or through a combination of sound, vision, touch, and emotions, which are in part cued by the hawk's actions, the sensuous, that is, aesthetic, perceptions help me make sense of the hawk's movements and appearance, its position in space, its sounds. In Vischer's thinking, there is a repertoire of kinesthetic behaviors which the hawk and I share, which is to say, the particulars of its actions are not completely foreign to me. As the hawk suddenly launches from a tree branch to sweep over a hedge, my eyes, ears, my proprioceptive sense – that is my self-movements and body position – and my emotions are making sense of the animal, its movements, its bodily properties and materiality, and what they all mean for the hawk and me. We might observe that the aesthetic here functions in a double sense. It connotes the way in which our senses produce knowledge of the animal without necessarily referring it to concepts; it also concerns the way in which the animal is

---

35 Vischer, *Kritische Gänge*, 143.

constructed, to use Vischer's metaphor, in the image of our mobilized embodied emotions. Drawing on his father's work, Robert Vischer later described this as "imagined self-motion," wherein we project into the object the feeling that we derive or would derive from this motion.[36] Finally, it is worth noting that the (human) emotion that I lend to the hawk is not purged of the qualities of the hawk. To put it differently, these emotions are not so saturated with the human that there is nothing of the hawk to them. On the contrary, F. T. Vischer's view would be that the materiality and the content of the animal is already filtering our likely perceptions, emotions, and reactions as they take shape.

One of the ways in which *Einfühlung* for animals differs from empathy as it is used by contemporary scholars in animal studies is that *Einfühlung* was typically not a form of sympathy with the emotional state of animals. *Einfühlung* did not assume that if, for instance, an animal mourns, we mourn with it or that we intervene to reduce its suffering. Instead, it sought to explain why animals appear for us in a manner that is sensuous and immediately recognizable through symbolic patterns of human acts. That is to say, animals appear in a way that is meaningful to us as we infuse something of ourselves into what we observe.

For all its emphasis on the subjective transposition of human emotion and activity into things and forms – this applies above all to works of Theodor Lipps – *Einfühlung* could nonetheless not escape a reliance on the assumption that animals have meaning for us. In this sense, we might regard animals as those beings that resist the totalizing subjective bent to be found in much of the thought about *Einfühlung*. This is nowhere clearer than in F. T. Vischer's writings, where animals form the one group of beings in nature that manifest intentionality. Moreover, their material, emotional, and phenomenological properties assert themselves and confront human perception. In other words, animals are those forms of nature that complicate the subjective projection of the human *I*.

Vischer would not envision this as "anthropomorphism," if we mean by that the attribution of human personality or characteristics to an animal. For that would be to understand *Einfühlung* as a mere transference from one autonomous domain to another. Though Vischer's main concern was with human-driven *Einfühlung*, he clearly assumed that animals also engaged in the same processes. This distinguishes it not only from empathy as it is used today, where it is almost synonymous with sympathy, it also distinguishes it from anthropomorphism. Anthropomorphism had long been considered the poetic attribution of human qualities to gods, before it was repurposed to refer to their attribution

---

36 Robert Vischer, "On the Optical Sense of Form: A Contribution to Aesthetics" in *Empathy, Form, and Space, Problems in German Aesthetics, 1873–1893*, eds. and trans. Harry Francis Mallgrave and Eleftherios Ikonomou (Santa Monica: Getty Center, 1994), 107.

to animals. We might coin a term and consider Vischer's notion of *Einfühlung* more akin to a kind of "zoopomorphism" than anthropomorphism. Vischer's reference to the qualia of things and beings, the psycho-physiological nature of perception and emotions draws on assumptions regarding what we might today call the embodied emotions of all animals, including human animals.

Animal aesthetics

Many scientists engaged with the circumstances under which different animals could be perceived aesthetically. The basic assumption of the relevance of *Einfühlung* for studies of animals was sufficiently pervasive that it appeared in the work of scholars who wrote for a popular readership, such as the biologist Karl Möbius. Author of *Ästhetik der Tierwelt* (The aesthetics of the animal world, 1908), Möbius assumed the validity of *Einfühlung* for an investigation of animals and human feelings toward them. Möbius asked: "What is the content of our empathy for [*Einfühlen in*] animals, whose beauty enthralls us? This feeling into a magnificent lion; in a high-spirited horse; in an eagle hovering above our heads; in the adroit flight of swallows; in colorful butterflies, which flit from blossom to blossom; in a spider spinning its web; in a jellyfish that inches forward in bright sea water?"[37] Even in this book for readers of popular science, one can see that the mode of the aesthetic assumed here differs from either a Kantian view, which emphasized the schemata of consciousness as they experienced the feeling of contemplating the beautiful, or modernist *l'art pour l'art* sensibilities, which could be said to disregard the meaning of the object's properties. Möbius mentioned a range of animals with which humans could aesthetically empathize. In doing so, he stressed the ways in which we do not lose sight of the particular life of the animal, nor do we regard ourselves as completely distinct from them, for we imagine that we slip into their bodies through *Einfühlung*.

This led to a parallel and related discussion of the late nineteenth century regarding whether we can understand the specific emotions that animals display through their expressive acts. In the wake of Charles Darwin's *The Expression of the Emotions in Man and Animals* (1872), many thinkers in the German scene wondered whether one can assert that animals are aware of their own aesthetic reactions to animal displays, for example in mating rituals. For instance, the art historian Karl Woermann, writing in 1900, drew on the example of birds that decorate their houses to secure a mate, and asserted that animals

---

37 Karl Möbius, *Ästhetik der Tierwelt* (Jena: Gustav Fischer, 1908), 10.

have an aesthetic sense: "we can say that these little creatures would not achieve their ends if they took no joy in these colorful creations of their imagination."[38]

A major figure in the discourse on *Einfühlung*, Johannes Volkelt, intervened in the debates regarding an "Ästhetik der Tiere" (an aesthetic of animals). In his *System der Ästhetik* (Aesthetic system) of 1905, he asked, how should we know what effect the sensuous qualities of animals have for their feelings and appraisals: "How should anyone decide which emotions or ideas move birds, fish, or butterflies when they glimpse the radiant, richly colored appearance of their fellow creatures, or when they indulge in all manner of games?"[39] Along with Möbius, Volkelt expressed skepticism about humans' ability to understand the aesthetic empathy of animals. Yet to imagine that non-human animals, in addition to humans, may rely on emotions, as Vischer indicated, to make sense of the meaning of external stimuli for themselves, and also to derive a sense of the emotions of external entities – other animals or humans – is not something with which Volkelt directly engaged.

Adolf Göller, a professor of architectural history and aesthetics at the Stuttgart Technische Hochschule, author of works on architectural style as well as the posthumous *Das ästhetische Gefühl* (Aesthetic feeling, 1905), asserted an emotional basis common to humans and animals making it possible for us to tap into the sensuous worlds of animals. Göller drew on the tenets of *Einfühlung* to assert, for instance, that cats and dogs experience aesthetic pleasure at the sight of faces and the feeling of interior spatial forms. He claimed we could locate the "animal soul's gentle aesthetic excitation at the sound of music," and postulated that an eagle has a sense for "the magnificence of the mountainscape beneath him."[40] For Göller, "in its attachment to the way in which it inhabits its life, every animal has a feeling reminiscent of the aesthetic feeling that humans have for their own."[41] Göller clearly located a value in an assumption that humans shared with animals some sort of aesthetic substrate, which enabled them to experience similar basic emotions.

---

38 Karl Woermann, *Geschichte der Kunst aller Zeiten und Völker*, vol. I (Leipzig: Bibliographisches Institut, 1900), 4.

39 Johannes Immanuel Volkelt, *System der Ästhetik*, vol. 1 *Grundlegung der Ästhetik* (Munich: Beck, 1905), 60.

40 Adolf Göller, *Das ästhetische Gefühl: Eine Erklärung der Schönheit und Zergliederung ihres Erfassens auf psychologischer Grundlage* (Zeller & Schmidt vorm. E. Rupfer, 1905), 108.

41 Göller, *Das ästhetische Gefühl*, 109: ("Jedes Tier hat in seiner Anhänglichkeit an seine Lebensgewöhnung etwas, das an das ästhetische Fühlen des Menschen für die seinige anklingt").

Projection and expression

If *Einfühlung* was to have value as an account of perception, it would have to come to terms with everything to which humans claim to relate. For, as we have seen with F. T. Vischer, the discourse assumes at once that a gap exists between human perception and the world, and at the same time that this gap must be bridged. *Einfühlung* needed to comprehend how an embodied human consciousness could extend itself into not only features of natural landscapes, such as mountains or trees, not just other humans, but also animals. Furthermore, it would have to outline why it was even possible for humans to empathize with animals. Empathy aesthetics would need to account for the possibilities and limitations of similar feelings between humans and non-human animals.

Thinkers of *Einfühlung* assumed a model of similarity with a difference. They believed that animals and humans have similar make ups in terms of their bodily lives, which permits us to transfer ourselves imaginatively into the embodied selves of non-human animals. But at the same time, the self that we project into animals is different from the human self in play in human-to-human interaction. It derives in part from the very different modes of being and different expressive movements made by animals. Munich professor Theodor Lipps became the best-known proponent for the new theories of *Einfühlung* around 1900. Lipps shared similar assumptions with Volkelt and F. T. Vischer regarding human and animal similarities: "Why the outer appearance of the human alongside that of the animal can be a direct object of our empathy is clear. The expressions of animal life and the forms of animal bodies are most comparable to those of our own."[42]

Lipps thus allowed that, regarding the manifestations of life as well as the bodily interactions with the world, a kinship existed between those of humans and animals. Of all real and possible other forms of life, humans and animals shared bodily features to make this happen. This embodied way of living and perceiving enabled humans to empathize with animals. Nonetheless, Lipps assumed crucial differences: "The *I* that we feelingly project into the external appearances of animals is not of the same kind that we project into the appearance of humans. Instead, we modify this *I* pursuant to the different configuration of animal forms."[43] In other words, empathy with animals requires the creation of a modified *I*, one that takes into consideration the formal features of animals. Robert Vischer, perhaps the most perceptive practitioner of the theory, asserted something similar regarding the human that empathizes with an animal: "With organic

---

42 Theodor Lipps, *Psychologie des Schönen und der Kunst*, vol. I, "Ästhetik: Grundlegung der Ästhetik" (Hamburg: Leopold Voss, 1903), 160.
43 Lipps, *Psychologie des Schönen und der Kunst*, 160.

nature, empathy [*Einfühlung*] functions symbolically to animate a plant and to anthropomorphize an animal; only toward other human beings does it act as a doubling of self."[44] In human-to-human empathy, a second self or subject is projected. Yet for humans to symbolically inhabit the life of an animal, the self would need to undergo a modification instead of a doubling.

Einfühlung was critiqued, repudiated, and largely abandoned in the years after the First World War. In particular, the assumption that the self can be un-problematically projected into other people, things, nature, and animals came in for heavy criticism. One factor that led to the demise of *Einfühlung* was the general turn in modernism toward an aesthetic of distance, whereby the avoidance of distance and the inclination toward immediacy and identification came to be regarded as a "hallmark of 'German kitsch.'"[45] Neo-Kantianism and phenomenology assimilated aspects of *Einfühlung* or relegated it to the status of one element of aesthetic experience though not its defining feature. Wilhelm Worringer's assertion, in his *Abstraktion und Einfühlung* (*Abstraction and Empathy*, 1907), that the mode of aesthetic apprehension central to *Einfühlung* was unsuited to the comprehension of non-Western art forms, further weakened its usefulness. Nazi thinkers such as Alfred Rosenberg criticized *Einfühlung* for its reliance on psychology, the body, and its neglect of a racialized framework.[46] Yet what has been overlooked is that the scholars and scientists of aesthetic empathy realized that the particulars of nature, things, and animals impact the human, resulting in changes to people in specific situations. The notion of a self that is modified to mimic, as it were, the contours of the other, in this case, the animal that is perceived, could act as a constraint on any notion that the self can "animate" another being as some form of domination. For the theory assumed in one way or another that the particulars of the object shape our projected feelings.

It is on the basis of this modified *I* that animals can be the object of our *Einfühlung* and be aesthetically meaningful to us. For Lipps, by experiencing within myself the emotional (*seelisch*) life of the animal, it becomes comprehensible to me. As we seek to uncover the meaning of animals, for Lipps, we are constantly referred back to "human movements and forms, particularly visible acts [*Leistungen*] of the human body, as symbols for a manner of inner life [*Lebensbetätigung*]."[47] Similarly, Johannes Volkelt asserted that only on the basis of a range of intelligible *Ausdrucksbewegungen*, (literally, "expressive movements,"

---

44 Vischer, "On the Optical Sense of Form," 106.
45 Fontius, "Ästhetik/ästhetisch," 125.
46 Fontius, "Ästhetik/ästhetisch," 136.
47 Lipps, *Psychologie des Schönen und der Kunst*, 160.

but one could also refer to "emotional gestures"), shared by humans and animals, can we locate animal emotions.

That idea that "expressive movements" make it possible for humans to empathize themselves into the worlds of animals was a basic assumption for *Einfühlung*. Numerous scientists and cultural figures, including psychologists, psychiatrists, philosophers, art historians, as well as an array of artists were attracted to the relationship of physical acts to feelings. The psychologist Wilhelm Wundt was the most significant architect of a psychophysical notion of expressive movements, a concept widely accepted by psychologists, graphologists, philosophers, and critics.[48] It became an indispensable motif as scholars sought to understand and account for various dimensions of the mind/body relationship and the place of emotions, in particular.

These physical signals, which included language, had their origins, scholars asserted, in emotions.[49] Though relevant for various kinds of communication, *Ausdrucksbewegungen* were all about emotions: "the primary cause of natural gestures does not lie in the motivation to communicate a concept, but rather in the expression of an emotion. Gestures are first and foremost affective expressions."[50] As a foundation for the *Ausdrucksbewegung*, Wundt assumed a psychophysical parallelism, according to which psychical events and systems have correlates in physical events and systems. Any inner feeling, which he frequently distinguished with reference to the figure of *Gemütsbewegung* (movement of temper), has a correlate in potentially perceivable, sensory or nervous, physical acts.[51] Wundt indicated the complexity of these considerations when he asserted that "the emotion and its physical correlative manifestation begin simultaneously" as part of one process.[52] Regarding emotions and animals, thinkers such as Volkelt placed great stock in expression, positing "that empathy is only possible on the basis of our ability to make expressive movements." Yet Volkelt was less concerned with the certainty that animal expressions accurately conveyed emotions than he was with the way

---

48 Wundt's basic observation regarding emotions and expression was laid out already in 1863: Wilhelm Max Wundt, *Vorlesungen über die Menschen- und Thierseele* (Leipzig: Voss, 1863), 387. For further discussion of expressive movements, see Derek Hillard, "Reading Embodied Emotions in Rilke's *Die Aufzeichnungen des Malte Laurids Brigge*," in *Feelings Materialized: Emotions, Bodies, and Things in Germany, 1500–1950*, eds. Derek Hillard, Heikki Lempa, and Russell Spinney (New York: Berghahn Books, 2020), 62–76.

49 Wilhelm Max Wundt, *Grundzüge der physiologischen Psychologie* (Leipzig: W. Engelman, 1874), 429.

50 Wilhelm Max Wundt, *The Language of Gestures*, ed. George Herbert Mead (Berlin: De Gruyter Mouton, 1973), 146.

51 Wilhelm Max Wundt, *Völkerpsychologie*, vol. I (Leipzig: W. Engelmann, 1900), 84–85.

52 Wundt, *Völkerpsychologie*, 84.

in which they invited our own affective welling over into animal beings via expressions, which relied on a shared sensuous condition.

The symbolic

Again and again, theorists of empathy aesthetics claimed that more humanlike mammals with their "developed consciousness" lend themselves most easily to being objects of *Einfühlung*.[53] For Volkelt, because animals have emotions and a highly developed consciousness, they require little anthropomorphizing. Indeed, they already demonstrate emotional expression, enabling humans to see themselves in animals: "When we see a bolting horse and regard it as driven by courage and pride, we can easily understand this as empathy without any personification."[54] In other words, the act of projection through *Einfühlung* is almost unnecessary, because emotions are so immediately present in physical movements.

Volkelt considered human empathy for animals to be that mode that exists between the one felt for other humans on the one hand and for objects on the other: "The empathy into animal movements and gestures stands in the middle between (actual) empathy into the expressive human form and the (symbolic) empathy into expressive inanimate things." For Volkelt, our own kinesthesia, or sensations of movement (*Bewegungsempfindungen*), come closest to those felt by animals.[55] Though he stresses the symbolic in this projection – because we attribute to animals an affective stimulus similar to ours – he nonetheless insists that the human self that is projected into animals is less symbolically charged than for other natural phenomena or things, such as mountain ranges, because of our nearness to animals. By distinguishing human-animal *Einfühlung* as "symbolic" from the "actual" *Einfühlung* between humans, Volkelt suggests that it must be done with a distance, with heightened level of tact and sensitivity, because of the differences between humans and animals.

The distinction that Volkelt makes between "objectivists" and "subjectivists" with regard to *Einfühlung* is relevant for the discussion of animals. Volkelt was aware that the knowledge we have of animals enabling us to relate emotionally or sensuously to them is not scientific. Instead, it is practical or experiential: "One does not need to be a zoologist to aesthetically appreciate horses, dogs,

---

53 Volkelt, *System der Ästhetik*, 456.
54 Volkelt, *System der Ästhetik*, 456.
55 Volkelt, *System der Ästhetik*, 267.

cows, chickens in paintings or in reality."[56] Familiarity and practical knowledge of animals is productive, because it forms, perhaps paradoxically, the basis for the "humanizing empathy" (*vermenschlichende Einfühlung*).[57] Without our feelings for animals, without animals experiencing emotions themselves, indifference or callousness would be the mode through which we relate to animals.[58] What Volkelt terms an "objective" approach to non-human emotions is, in his eyes, essentially a mistaken view. It is mistaken because it perceives animals in regard to categories of science or idealist (Kantian or Hegelian) philosophy. We can understand them scientifically, in which we catalog animals. Or we appreciate them as beautiful specimens in all their perfection and as realizations of ideas we have of them. In this Hegelian view, animals or nature are beautiful to us because they are the direct sensuous manifestations of our idea. That is, a unity for the beholder is achieved between, for instance a real horse, in all its perfect beauty and the idea of what a horse is. By contrast, the "subjective" view acknowledges how humans rediscover parts of themselves in animals. The subjective view folds the animal into a more complex approach, one that reserves an essential role for the "emotional-symbolic animation, the human-analogical content felt in to animals."[59]

By perceiving animals emotionally and aesthetically, in Volkelt's view, we both assert a relatedness and a distance: "The nearness, warmth, and immediate appeal in our aesthetic impression of animals, which we feel in such a beneficial way, derives from this involuntary humanizing [*Vermenschlichung*]."[60] Our empathetic connection to animals can be viewed as a strictly ethical one. Yet, as Lipps, Vischer, and Volkelt posit, it can also be an aesthetic one, that is to say, an empathy that is considered emotional and corporeal. For Volkelt, only aesthetically can we *become aware* of animals. For being aware here rests not, as contemporary theory stresses, on Otherness and radical difference, but on a meaningful relatedness, which exists because of shared features of human and animal worlds.[61] This similarity permits us to surrender ourselves to the belief that we are on the same emotional wavelength as animals, that there is a sensuous meeting of beings, at the same time that we may regard this merging of the human and the non-human as an illusion (although we may be motivated to participate in this illusion).

---

56 Volkelt, *System der Ästhetik*, 444.
57 Volkelt, *System der Ästhetik*, 446.
58 Volkelt, *System der Ästhetik*, 449.
59 Volkelt, *System der Ästhetik*, 441: "stimmungssymbolische Beseelung, den eingefühlten analog-menschlichen Gehalt."
60 Volkelt, *System der Ästhetik*, 441.
61 Volkelt, *System der Ästhetik*, 441.

Let us pursue an implication of Volkelt's comment above: humans have the universal urge to perceive themselves symbolically-emotionally in animals. Yet science and modernity have altered this naïve, immediate orientation. The naïve embrace of animals in the shape of the human is replaced by an emotionally symbolic transfer of sensuousness and sensibility into animals. The impulse to animate or emotionalize nature (*Naturbeseelung*) no longer takes place according to mythology. Although science has disenchanted (to use Max Weber's concept) animals, along with the rest of the world, we nonetheless at times let down our guard, so to speak, and automatically become immersed in animals. The immersion into animals remains, for Volkelt, an *Als-Ob* ("as if"), that is, the "play of illusion" with its "character of appearance and symbolism."[62] The notion of the aesthetic here is under the spell of a sort of disenchanted but "gladdened" relation to the world. This core theme of illusion or the "as-if," present in Volkelt, F. T. Vischer, and Robert Vischer, often gets overlooked when researchers assert that *Einfühlung* was a form of pantheism. Yet this is an essential element of the aesthetic with regard to human/non-human animal empathy.

What follows from Volkelt's assumptions – though he does not explicitly state this inference – is that while the act of projection remains exceptionally human, the human nonetheless surrenders something to the animal in its careful attentiveness to animal life. Here we see how Volkelt develops Vischer's notion of attending to the material effect of nature and animals. To aesthetically empathize with animals is not merely to intentionally transpose human emotions into an animal. It is an unconscious process where the strictly human content is weakened in projection. Remaining centered on human emotions, his view nonetheless recognizes and accepts the limitations of the human. It raises the question how can we posit non-human emotions given our situatedness as humans? How can we observe them from our location within the human? Yet what if we do not know whether our lived experience of emotion is so saturated with the human that it does not already include something non-human?

Volkelt's assumptions create a possibility that he seems not to have explicitly considered: that the starting point for human-animal relationships need not be a basic difference that is then bridged by emotions according to *Einfühlung*. Instead, as we saw in the discussion of F. T. Vischer, it is possible to contend that we have already been impacted by animals before we consciously perceive them. As Vischer contended, *Einfühlung* is not a feature exclusively reserved for the human. Perhaps Volkelt gets at this question, when he claims that in the transfer of human sensuous perceptions to animals, "something of the human

---

62 Volkelt, *System der Ästhetik*, 446–447.

undergoes a certain attenuation, a transposition into a different, more basic level, a transference to another, deeper form of life."[63] Thus in the moment that the human finds itself in nature and in animals, it experiences a reduction of the human. It seems to suggest that in *Einfühlung* humans become less human. So that *Einfühlung* is not just the urge of the human to place itself emotionally in the world of animals and nature. Instead, *Einfühlung* was understood to bracket out elements of the human.

In this essay, I have analyzed how the particular type of empathy envisioned in psychological *Einfühlung* was discussed with regard to non-human animals. The goal was not to debunk or embrace it. The discussion suggests that there are benefits in rehabilitating "aesthetic empathy." *Einfühlung* describes discovering what animals mean to us and how we feel about them through emotions occurring in human/non-human animal interaction. Feeling about animals one way or another need not be preceded by a cognitive assessment or appraisal. Instead, our emotions are the ways through which animals become intelligible to us. In this, we likely cannot and perhaps should not aim to refrain from seeing emotional content in animals, from which it is likely impossible to drain from it everything "human."

In Volkelt's thought, features of animals' corporal being and animal "expression" (i.e., how we perceive the sensuous qualities of an animal and its environment, through touch, sound, sense of speed, etc.) are combined with the human bent to impart an emotional stance to the animal. We can view this as an illusion with a difference. Reading human emotions, human symbolism into animals may mean engaging in an illusion, one that we practice with a mix of the conscious and unconscious mind. Yet emotional cues given by animals are, because of our common condition of embodied life, not meaningless to us. Embodied and situated emotions are a feature of animals and humans. For both animals and humans, they are essential for our discovery of what has meaning for us. Combining expressive elements perceived by humans with the distinct attributes of the animal may lead us to the sense that animal emotions are legible for humans in "that singularly divided and playful attitude that we have come to see as illusion."[64]

---

63 Volkelt, *System der Ästhetik*, 449–450: "es findet an dem Charakter des Menschlichen eine gewisse Abschwächung, eine Umsetzung in eine andere, niedrigere Stufe, eine Übertragung in eine andere, tiefer stehende Daseinsform statt."
64 Volkelt, *System der Ästhetik*, 451: "kommt das Bewußtsein in jene eigentümlich gespaltene und spielende Haltung, die wir als Illusion kennen gelernt haben."

Bibliography

Aaltola, Elisa. *Varieties of Empathy: Moral Psychology and Animal Ethics* (London: Rowman & Littlefield, 2018).

Acampora, Ralph R. *Corporal Compassion: Animal Ethics and Philosophy of Body* (Pittsburgh: U of Pittsburgh Press, 2006).

Böhme, Hartmut. *Fetishism and Culture: A Different Theory of Modernity* (Boston: De Gruyter, 2014).

Campe, Rüdiger, and Julia Weber, eds. *Rethinking Emotion: Interiority and Exteriority in Premodern, Modern, and Contemporary Thought* (Berlin: De Gruyter, 2014).

Curtis, Robin, and Gertrud Koch, eds. *Einfühlung: Zur Geschichte und Gegenwart eines ästhetischen Konzepts* (Munich: Fink Verlag), 2009.

de Waal, Frans. *Mama's Last Hug: Animal Emotions and What They Tell Us about Ourselves* (New York: W. W. Norton, 2019).

de Waal, Frans. "Putting the Altruism Back into Altruism: The Evolution of Empathy," *Annual Review of Psychology* 59 (2008): 279–300.

Donovan, Josephine. "Attention to Suffering: Sympathy as a Basis for Ethical Treatment of Animals," in *The Feminist Care Tradition in Animal Ethics*. Eds. Josephine Donovan and Carol Adams (New York: Columbia UP, 2007), 58–86.

Downes, Stephanie, Sally Holloway, and Sarah Randles, eds. *Feeling Things: Objects and Emotions through History* (Oxford: Oxford UP, 2018).

Eitler, Pascal. "'Weil sie fühlen, was wir fühlen.' Menschen, Tiere und die Genealogie der Emotionen im 19. Jahrhundert," *Historische Anthropologie* 19, no. 2 (2011): 211–228.

Göller, Adolf. *Das ästhetische Gefühl: Eine Erklärung der Schönheit und Zergliederung ihres Erfassens auf psychologischer Grundlage* (Stuttgart: Zeller & Schmidt vorm. E. Rupfer, 1905).

Gruen, Lori. *Entangled Empathy: An Alternative Ethic for Our Relationships with Animals* (New York: Lantern Books, 2015).

Hillard, Derek, Heikki Lempa, and Russell Spinney, eds. *Feelings Materialized: Emotions, Bodies, and Things in Germany, 1500–1950* (New York: Berghahn Books, 2020).

Hillard, Derek. "Reading Embodied Emotions in Rilke's *Die Aufzeichnungen des Malte Laurids Brigge*." *Feelings Materialized: Emotions, Bodies, and Things in Germany, 1500–1950*. Eds. Derek Hillard, Heikki Lempa, and Russell Spinney (New York: Berghahn Books, 2020), 62–76.

Kohut, Thomas A. *Empathy and the Historical Understanding of the Human Past* (London: Routledge, 2020).

Lipps, Theodor. *Psychologie des Schönen und der Kunst*, vol. I, *Erster Teil, Ästhetik: Grundlegung der Ästhetik* (Hamburg: Leopold Voss, 1903).

Mallgrave, Francis. *Architecture and Embodiment: The Implications of the New Sciences and Humanities for Design* (London: Routledge, 2013).

Möbius, Karl. *Ästhetik der Tierwelt* (Jena: Gustav Fischer, 1908).

Perty, Maximilian. *Über das Seelenleben der Thiere* (Leipzig: C. F. Winter: 1865).

Ryan, Derek. *Animal Theory: A Critical Introduction* (Edinburgh: Edinburgh UP, 2015).

Schasler, Max. *Ästhetik. Grundzüge der Wissenschaft des Schönen und der Kunst, Erster Teil* (Leipzig: G. Freytag, 1886).

Sommer, Robert. *Grundzüge einer Geschichte der deutschen Psychologie und Aesthetik von Wolff-Baumgarten bis Kant-Schiller* (Stuttgart: Stahel, 1892).

Vischer, Friedrich Theodor. *Kritische Gänge, Neue Folge*, vol. 5 Kritik meiner Ästhetik (Stuttgart: Cotta, 1866).

Vischer, Friedrich Theodor. "The Symbol," trans. Holly A. Yanacek, *Art in Translation* 7, no. 4 (1 December 2015): 417–448. https://doi.org/10.1080/17561310.2015.1107314.

Volkelt, Johannes Immanuel. *System der Ästhetik*, vol. 1, *Grundlegung der Ästhetik* (Munich: Beck, 1905).

Weltrich, Richard. *Christian Wagner, der Bauer und Dichter zu Warmbronn: eine ästhetisch-kritische und sozialethische Studie* (Stuttgart: Strecker & Moser, 1898).

Woermann, Karl. *Geschichte der Kunst: aller Zeiten und Völker*, vol. I (Leipzig: Bibliographisches Institut, 1900).

Wundt, Wilhelm Max. *Grundzüge der physiologischen Psychologie* (Leipzig: W. Engelman, 1874).

Wundt, Wilhelm Max. *The Language of Gestures*. Ed. George Herbert Mead (Berlin: De Gruyter Mouton, 1973).

Wundt, Wilhelm Max. *Völkerpsychologie*, vol. I (Leipzig: W. Engelmann, 1900).

Wundt, Wilhelm Max. *Vorlesungen über die Menschen- und Thierseele* (Leipzig: Voss, 1863).

Jared Poley
Biology, Behavior, and Emotion
Control and Companion in the Work of Jakob von Uexküll and Konrad Lorenz

Scientists have debated the underlying biology and physiology of emotion since the 1872 publication of Charles Darwin's *The Expression of the Emotions in Man and Animals*. One view, anchored in the work of physiologists like Ivan Pavlov and Walter Cannon, located the origins of emotion in the work of hormones released into the blood and conveyed through the sympathetic nervous system. A different view, one associated with the work of the Baltic German biologist Jakob von Uexküll, proposed that emotion and behavior originated in the complex interplay between an organism's perception of, and attempts to shape, its environment.

Situating the individual within a larger environmental context and working intensively on the ways that stimuli and perception affected behavior, Uexküll created the foundation for broader ways of understanding behavior that applied to all animals – human and not. In this essay I consider the ways that Uexküll's framework for understanding the actions of an organism in its environment was translated into the work of later animal behaviorists, notably Konrad Lorenz. We will see that Uexküll's conceptualization of animal subjectivity and his use of categories like *Kumpan* – or companion – recalled but undermined the gendered use of the term in other contexts.

Uexküll's fame among biologists has waned even as his reputation among semioticians, cultural and media studies scholars, and historians of science has waxed. His scientific work, which emerged in a late nineteenth-century academic setting framed by debates about mechanical and biological (even vitalist) forces, reached a pinnacle in the 1920s. His conservative political outlook did not prevent him from maintaining his stature during the Third Reich. While his reputation as a scientist was compromised by this context, his ideas about the circuitry of animal perception has prompted continued engagement with Uexküll's work.[1] This chapter reframes aspects of Uexküll's work in the context of

---

1 Jussi Parikka, *Insect Media: An Archaeology of Animals and Technology* (Minneapolis: U of Minnesota Press, 2010); Alain Berthoz and Yves Christen, *Neurobiology of "Umwelt": How Living Beings Perceive the World* (Berlin: Springer, 2009); Brett Buchanan, *Onto-Ethologies: The Animal Environments of Uexküll, Heidegger, Merleau-Ponty, and Deleuze* (Albany: SUNY Press, 2008); Timo Maran, Dario Martinelli, and Aleksei Turovski, eds., *Readings in Zoosemiotics*

https://doi.org/10.1515/9783110753677-004

the history of ideas and the history of science in order to take up the question of how ideas regarding the biology of animal perception, behavior, instinct, and emotion unfolded in the interwar period.

Since the publication of Darwin's *The Expression of the Emotions in Man and Animals*, analyses of emotion have historically revolved around the degree to which emotional displays were informed by the process of natural selection.[2] In short, behavior, inheritance, and semiotics have oriented our understanding of the emotional life of animals for the past 150 years. The problem of how emotions are expressed, and the degree to which those expressions are instinctual or learned, continues to influence ethology today. Historian Robert Richards notes that "while modern ethologists attribute vital communicative functions to expressions in animals, Darwin denied that emotional responses had any use at all, which is why he did not invoke natural selection to explain them."[3] Historians of science have understandably oriented their analyses of these issues through an exploration of Darwin and Darwinian thought as it proliferated in an Anglo-German context.[4] This essay takes a different tack, looking not at the influence of Darwin on German thinkers, but rather at the arguments and rhetorical impulses two influential German scientists used to discuss animal emotion.

Jakob von Uexküll, in the view of historian of science Anne Harrington, rejected mechanistic views of behavior like those advanced by Ivan Pavlov or Walter Cannon.[5] Embracing instead a holistic, even neo-vitalist, perspective Uexküll framed the central problems of biology within a German academic context defined, as Harrington explains, by the debates about mechanical vs. material explanations for the potency of biological life. In his work *Theoretische Biologie* (*Theoretical Biology*, 1920), Uexküll made the distinctions between physiology and biology clear: "a new scaffolding is needed for biology: the old scaffolding, borrowed from chemistry and physics, will suffice no longer. For chemistry and

(Berlin: De Gruyter Mouton, 2011); Floyd Merrell, *Sensing Corporeally: Toward a Posthuman Understanding* (Toronto: U of Toronto Press, 2016); Giorgio Agamben, *The Open: Man and Animal*, trans. Kevin Attell (Stanford: Stanford UP, 2004).

2 Charles Darwin, *The Expression of the Emotions in Man and Animals* (London: J. Murray, 1872); Robert J. Richards, *Darwin and the Emergence of Evolutionary Theories of Mind and Behavior* (Chicago: U of Chicago Press, 1987), 230.

3 Richards, *Darwin and the Emergence of Evolutionary Theories of Mind and Behavior*, 230.

4 Robert J. Richards's *Darwin and the Emergence of Evolutionary Theories of Mind and Behavior* (1987) remains the definitive work on the reception of Darwin and Darwinian thinking in the German context. See also Greg Moore's essay "Darwinism and National Identity, 1870–1914," in *The First World War as a Clash of Cultures*, ed. Fred Bridgham (Rochester, NY: Camden House, 2006).

5 Anne Harrington, *Reenchanted Science Holism in German Culture from Wilhelm II to Hitler* (Princeton, NJ: Princeton UP, 1996).

physics do not recognise conformity with plan in Nature. Biology, however, consists in the setting up of a scaffolding of doctrine that takes account of this conformity as the basis of life."[6] Rejecting what he perceived as a coldly mechanical physiology, Uexküll promoted biology – with an organic and holistic view of the organism in its environment as a way to advance our understanding of the natural world:

> This way of regarding the world [a focus on the chemical and physical properties of the reflexes] reduces man to a machine, endowed by chance with consciousness, while all other animals are able to get along quite well without it. Instinct would find no place either, and, in spite of the non-demonstrable nervous organisation, would have to be interpreted as a highly complicated reflex action. It all depends on whether we can explain the life of animals by the presence of a framework conformable with plan and analogous to that of a machine.[7]

Uexküll is important because his work lets us probe the ways that emotions – animal or human – were understood in early twentieth-century German science. But what does Uexküll tell us about the distinctions between human and animal as they were understood at the time? What does he teach us about what cognition was thought to be?

Jakob von Uexküll, born in 1864 in Estonia, was a Baltic German, a member of an ethnic enclave within the Russian Empire. Anne Harrington explains that the anti-democratic context of his Baltic German heritage was derived from this aristocratic milieu, and she proposes that aspects of this worldview colored his scientific work over the course of his career. Uexküll's scientific education unfolded under the tutelage of physiologist Wilhelm Kühne at the University of Heidelberg. Kühne's research focused in part on the biological implications of enzymes, and he steeped his students in an anti-materialist and anti-Darwinist intellectual tradition.[8] After Kühne's death in 1890, Uexküll continued research on marine invertebrates, leading him to the idea of the *Bauplan* (Harrington translates the term as "blueprint"), "the cornerstone of a comprehensive world view operating at once as a biological, political, and spiritual principle."[9] The *Bauplan* connected an organism's physical structure to its environment in ways that avoided evolutionarily-determined developmental pathways, and represented in Harrington's view, a "preestablished teleological coordination."[10] In short, an organism's physiology was suited to its environment.

---

6 Jakob von Uexküll, *Theoretical Biology*, trans. Doris L. Mackinnon (London: K. Paul, Trench, Trubner & Co. Ltd., 1926), xi, http://archive.org/details/theoreticalbiolo00uexk.
7 Uexküll, *Theoretical Biology*, 120.
8 Harrington, *Reenchanted Science*, 39.
9 Harrington, *Reenchanted Science*, 40.
10 Harrington, *Reenchanted Science*, 40.

Harrington explains that by 1905, Uexküll – through his provocative use of the terms *Anschauung* (illumination or illustration) and *Bauplan* – was beginning to differentiate between the work of physiology and biology.[11] "Physiologists," Harrington argues Uexküll came to believe, "concerned themselves with the material, causal substances, and forces operating within the organism. Biologists [. . .] were interested in accounting for the activities of a particular animal in terms of its functional logic and underlying plan."[12] This distinction is important, because as Harrington notes, it set the stage for a rethinking of what an organism was. Uexküll's vision of the organism existing in intimate symbiosis with its environment set the stage for his later analysis of the relationships between a creature and the *Umwelt* (environment) in which it existed. Harrington argues that Uexküll came to see that "every animal, every living thing, far from being a passive product of an external world [. . .] was also, in fact, an active *creator* of its own 'external reality.'"[13] Biological analysis, then, is a function of the intense subjectivity of the observer-scientist, compounded by the fact that the external world is actively created by the subject through sensory input.

Uexküll developed these ideas over many years, but they attained a hardened status in his 1909 work, *Streifzüge durch die Umwelten von Tieren und Menschen* (translated as *A Foray into the Worlds of Animals and Humans*, and reissued in 1933), in which Uexküll developed a vision of *Umwelt* as a biological – and therefore an anti-mechanistic – set of relationships.[14] Sense impressions for Uexküll would perform a totally different function than the mechanistic senses of physiologists like Ivan Pavlov and Walter Cannon. Perhaps the most well-known feature of the text is Uexküll's description of a tick, triggered by the scent of butyric acid released by a mammal, that drops from its perch in search of a source of blood. Uexküll proposed that the tick existed within a cycle of *Merkmale* (sensory cues) that provoked *Wirkmale* (responses). Uexküll imagined a type of feedback loop, and represented the cycle of input/output, action/reaction as a set of circular connections that unfolded within a particular contextual space (unlike those reactions that might be merely physiological and were not conditioned by the surrounding environment). Uexküll's connected sequence of sensory input to behavioral output, represented in the form of a feedback loop, has since been viewed as a forerunner to cybernetics.

---

11 Harrington explains that Uexküll's use of the term was a complex one that centered on the ability of the biologist to illustrate through provocative example the plan or blueprint that an organism followed. Harrington, *Reenchanted Science*, 40.

12 Harrington, *Reenchanted Science*, 40.

13 Harrington, *Reenchanted Science*, 41.

14 Jakob von Uexküll, *A Foray into the Worlds of Animals and Humans: With A Theory of Meaning*, trans. Joseph D. O'Neil (Minneapolis: U of Minnesota Press, 2010).

Yet it is important to note that Uexküll remained fixated on the biological. The organism in its *Umwelt* might look mechanical, but it was fundamentally some other order of life. "Whoever wants to hold on to the conviction that all living things are only machines," Uexküll wrote in the preface to the 1933 edition of *Foray*, "should abandon all hope of glimpsing their environments."[15] The cycle of cause and effect was not just a mechanical process, and Uexküll was clear in noting the existence of a "machine operator," the subject, which united the various elements of the process. "Whoever still holds the view that our sensory organs serve perception and our motor organs serve the production of effects will also not see in animals simply a mechanical assemblage; they will also discover the machine operator who is built into the organs just as we are into our body."[16] The implications of this line of thinking were, for Uexküll, profound, allowing him to "address himself to animals not merely as objects but also as subjects, whose essential activities consist in perception and production of effects."[17]

If even relatively simple animals possessed a form of subjectivity characterized by their ability to regulate the interrelationships between sensory perceptions and physical results, then the biological foundations of life needed to be rethought. By 1933, Uexküll indicated that the category of the animal had shifted. An animal was no longer simply some processor of causes and producer of effects. When "animals are made . . . into pure objects," Uexküll argued, "[. . .] one forgets that one has from the outset suppressed the principal factor, namely the *subject* who uses these aids, who affects and perceives with them."[18] The animal exists within the *Umwelt*, the "closed unit" consisting of the "perception world" and "the effect world," and it actively constructs the world around it.[19] Uexküll offered a new way of understanding the cognitive and sensory worlds of animals. An animal was not just a processor – it also possessed a transcendent ability to shape reality.

Uexküll's positioning of the animal within the *Umwelt* was a novel way of presenting some of the distinctions between biology and physiology that he asserted governed the life sciences in the late nineteenth and early twentieth centuries. In Uexküll's formulation, the tick might be an object – a machine that possessed various component parts that could be studied by the physiologist. But more importantly, the tick was also a subject – the controller of the machine – that might be studied by the biologist. The biologist was committed to a

---

15 Uexküll, *A Foray into the Worlds of Animals and Humans*, 41.
16 Uexküll, *A Foray into the Worlds of Animals and Humans*, 42.
17 Uexküll, *A Foray into the Worlds of Animals and Humans*, 42.
18 Uexküll, *A Foray into the Worlds of Animals and Humans*, 42.
19 Uexküll, *A Foray into the Worlds of Animals and Humans*, 42.

holistic analysis of life: "The biologist [. . .] takes into account that each and every living thing is a subject that lives in its own world, of which it is the center."[20] Uexküll's recasting of subject-object distinctions is significant. He suggested a transformed view of nature and its component parts. And perhaps most important, Uexküll's positioning of animals as subjects – "machine operators" rather than mere machines – indicates a reimagining of the biology of animals in ways that promoted animal subjectivity. He expanded on this point in later writings. In *Theoretical Biology*, Uexküll proposes that sense perception and the creation of subjective reality in animals permitted the creation of a type of "inner world" fabricated by the organism:

> The sum of the stimuli affecting an animal forms a world in itself. The stimuli, considered in connection with the function-circle as a whole, form certain indications, which enable the animal to guide its movements, much as the signs at sea enable the sailor to steer his ship. I call the sum of the indications the *world-as-sensed*. The animal itself, by the very fact of exercising such direction, creates a world for itself, which I shall call the *inner world*.[21]

This "function circle" connecting perception and action constituted the spatial and experiential dimensions of *Umwelt*.

The nexus of perception and effect that was the center of Uexküll's understanding of biology did not simply exist at the level of the organism. Indeed, the organism was a collection of independent entities that came to be organized – Uexküll uses the term "coordination" – by the organism. "Every living cell," he writes, "is a machine operator that perceives and produces and therefore possesses its own particular (specific) perceptive signs and impulses or 'effect signs.'"[22] The coordination of these diverse perceptive machine operators was achieved in the brain: "the organism uses brain cells (which are also elementary machine operators), grouping half of them in differently-sized groups of 'perception cells' in the part of the brain that is affected by stimuli, the 'perception organ.'"[23] The result is an organism that could attain subjectivity without possessing consciousness; one that could perceive – even actively construct – both space and time. In his later work *Theoretical Biology*, Uexküll reinforced this argument, suggesting that organs achieved a functional value in the course of development. "The organs of animals are always the perfect expression of one function or of several, and consequently changes that take place in them point to a change of function. The

---

20 Uexküll, *A Foray into the Worlds of Animals and Humans*, 45.
21 Uexküll, *Theoretical Biology*, 126.
22 Uexküll, *A Foray into the Worlds of Animals and Humans*, 47.
23 Uexküll, *A Foray into the Worlds of Animals and Humans*, 47.

functions themselves, however, are always unities, and not subject to change. One function, it is true, may more or less force another into the background or even cause it to disappear altogether; but functions themselves do not change."[24]

Uexküll recognized that the connection between perception and action could be severed, or an organism could suffer from a misperception that nonetheless generated a particular set of actions. In *Theoretical Biology*, Uexküll addressed this problem by noting the differences between instinct and experience. "There are animals that execute quite definite movement-sequences, in which control by the sense-organs is lacking. Actions of this kind can come about through a special kind of nerve-linking; they are called reflexes. When, on the other hand, regulated movement-sequences are performed by an animal that is without control by sense-organs, and such movements are not linked together and conditioned by any demonstrable structure, we speak of *instinctive actions*."[25] Having defined a reflex or an instinct, Uexküll addressed the distinction between human and animal through this lens. "The difference between animals that learn through experience, such as human beings, and instinctive animals like birds and insects, depends mainly on the latter having for their functions inborn impulse-sequences which proceed faultlessly without any further control. Intelligent animals require schemata in order to form the correct functions and maintain these by their control."[26]

Uexküll's identification of the brain as the location of the master "machine operator" is not especially surprising, of course. But it is important to work out what he imagined the brain was, and what its larger capability and function might be in order to understand how non-human animals might ascend to subjectivity. In *Bedeutungslehre* (*A Theory of Meaning*, 1940), Uexküll admitted that the state of knowledge about the brain was currently limited. "It goes without saying that the whole account of Nature built on meaning requires thoroughgoing research, for we cannot do very much yet with the brain, which must possess a 'thinking tone.' But, here too, meaning bridges the gap between physical and nonphysical processes, just as it did between the sheet music and the melody."[27] In his book *Theoretical Biology*, Uexküll introduced a set of other ideas about the structure and function of the brain. Returning to the larger differences between the work of physiologists and biologists, Uexküll indicates that there are important methodological distinctions that arise when considering the functioning of the brain. "In contrast to physiology, biology considers the

---

24 Uexküll, *Theoretical Biology*, 116.
25 Uexküll, *Theoretical Biology*, 118.
26 Uexküll, *Theoretical Biology*, 119.
27 Uexküll, *A Theory of Meaning*, in *A Foray into the Worlds of Animals and Humans*, 157.

manifestations of the central nervous system, not as processes going on inside of apparatus, but as processes within *organs*."[28] Commenting on the role of protoplasm, which "has the important task of continuously regulating the framework of the central nervous system," Uexküll argues that "[t]his super-mechanical activity raises the organ to a higher level than mere apparatus, and endows it with the peculiar property of life."[29] When the brain is elevated to the level of biological organ and is no longer constrained by the physiologist's fixation on the study of mere "apparatus," it can begin to do a different type of cultural work. "Consideration of the function-world of organisms," Uexküll writes, "showed that the animal-subject is not to be sought in an ego localised in the brain, but that the subject governs the entire framework of the animal body."[30]

Uexküll's "machine operator" vision of the neurobiology of an organism provides a useful way to examine the functioning of gender in the construction of scientific knowledge in the early twentieth century. While the term corresponds to a vision of technological masculinity that connotes mastery not just over one's self but also over the construction of the environmental surroundings of the organism, there is a different way to understand Uexküllian biology. In his consideration of perception and effect, Uexküll focused his analysis on animal behaviors that revolved around threat perception, maternal "instinct," and affective bonding. To the degree that these behaviors were layered with gendered significance, we can pick apart how gender may have functioned in Uexküll's system. His understanding of threat perception – typified in *Foray* in the reactions of a jackdaw to the appearance of a cat with another bird in its mouth – extended into a larger analysis of companionship. Rather than joining threat perception to masculine protective mechanisms, Uexküll connected the behavior to communal feeling. In his descriptions of the protection a mother hen exhibited toward a fettered chick, Uexküll did not indicate a primarily feminine set of instinctual effects. In each of these cases – affective bonding, companionship, and protective behaviors – Uexküll's machine operator exhibited behaviors typically coded as feminine at the time, regardless of the physical sex of the individual organism.

Gender was not the only way Uexküll joined behavior and subjectivity in his descriptions of animal biology. His emphasis on the subjectivity of animals also has important implications for how he imagined animals experiencing emotions. Especially when connected to the close interrelationships between perception and effect, animal emotion was expressed in a set of behaviors that could be observed.

---

28 Uexküll, *Theoretical Biology*, 152.
29 Uexküll, *Theoretical Biology*, 152–153.
30 Uexküll, *Theoretical Biology*, 234.

In the section of *Foray* in which Uexküll explores companionship, he not only describes the attempts of some bird species to induce their companions to participate in shared behaviors, but he also devotes his attention to affection and love. In one especially provocative section of the chapter, Uexküll relates the story of the director of the Amsterdam Zoo, who became the love-object of a male bittern (a species of heron). In order to encourage the bittern to breed, the director stayed out of sight. When reappearing, "the male saw his former love companion again [and] chased the female off of the nest and seem to signal by repeated bows that the director should take his proper place and carry on the business of incubation."[31]

The passage is a strange one: at once suggesting that animals experience emotion but also depicting those emotions as inauthentic or erroneously triggered by misperception, Uexküll advances a dual image of how animals feel. This duality is compounded with his queering of the example, perhaps suggesting that he considered same-sex desire to be just as inappropriate as a cross-species liaison, a situation he described in another passage as the result of a "confusion" on the part of an animal. And here too, the connections between gender and emotion may be glimpsed. We see in the passage a brief description of the psychodrama underlying mate selection and the experience of parenthood. Why does the bittern love the human? Is it because the zoo director might be a better mother than the female bittern? Or perhaps the bittern is simply recalling the pleasures of a past love. Uexküll is silent on the issue, but by deploying the episode as a winking punchline to a larger argument about the validity of animal emotion, one can draw the conclusion that animal emotions – to the degree that they were real – might be nothing more than a consequence of the perceptual misapprehension of the world.

After he established the Institut für Umweltforschung (Institute for Environmental Research) at the University of Hamburg in 1926, Uexküll's prominence in German biology was enhanced. One researcher who was profoundly influenced by Uexküll's ideas was Konrad Lorenz, a "father of ethology," who was awarded the Nobel Prize for Physiology or Medicine in 1973.[32] Lorenz's early work was focused on the behavior of birds, and his fame was cemented in July 1935 with the publication of his study of imprinting, "Der Kumpan in der Umwelt des Vogels" ("The Companion in the *Umwelt* of Birds") in *Journal für Ornithologie* (Journal of ornithology).[33] The essay, dedicated to Uexküll, was quickly translated into English and

31 Uexküll, *A Foray into the Worlds of Animals and Humans*, 112.
32 Richards, *Darwin and the Emergence of Evolutionary Theories of Mind and Behavior*, 530–531.
33 Konrad Lorenz, "Der Kumpan in der Umwelt des Vogels," *Journal für Ornithologie* 83, no. 2 (1 April 1935): 137–213, https://doi.org/10.1007/BF01905355; Konrad Lorenz, "Der Kumpan in

published for an Anglophone audience in *The Auk*.[34] The focus of the essay is on the connections between environmental triggers – "releasers" in Uexküllian and Lorenzian terminology – and behavior. Lorenz looked especially at how an environmental cue – an image, a scent, a sound – might provoke the expression of an "instinctual" behavior. In the essay he recalls Uexküll's tick seeking blood, and relates the story of his pet bird, a jackdaw, attacking him when the animal saw him carrying a black cloth that visually approximated the size and shape of a bird that had been killed by a predator. Lorenz noted the evolutionary value of these behaviors and looked to Darwin's *The Expression of the Emotions in Man and Animals* for clues as to their development. As Lorenz explains, an animal does not "master its environment by insight or learning but is innately adapted to it by possessing highly differentiated instinctive powers of response."[35]

One of Lorenz's insights in the essay is to shift analysis of animal behavior away from individual organisms to consider social or group behaviors. Given his interest in ornithology and the behavior of flocking birds, this is perhaps not surprising. He expressed interest in the problem of behaviors that appear to be conveyed socially – he notes how laughing or yawning may be transmitted contagiously – and raises questions about the significatory power of the behaviors.[36] Ultimately, Lorenz returned to basic questions about the forces governing social or group behaviors. Flocking, herding, and stampeding – behaviors with a strong social or contagious element – drew his attention to the ways these behaviors were at once instinctual and learned. The essay is a wide ranging one, and its emphasis on individual/group dynamics is a turning point in the history of our understanding of animal behavior.

Lorenz's analysis revolved around the category of the "companion," or *Kumpan*, a framework that he absorbed from Uexküll's work. Behavioral triggers provided an opportunity to investigate the formation and perception of subject-object distinctions. Crucially, Lorenz suggested that these developmental processes were divorced from the need for mere survival. "The agent as a subject need not," Lorenz writes, "even in the vaguest way, be conscious either of the survival value of his actions, or of the identity of their neutral object. The object in the agent's world need not be represented as that kind of unit in space and time which we are accustomed to call a 'thing,' if only it is sending out the specific set of stimuli and

---

der Umwelt des Vogels," *Journal für Ornithologie* 83, no. 3 (1 July 1935): 289–413, https://doi.org/10.1007/BF01905572.

34 Konrad Lorenz, "The Companion in the Bird's World," *The Auk* 54, no. 3 (1 July 1937): 245–273, https://doi.org/10.2307/4078077.

35 Lorenz, "The Companion in the Bird's World," 246.

36 Lorenz, "The Companion in the Bird's World," 256.

releasing every one of the actions which must be executed toward it."[37] Conceptually rooted in Uexküll's understanding of the *Umwelt* and the creation of a subject-like organism, Lorenz argued for a new way to understand the origins of animal behavior that emphasized the instinctual: "Complicated and far-fetched though this devious method of object-treatment may seem to the human mind, it is certain that for animals on the mental level of birds this has been easier to attain through evolution than have the mental powers necessary to effect an object-treatment of equal complication and consistence by insight and purpose."[38] The companion, which through its existence in an organism's *Umwelt* might be the cause of various behaviors, was therefore a central element in the developing theory of animal behavior.

Companionship connotes the possibility of an affective bond, and Lorenz's field observations about the interactions between an organism and its companions are sometimes thought to include deeply emotional connections between different organisms. The pair-bonds that drew Lorenz's attention, for instance, are often anthropomorphized in ways that highlight the affective qualities of the bonding process, and further integrated into gendered characterizations about bourgeois childhood and motherhood, for instance, that fit the assumptions commonly expressed in European society in the first part of the twentieth century. Companionship expresses a baseline of feeling, in other words. As Lorenz writes, "The most peculiar role which the fellow-member of the species thus plays in the agent's world, being perceived as one thing when representing the object of one reaction and as a different one when being that of another, has been termed that of a 'Kumpan' by Professor J. von Uexküll."[39]

But Lorenz articulated a much different vision of the companion in his translation and use of Uexküll's word *Kumpan* in his English-language work, "The Companion in the Bird's World." Lorenz attempted to signal to his Anglophone audience that the term did not include an affective element. "The German word, *Kumpan*, means a fellow who is our companion so far as concerns but one particular kind of occupation, such as hunting or drinking (*Jagdkumpan*, *Saufkumpan*). It implies that no deeper and nobler bonds link us to our fellow in this kind of companionship. The word certainly meets the case exceptionally well, although it is hardly translatable into English. The word 'companion' certainly lacks the detracting implication which is so essential for the wonderful way in which Uexküll's term describes this lowest type of animal companionship."[40] In short, Lorenz sought to minimize the degree and type of

---

37 Lorenz, "The Companion in the Bird's World," 259.
38 Lorenz, "The Companion in the Bird's World," 259–260.
39 Lorenz, "The Companion in the Bird's World," 260.
40 Lorenz, "The Companion in the Bird's World," 260.

affect implicit in an organism's subject-object bonds. The *Umwelt* might be the stage for a lot of different interactions, but deeply emotional ones were not necessarily present – even in circumstances that might appear to the human observer to be enchained in emotionality. Lorenz's fame rested in part on his path-breaking studies of imprinting, a set of parent-offspring bonds. And while the basis of the behavior was instinctual, Lorenz recognized the importance of conditioning the reflex, especially through social behaviors. The *Kumpan* – especially when related to imprinting – did not necessarily imply the presence of an affective bond.

Animal models have for centuries been held up as ideal types upon which human society should be founded. The presumed dichotomy between animal and human, and the innate naturalness exhibited by the former, provided a canvas upon which discursive descriptions of ideal human societies were painted. In *The Fable of the Bees* (1714), Bernard Mandeville described an ideal animal society that expressed the inner logic of a social division of labor in the early eighteenth century. Ernst Jünger's *Gläserne Bienen* (*Glass Bees*, 1957) did a similar type of cultural work in the twentieth. Ant stories like Carl Stephenson's "Leinigens Kampf mit den Ameisen" ("Leiningen Versus the Ants," 1938) or Hanns Heinz Ewers's *Die Ameisen* (*The Ant People*, 1927) examined ant colonies in a similar fashion. In short, the animal world has a long history of being deployed as an ideal type – both of virtue and of danger – that has made it a significant element of cultural understandings of human society. And while the various ideals projected through representations of the animal world were certainly not free of politics, the political content expressed was never fixed. Representations of animal life functioned as blank canvases upon which an author's fantasies were projected. That said, what elements of animal life – and of the emotional lives of animals – were Uexküll and Lorenz isolating? And how might those depictions of animal behavior serve as a model for human society?

Both Uexküll and Lorenz were biologists, with all the shaded meanings that that term conveyed for Uexküll as a counterpoint to mechanical physiology. Uexküll was perplexed by the Weimar Republic and notions of democracy and equality more generally. Anne Harrington argues that

> In the natural sciences, it had long been clear that truth was not something that could be decided through majority consensus; and for this reason, modern science was necessarily an aristocratic enterprise in which the assertions of one genius could topple the untutored opinions of the would-be knowers. Politics had yet to learn this obvious lesson, and much of Uexküll's energy after the establishment of the Republic in 1918 would be devoted to developing biologically based arguments to demonstrate the unnaturalness and absurdity of the new democratic system in Germany.[41]

---

41 Harrington, *Reenchanted Science*, 38.

Lorenz's vision of companions without friendship, protective parenting without love indicated a different take on the emotional lives of animals and humans alike. The combined vision of an organism existing in its environment, coolly responding to perception and stimuli with a measured and predictable response governed by command and control circuitry provides a window into how perceptions of the natural world could be shaded with political overtones in the 1930s. It is clearly too simple to argue that Uexküll and Lorenz provided a biology suited to the fascist state.[42]

Unfolding in the cultural and political context of a Nazi deification of nature, the work of these biologists remains significant.[43] Historian Robert Pois noted that the "line drawn between humankind and nature by the Judaeo-Christian tradition is due primarily to the influence of the Mosaic Code"[44] that distinguished between human and animal, and raised the possibility that "Man was part of nature, and there was nothing that suggested that there was any essence which elevated him above it."[45] Pois argues that National Socialism enjoined two critical elements that transformed this older logic. The Nazis participated in a "sanctification of nature" and "supremacy of science over any form of religious belief."[46] Indeed, Hitler described the "necessity to apply ['stern and rigid' natural laws] to areas of human existence."[47] In a natural world in which animals do not really think, do not really learn, and do not really experience emotional connections to the other objects in their environment, we perhaps glimpse a hint of what the natural world could express as a model of fascist society. While neither Uexküll nor Lorenz was a fascist, they also each perhaps tapped into some inexpressible mode of interacting that fascists were in fact committed to creating.[48] Expressions of an emotionless nature, in other words, might serve a sinister political program.

I have argued in this chapter that aspects of German biological sciences in the early twentieth century provided a novel understanding of animal behavior. Jacob von Uexküll's elaborate theory of the interactions between the *Umwelt* and "machine-operator" organism provides insight into the ways that non-human organisms possessed a form of subjectivity. Uexküll's imaginative view of perception,

---

42 For the complex relationships between Lorenz, his ideas, and National Socialism, see Richards, *Darwin and the Emergence of Evolutionary Theories of Mind and Behavior*, 534–536.
43 Robert A. Pois, *National Socialism and the Religion of Nature* (New York: St. Martin's Press, 1986).
44 Pois, *National Socialism and the Religion of Nature*, 37.
45 Pois, *National Socialism and the Religion of Nature*, 38.
46 Pois, *National Socialism and the Religion of Nature*, 39.
47 Pois, *National Socialism and the Religion of Nature*, 40.
48 Klaus Theweleit, *Male Fantasies, Volume 1: Women, Floods, Bodies, History*, trans. Chris Turner (Minneapolis: U of Minnesota Press, 1987).

behavior and instinct, of the intricate differences between the work of biologists and physiologists, and of the oscillating nature of sensation and action shaped a view of non-human life that built a new foundation for understanding how animals processed information, experienced their environments, and shaped their own realities. Konrad Lorenz applied aspects of Uexküll's theories to issues of instinct and behavior, orienting aspects of his analysis around the category of the "companion." Significantly, the Lorenzian companion was divorced from any inherent affective bond; it was an object in the environment and not inherently a source of emotional connection. These views cohere into a representation of non-human animal life that is centered on an organism that shapes its own reality but also lends expression to instinctual urges formed in relationship to the environment in which it is situated. In this way, nature's "plan" could be fulfilled. This view of nature, shaped during the *Kaiserreich* but rising to institutional dominance during the Weimar Republic and the Third Reich, remains important to biology and ethology to this day. And this vision of animal subjects that perceive, act in, shape, and react to their environments, interacting with other organisms in ways that objectify them, illuminates that historical context as it continues to influence our own.

Bibliography

Agamben, Giorgio. *The Open: Man and Animal*. Trans. Kevin Attell (Stanford: Stanford UP, 2004).

Berthoz, Alain, and Yves Christen. *Neurobiology of "Umwelt": How Living Beings Perceive the World* (Berlin: Springer, 2009).

Bridgham, Fred, ed. *The First World War as a Clash of Cultures* (Rochester, NY: Camden House, 2006).

Buchanan, Brett. *Onto-Ethologies: The Animal Environments of Uexküll, Heidegger, Merleau-Ponty, and Deleuze* (Albany: SUNY Press, 2008).

Darwin, Charles. *The Expression of the Emotions in Man and Animals* (London: J. Murray, 1872).

Harrington, Anne. *Reenchanted Science Holism in German Culture from Wilhelm II to Hitler* (Princeton, NJ: Princeton UP, 1996).

Lorenz, Konrad. "The Companion in the Bird's World." *The Auk* 54, no. 3 (1 July 1937): 245–273. https://doi.org/10.2307/4078077.

Lorenz, Konrad. "Der Kumpan in der Umwelt des Vogels." *Journal für Ornithologie* 83, no. 2 (1 April 1935): 137–213. https://doi.org/10.1007/BF01905355.

Lorenz, Konrad. "Der Kumpan in der Umwelt des Vogels." *Journal für Ornithologie* 83, no. 3 (1 July 1935): 289–413. https://doi.org/10.1007/BF01905572.

Maran, Timo, Dario Martinelli, and Aleksei Turovski, eds. *Readings in Zoosemiotics* (Berlin: De Gruyter Mouton, 2011).

Merrell, Floyd. *Sensing Corporeally: Toward a Posthuman Understanding* (Toronto: U of Toronto Press, 2016).

Parikka, Jussi. *Insect Media: An Archaeology of Animals and Technology* (Minneapolis: U of Minnesota Press, 2010).

Pois, Robert A. *National Socialism and the Religion of Nature* (New York: St. Martin's Press, 1986).

Richards, Robert J. *Darwin and the Emergence of Evolutionary Theories of Mind and Behavior* (Chicago: U of Chicago Press, 1987).

Theweleit, Klaus. *Male Fantasies, Volume 1: Women, Floods, Bodies, History*. Trans. Chris Turner (Minneapolis: U of Minnesota Press, 1987).

Uexküll, Jakob von. *A Foray into the Worlds of Animals and Humans: With a Theory of Meaning*. Trans. Joseph D. O'Neil (Minneapolis: U of Minnesota Press, 2010).

Uexküll, Jakob von. *Theoretical Biology*. Trans. Doris L. Mackinnon (London: K. Paul, Trench, Trubner, 1926). http://archive.org/details/theoreticalbiolo00uexk.

Emotional Functions of Non-Humans

Sarah L. Leonard

Expressive Creatures

Animals in Early German Photographic Portraits

In the German states, the photographic process did not exist long before it was pressed into the service of human portraiture. After the publication of Louis Daguerre's method in 1839, it was only a handful of years before experimental and entrepreneurial daguerreotypists established portraiture studios and rigged themselves with mobile daguerreotype equipment so they could travel from town to town, offering their services. We know from the client books of early photographers like the prolific Leipzig-based portraitist Bertha Wehnert-Beckmann that people from many walks of life pursued the singular little silver images. German artists, mechanics, and scientists were quick to take up the new form, and people were ready to embrace it.[1]

Enthusiasm for the photographic portrait from the very beginning of the medium suggests that these images met compelling human needs, and some of those needs were certainly emotional. Surveying the daguerreotypes and early photographs created by Wehnert-Beckmann and talented contemporaries like Hermann Krone and Carl Ferdinand Stelzner, one sees their early efforts to use the affective power of the medium.[2] Krone's early daguerreotypes, for example, included playful, tender portraits of him and his wife and relaxed images of his dapper brother. The vast majority of early photographic portraits captured carefully composed faces and elegantly curved portraits of individuals and (less often) families; however, a small but striking body of images documented dead children held by women who were presumably their mothers as well as dignified portraits of the dead. As Roland Barthes has famously written, photographs document life and loss simultaneously. Their mode of address, he explains, is "this has been."[3] Photographs capture what *was* by bringing it into the present tense. And yet, from the very moment they are created, they document something

---

1 Bertha Wehnert-Beckmann's Client Book is held in the archives of the Stadtgeschichtliches Museum Leipzig, which also holds a large collection of her photographs and papers.
2 These reflections on early photographers like Hermann Krone, Carl Ferdinand Stelzner, and Wehnert-Beckmann are based on my research on all three in the Krone Archiv in Dresden, the Museum für Kunst und Gewerbe in Hamburg (which has important records relating to Stelzner), and the Stadtgeschichtliches Museum Leipzig (Wehnert-Beckmann).
3 Roland Barthes, *Camera Lucida: Reflections on Photography*, trans. Richard Howard (New York: Hill and Wang, 1981), 96.

https://doi.org/10.1515/9783110753677-005

that is inevitably past – even if it is simply the moment. This affective temporality informed the power of photography from the beginnings of the medium.

Some early photographic portraits also featured non-human animals – either alongside humans or at the center of images. Dogs, birds, and horses were the animals that showed up most often in daguerreotypes, and the creatures were almost always singular, unaccompanied by other members of their species. Dogs and small birds appeared in the spaces of the photographic studio, which were designed to mimic the interiors of middle-class homes. In keeping with this, animals were presented as fully domesticated. Portraits of horses were taken outdoors by necessity, but these images were highly formalized, with horses and riders fully outfitted with riding tack and attire. Like human bodies in daguerreotype portraits, the bodies of animals were tightly managed; whatever affective power they held, it had little to do with wildness, representations of "nature," or spontaneity.

Producing a proper photograph of a non-human animal was a technical challenge at the beginning of the medium. Humans struggled to hold postures for extended exposure times; coaxing a dog to remain still was harder yet. Scholar David Lulka speculates that extant daguerreotypes of animals, created despite the technical difficulties involved, attest to the importance of human-animal relationships: "Unlike inanimate props, animals embodied a potential cost in time and money, and this cost had to be outweighed by the value of the animal's presence. This situation points to the highly personal connection between the human subjects and animals in daguerreotypes, for it suggests an affinity that made this risk worthwhile and that was unmatched by generic props [. . .]."[4] While Lulka is probably correct that most non-human animals included in portraits held emotional value for the human sitters, this was not always the case. Wehnert-Beckmann had a studio dog that made appearances in multiple portraits, particularly of children.[5] The dog may have been used to calm child sitters or to suggest that the humans in the portraits possessed certain attributes.

The aim of this chapter is to understand what it meant to include non-human animals in early photographic portraits in the German states. This was a genre that quickly became formalized. It was also connected to affect; scholar Geoffrey Batchen argues that daguerreotype portraits were bound up with touch,

---

4 David Lulka, "Animals, Daguerreotypes and Movement: The Despair of Fading and the Emergence of Ontology," *Journal of Material Culture* 19, no. 1 (2014), 40.
5 The vast collection of Wehnert-Beckmann's photographic negatives held at the Stadtgeschichtliches Museum Leipzig includes multiple portraits taken with the same dog. It therefore seems that this dog was associated with the studio, not the pet of individual sitters.

and therefore with emotions anchored in physical presence.[6] Everything included in these carefully constructed images had a particular role to play, and non-human animals were no exception. In particular, their presence seemed to provide information about the emotional attributes of the human being in the portrait. At a moment when contemporaries were preoccupied with human interiority, the medium of the early photograph was expected to reveal the quality of sitters' inner lives. Sometimes the presence of animals provided evidence of sitters' material status. Horses, for example, demonstrated material comfort and athleticism. Images of dogs and birds provided opportunities for sitters to demonstrate their capacities for calm and affection. Early photographers also made portraits of their own dogs, demonstrating another form of encounter between species shaped through the technology of the camera.

Questions from animal studies

The field of animal studies provides concepts that help guide this analysis. Confronted with examples of human-animal relations, scholars resist the tendency to center their analysis on humans.[7] As historian Sonya Lipsett-Rivera writes, "The anthropological concept of 'co-being' provides a way into a new approach to social history, one in which the divide between human and non-human is erased. [. . .] If applied to the past, the idea of co-being can shed light on the ways that humans interrelated with non-humans."[8] In looking at early photographic portraits of humans and animals, as well as portraits of animals created by their human companions, it is important to attend to the co-existence and co-being of animal and human – what is expressed in the gestures, faces, and bodies of human sitters? And further, what can we gather about the state of the animals captured in these portraits? What images of animals – and of animals and humans together – were deemed worthy of the time, effort, and expense necessary to produce these tiny, unreproducible objects?

Historian Erica Fudge argues that it is important to write histories of animals because of the role they have played in defining what it has meant to be

6 Geoffrey Batchen, *Forget Me Not: Photography and Remembrance* (New York: Princeton Architectural Press, 2004), 31.
7 Matthew Brower, *Developing Animals: Wildlife and Early American Photography* (Minneapolis: U of Minnesota Press, 2011), xviii.
8 Sonya Lipsett-Rivera, "A New Challenge: Social History and Dogs in the Era of Post-Humanism," *Sociedad Indiana* (2015), https://socindiana.hypotheses.org/320.

human. She writes, "The centrality of the animal in our own understanding of ourselves as humans forces us to reassess the place of the human as neither a given nor a transcendent truth."[9] Non-human animals played multiple roles in early German photographs. Even through their generic standardization, photographers worked in the 1840s and 1850s to represent the inner lives of sitters in distinct (though not necessarily diverse) ways. Books were ubiquitous props; they suggested that the sitter was literate and cultivated, that they were capable of learning and solitary thought. The presence of a book did not guarantee depth of feeling, of course, but the genre aspired to transcend surfaces.

Scholars of emotions like Monique Scheer argue that emotions are *done* rather than had. People's practices in the world produce, rather than simply reflect, affective states. Furthermore, these states are produced and experienced through the body, not simply located in the mind.[10] Sitters brought objects with them to the studio, among them photographic albums and images of individuals, which were held in the final image. They also brought animals, which they held or positioned at their feet. It may be that these objects were included in photographic portraits because they held emotional value and helped them perform affective experiences in front of the camera.

Scholars have also asked what is at stake in representations of non-human animals. What have humans tried to express, across time and space, through images of animals? The presence of animals in cave paintings is just one example of the centrality of animals in human representative efforts. Art critic John Berger initiated this question in his 1977 article titled, "Why Look at Animals?" In it, Berger argued that before the modern era, images of animals had played an important role in human efforts to make sense of the world. "If the first metaphor was animal, it was because the essential relation between man and animal was metaphoric."[11] Images of animals were essential to the ways humans navigated the world. He wrote, "What we are trying to define, because the experience is almost lost, is the

---

9 Erica Fudge, "A Left-Handed Blow: Writing the History of Animals," and Kathleen Kete, "Animals and Ideology: The Politics of Animal Protection in Europe," both in Nigel Rothfels, ed., *Representing Animals*, Kindle Version, Location 301–307 of 3650.

10 Monique Scheer, "Are Emotions a Kind of Practice (And Is That What Makes Them Have a History)? A Bourdieuian Approach to Understanding Emotion," *History and Theory* 51, no. 2 (2012): 193–220.

11 John Berger, "Why Look at Animals?," in *About Looking* (New York: Vintage, 1980), 7. The essay was originally published in three parts in 1977 in the journal *New Society*. For a recent rereading of this influential essay, see Jonathan Burt, "John Berger's 'Why Look at Animals?': A Close Reading," *Worldviews* 9, no. 2 (2005): 203–218.

universal use of animal-signs for charting the experience of the world."[12] The experience was almost lost, he explained, because nineteenth-century industrialization and the rise of modern capitalist societies (presumably in the West) had produced distance between humans and animals. In premodern contexts, animals and humans interacted daily, often through production and agricultural work. With industrialization, animals were looked at – in zoos, circuses, and photographs; humans ceased to work alongside them. Berger argued that these rich relationships between humans and animals all but disappeared with the rise of industrial capitalism. What remained was a denatured gaze at animals, who had become privatized and made into pets, toys, and objects of observation. For Berger, the reduction of animals accompanied a similar process of estrangement for human beings.

Scholars have noted that Berger's narrative is overly schematic and built on a vision of preindustrial co-existence between humans and animals that ignores historical realities. Yet it was important that Berger historicized the process of looking at animals and established the idea that there was something to learn from charting changes in human-animal relations. Animal studies scholars consistently return to Berger's essay, even as they critique it. As scholar Jonathan Burt writes in his recent rereading of the essay, "one cannot have the idea of looking without the idea of being looked at in turn [. . .]."[13] Even in nineteenth-century photographic portraits, the gaze goes both ways, or perhaps even three or four ways, depending upon who looks at whom in the configuration of the portrait. Scholar Matthew Brower does not follow Berger's historical schema in his recent book on wild animals in early American photography, but he does affirm Berger's insight that images of animals structure our understandings of them.[14]

Historians like Kathleen Kete and Erica Fudge have written more fine-grained studies of human-animal relations in early modern and modern Europe. Kete's work on the nineteenth century is particularly useful for understanding the emotional contexts in which photographic portraits of animals landed. The period between 1820 and 1840, she writes, was marked by a wave of humanitarian reforms and accompanying sentiments, which included prison reform, changes in the care of the mentally ill, anti-slavery activism, and organized movements against cruelty to animals. In the German States, the cities of Dresden, Nuremberg, Berlin, Hamburg, Frankfurt, Munich, and Hannover established societies for the protection of animals. In this context, Kete writes, "Kindness to animals came to stand high in

---

12 Berger, "Why Look at Animals?" 8.
13 Burt, "John Berger's 'Why Look at Animals?'" 207.
14 Brower, *Developing Animals*, xviii.

the index of civilization. It formed the project of civilization." Addressing cruelty to animals was part of a larger effort to "quarantine violence," something that was imagined as contagious, particularly to those who witnessed it.[15] These laws spoke to the fear that certain behaviors weighted with emotions – in this case cruelty to animals – would damage the affective lives of those who watched this behavior. Cruelty was thought to be contagious. Conversely, sympathetic co-existence with animals signaled kindness.

Eighteenth-century European notions of spectatorial sympathy associated with the psychology of sensation posited that humans must gaze upon the suffering of others to develop empathy. They believed that the humanitarian impulse rested upon the visual experience of viewing pain.[16] The trouble with this sensational psychology, historian Karen Halttunen writes, was that spectatorial sympathy also threatened to devolve into sensationalism and voyeurism.

In the late 1830s and 1840s in the German states, visual encounters with cruelty and pain were *not* considered as a means to develop empathy; indeed, the opposite was true. Jurists and early psychologists argued that viewing violence could permanently distort people's inner lives. In the late 1830s and 1840s, the new criminal codes of the German states of Saxony, Hesse, and Baden defined obscene texts and images as those that injured the viewer's sense of morality and modesty. The 1838 Saxon Criminal Code placed this new definition of obscenity alongside a law outlawing the torture of animals. A contemporary commentary on the relationship between these two laws by the respected legal scholar H. Josef Haubach explained that both laws worked to protect the emotional impulses of human witnesses to cruelty. According to the logic of the law, encounters with the torture of animals could render the viewer rough, insensitive, and prone to cruelty. "The human impulse of empathy is the object under attack and the object to be protected."[17] The equilibrium of inner life – its orientation toward the humane and the ethical – was defined as a social value that required legal protection.[18]

---

15 Kete, "Animals and Ideology," Kindle Version, location 569 of 3650, and 581 of 3650, respectively.

16 On spectatorial sympathy, see Karen Halttunen, "Humanitarianism and the Pornography of Pain in Anglo-American Culture," *American Historical Review* 100, no. 2 (April 1995): 303–334.

17 Sarah L. Leonard, *Fragile Minds and Vulnerable Souls: The Matter of Obscenity in Nineteenth-Century Germany,* (Philadelphia: U of Pennsylvania Press, 2015): 128–129.

18 Haubach quoted in Leonard, *Fragile Minds and Vulnerable Souls,* 129.

The role of objects

To understand the roles non-human animals played in early photographic portraits, it is important to consider the visual landscapes they joined and to understand who and what populated these images. Clothing, objects, furniture, books, and other photographs provided a relatively stable visual language that helped produce meaning. During the 1840s and 1850s, the daguerreotype portrait developed generic characteristics that would last these decades before new technologies and affective styles ushered in different conventions.

Like the painted portraits that preceded them, early photographs leaned upon faces, bodies, and objects to create the emotional resonance of images. Body postures and facial expressions settled into predictable patterns, forming the expectations of the genre. By the 1850s, portraits taken in well-regarded German studios created settings designed to look like respectable interior living spaces, outfitted with drapery, tables, plants, sitting chairs, and sofas. People having their portraits taken were meant to occupy these sets as though they were personal spaces rather than the impersonal environments of the studio. Photographs of women or men alone regularly showed them at a table, quietly contemplating a book or holding a photograph – presumably of a loved one. Downcast eyes were easier to maintain than a direct gaze when contending with slower shutter speeds. Yet this contemplative style was not technologically determined; many of the earliest daguerreotype portraits involved direct gazes at the camera by men and women. The quiet body and calm attention captured cultural aspirations. The interiors signaled respectability; the gaze fixed on the book suggested that the sitter enjoyed a developed inner life. Portraits of men, particularly in groups, were often physically and socially dynamic; images of women more often had them fixed in place, and holding a book provided a motive for their physical stasis.

Personal objects provided some relief from the recycled interior sets featuring standard tables, chairs, plants, and drapery. Those who sat for portraits in the 1840s and 1850s wore their own jewelry, and often a lot of it. Sometimes they would pay the extra cost to have the daguerreotype painted with gold to highlight the jewelry. Given the otherwise modest presentation of these portraits, the presence of jewelry probably said less about economic status than it did about connections between people created by gifts and inheritances. Worn close to the body, jewelry emphasized the importance of absent people.[19]

---

19 My thinking here about historical relationships between humans, objects, and affective ties is influenced by Leora Auslander, "Beyond Words," *American Historical Review* 110, no. 4 (October 2005): 1015–1045.

Non-human animals in early German photographs

Non-human animals brought to the portrait studio were equally important. Like clothing and jewelry, animals rested closely to the bodies of sitters. Dogs were the animals that appeared most often in mid-century German portraits, and they were featured in multiple ways. For example, dogs appeared regularly in portraits of children. In Wehnert-Beckmann's studio, famous for producing sensitive and compelling portraits of children, a particular dog appears with multiple sitters. The docile little black creature with pointy ears and a round belly was part of the complex process of capturing images of children. In the same studio, a far more substantial and elegant dog – perhaps an Irish Setter – graced dignified formal portraits of adult women, including a famous self-portrait of Wehnert-Beckmann herself. Dogs were also included in portraits of individuals, and even more often in family portraits. Presumably animals appeared in photographs because they were important. Most people had only a few images of themselves and therefore had to choose carefully what to include in portraits.

Even in the early years of the medium, photographers created singular portraits of dogs. German pioneers of photography such as Hermann Krone in Dresden, Carl Ferdinand Stelzner in Hamburg, and Wehnert-Beckmann in Leipzig, all turned their cameras on dogs that seem to have been their own. All three images we will consider here were *particular* dogs, and the photographs were personal rather than technical or documentary. The images by Krone and Stelzner, both daguerreotypes, were almost certainly produced in the 1850s. Krone's is dated 1851, and Stelzner's is dated between 1850–1865, but probably produced in the mid 1850s.[20] The third image, a self-portrait of Wehnert-Beckmann and her dog Pluto, is a photograph rather than a daguerreotype and probably dates to the late 1860s or 1870s. The portraits capture moments of human-animal interactions, mediated through the camera. Dog and photographer worked together to produce the image.

Krone's dog portrait is the earliest and most technically challenging of the three images. Taken outdoors in what looks like late spring or summer (there

---

20 Carl Ferdinand Stelzner, "Ulla, der Hund im Hause Stelzner," *Museum für Kunst und Gewerbe*, Hamburg, Pdo.J.222. The daguerreotype is dated by the Museum between 1850–1865, but Stelzner was producing daguerreotypes of his family and many people associated with his family in the mid 1850s, and it is likely that the dog was included in this detailed documentation of family life. Krone's daguerreotype, dated 1851, is from the Krone-Sammlung at the Technical University in Dresden. Krone's dog is discussed in Jochen Voigt, *Der gefrorene Augenblick: Daguerreotypie in Sachsen, 1839–1850* (Chemnitz: Edition Mobilis, 2004). It seems that the portrait of the dog is taken in front of the Japanese Pavilion in the Saxon city of Grimma, which is about 16 miles to the south of Leipzig.

are healthy leaves on the trees), Krone places his dog in front of a piece of Japanese-style architecture in a city park in the Saxon city of Grimma. The background is out of focus, but the outline of the roof suggests that this is not a European-style building. However, the dog, the fence, and the branch are all in full focus. The outline of the dog's body is carefully framed by the lines of the fence along the horizontal axis and by the triangles of lattice.

Famous for his technical innovations in photography, Krone is perhaps less recognized for the body of early, remarkably tender and playful daguerreotypes of those close to him, including his brother and wife. His self-portraits were similarly expansive; they included portraits of himself dressed in newspapers and others surrounded by elaborate collages of photographic equipment. Krone experienced the technical challenges of the early medium, working with slow exposure times and the challenges of natural light. Yet his daguerreotypes belie the refractory medium, which he was determined to press into the service of celebrating life. The emotional early daguerreotype of Krone and his wife, the playful images of Dresden's *Künstlerverein,* and the elegant portraits of his dandy brother reveal that Krone's relationship to the medium was emotive as well as technically and artistically ambitious.[21]

Krone's daguerreotype portrait of the dog may have served a number of purposes. For one thing, it was a technical challenge to set up the camera, focus the lens, and coax the dog to stay in place. Furthermore, he would have had to transport the camera and the developing equipment the 16 miles or so to Grimma. Historian Jochen Voigt reports that Krone was delighted that the picture took only one second to produce because of the abundant light.[22] But there is more to the image than execution and composition. Through the mediation of the camera, Krone casts a generous gaze on the animal. Daguerreotype cameras were big boxes, and it was technically difficult to meet the animal at its own level – yet we see the photographer has positioned himself at the level of the dog. Getting down on the ground suggests a kind of co-existence, if only momentarily. So too does the careful composition created by simple materials – pieces of wood pitched at different angles that emphasize the dog's shape without overpowering it. The effort to capture the animal in its own scale reflects thought and care. The animal responds with requisite stillness and composure, clearly comfortable enough to sit quietly. In the moment, photographer and dog surmount the technical difficulties and produce the portrait together.

---

21 These broader comments about Krone's daguerreotype work are based on my research into his work, including a research trip to the Krone-Sammlung in Dresden.
22 Voigt, *Der gefrorene Augenblick,* 151.

Figure 1: Hermann Krone, Hermann und Clementine Krone als Brautpaar, 1854, daguerreotype, Museum Ludwig, Köln, Ankauf/Acquisition Sammlung Agfa 2005/ Inventarnummer FH 00194.

It is less clear why Krone frames the dog against the grainy outline of the Japanese Pavilion. We can assume this was a deliberate choice, but one is left wondering how the humble wooden framing of the dog mixed with the (barely suggested) exoticism and monumentality of the building in the background. The Japanese Pavilion certainly serves to remove the dog from the *bürgerlich* domestic interiors that populated most photographic studios; and Krone does not decide to place his dog outside a European-style home, but rather in front of a

Figure 2: Hermann Krone, daguerreotype of a dog in front of the Japanese pavilion 1851. Hermann-Krone-Sammlung Dresden.

rather regal (and by no means ordinary) public building. Krone consistently played with the conventions of the photographic portrait; perhaps this explains his decision to picture the dog outside the conventions of the bourgeois interior.

A second daguerreotype portrait of a dog from an equally accomplished photographer, Carl Ferdinand Stelzner, provides a point of comparison for Krone's image. In this case, we know something about the dog in question, for the image is marked "Ulla, the dog from the Stelzner house." We can assume that Ulla belonged to the Stelzner family, and she merits her own dog-size pillow and exotic background. In this case, the background is a maritime scene with ships in the distance and a high mountain peak or maybe a volcano. None of this seems to mirror Ulla's domesticated existence in an established Hamburg household.[23]

---

23 Atelier von Carl Ferdinand Stelzner, "Ulla, der Hund im Hause Stelzner," c. 1850–1865, *Museum für Kunst und Gewerbe, Hamburg,* Sammlung Fotografie und neue Medien, PDo.J.222.

Figure 3: Carl Ferdinand Stelzner, "Ulla, der Hund im Hause Stelzner"/"Ulla, the dog from the Stelzner house" (1850-1865), daguerreotype, Museum für Kunst und Gewerbe, Hamburg.

One wonders why both Krone and Stelzner chose settings that refer to voyages abroad, to scenes of trade and to contacts with other cultures. Animal studies scholars emphasize enduring symbolic links between animals and colonized and enslaved peoples.[24] The dehumanization of people has long been related to the degradation of other creatures; talking about one is often also a way of talking about another. Stelzner and Krone probably did not intend to draw connections between dogs and the exploitation of colonial encounters, but both were sophisticated artists who made careful choices about how to create their photographs. In choosing atypical settings, they resisted the reigning convention to fold pet dogs into fully domesticated interiors. Yet both opted for backgrounds that involved human production; the animals were not cast in scenes of pristine nature.

Ulla the dog was one of several subordinate members of Stelzner's household captured in daguerreotypes. In the 1850s, the successful artist and portrait photographer committed time and resources to capturing his dog, his servant

---

24 Donna Haraway, *When Species Meet* (Minneapolis: U of Minnesota Press, 2008), 18.

Anna, and even the family's *Gemüsefrau* in photographic portraits.[25] These portraits of economic subordinates, like the portrait of Ulla, are all respectful. The photographer seemed intent on documenting the full range of creatures and humans who populated his household.

Like Krone, Stelzner collaborates with Ulla through the medium of the camera. The image they create together captures Ulla's obedience and ease. It took effort to position her on the cushion at just the right angle, which may have involved someone off to the side of the picture maintaining her gaze without luring her off the pillow and out of the frame. Her physical presence is on full display, taking up the center of the frame and unobstructed by the chairs and tables that occupied most human portraits. Brower's insight that images of animals structure how we see them seems important here. Ulla's careful placement on the pillow and at the center, the view of her straight on, humanize her. Even the backdrop provides a tranquil image, with schooners navigating gentle waters.

The final in this series of three by pioneers of early German photography is the self-portrait of Wehnert-Beckmann and her dog Pluto.[26] As a photograph – not a daguerreotype – taken in the late 1860s or early 1870s, the creation of this image posed fewer technical challenges. In addition, this is the one image in the series that places the collaboration between human and animal in full sight. Wehnert-Beckmann places herself, *with Pluto*, in front of the camera. Together, they form the subject of the image. While neither looks at the other, their bodies, expressions and gestures mirror one another. Pluto's presence suggests a certain joy in companionship, something that may have been deeply salutary for both sides of this animal-human pair.[27] Wehnert-Beckmann lost her husband, the accomplished daguerreotypist Eduard Wehnert, in 1847. She lived over three decades after his death – an active, professionally successful and probably full life – without remarrying. For a single, professional woman without children, Pluto's companionship may have been particularly welcome. The dog joined Wehnert-Beckmann in a smaller family unit than those of her male colleagues Krone and Stelzner, both of whom had wives. It is speculative to

25 Daguerreotype portraits of the Stelzner family's servant, Anna, are housed in the collection of the *Museum für Kunst und Gewerbe* in Hamburg; Stelzner also produced a rather famous daguerreotype portrait of a woman who was the fruit seller for the household.
26 "Bertha Wehnert-Beckmann in ihrem Atelier," c. 1870, *Stadtgeschichtliches Museum Leipzig*.
27 Jared Poley's essay in this volume argues that biologists Jakob von Uexküll and Konrad Lorenz, writing in the late nineteenth and early twentieth centuries, used the word *Kumpan* to describe animal companionship and caretaking "without the presence of an affective bond." I use "companion" here to describe the physical comfort expressed by both the human and the non-human animal in Wehnert-Beckmann's photograph.

Figure 4: Bertha Wehnert-Beckmann in her studio with her dog Pluto (c. 1870), photograph, Bertha Wehnert-Beckmann Sammlung, Stadtgeschichtliches Museum Leipzig, Inventarnummer: F/521/2004.

propose that all of this may account for why the photograph of Wehnert-Beckmann's dog is a double portrait – a visual documentation of their companionship. While Stelzner's and Krone's daguerreotypes represent important exchanges between humans and animals, Pluto and his photographer are framed together. Wehnert-Beckmann's dress and Pluto's coat harmonize perfectly; their expressions mirror one another. The bodily comfort of both creatures expressed in the photograph captures a moment of harmony and work shared between two.[28]

---

28 On Wehnert-Beckmann's life and career, see Jochen Voigt, *A German Lady: Bertha Wehnert-Beckmann, Leben und Werk einer Fotographiepionieren* (Chemnitz: Edition Mobilis, 2014).

Children and animals

Still, it was the other dog, smaller and less regal than Pluto, who performed the yeoman's work in Wehnert-Beckmann's studio in Leipzig. Over the course of a long career, she produced thousands of portraits, but those she made of children were (and still are) particularly well-regarded. Animals were integrated into many of these portraits – from the round little studio dog to live and stuffed birds, and a toy horse that found its way into many portraits of boys.

Creating sensitive, convincing photographs of small children was a matter of technique rather than affect, but the extensive collection of Wehnert-Beckmann's negatives housed at the Historical City Museum of Leipzig provides evidence of how she did it. As it turns out, she had help – on the one hand, from the chubby little dog who graced these portraits and from a woman who stood behind the curtains, gesturing to the children, propping them up if need be, and physically intervening in any shot that needed an extra (carefully concealed) hand.[29]

The same dog appears in multiple photographs of different children, which suggests that it was a regular fixture in the studio. As in the portrait above, this particular dog lent an additional presence, but was rarely seen interacting with the child. There were no portraits, for example, of the dog on a child's lap or by their feet. It occupied its own space – usually on a sofa or chair – providing an additional presence in the finished portrait. (While the woman behind the curtain was cropped out, the dog remained.) The lively little animal provided an animated presence, mirroring the youth of the sitter, and (perhaps importantly) kept the child from being alone in the portrait.

The vast majority of Wehnert-Beckmann's portraits of children incorporated non-human animals. These included the live and well-behaved studio dog, as well as a stuffed bird and toy horse that appeared in images of multiple children. In one series of images, a child is pictured holding and interacting with a pet bird. The photographs suggest how the presence of an animal could create an emotional narrative, and perhaps even a story about childhood.

In this lovely pair of images of a child and a small bird taken in Wehnert-Beckmann's studio, probably in the 1870s, we see a child dressed in jaunty attire holding and interacting with what appears to be a live small bird.[30] The presence

---

29 This glass negative of a child and dog is part of the large collection of negatives housed in the *Bertha Wehnert-Beckmann Sammlung* at the *Stadtgeschichtliches Museum Leipzig*. The dog and the woman behind the curtain appear in many portraits of children from Wehnert-Beckmann's studio.
30 This double portrait of a child and a bird is also housed amidst the hundreds of daguerreotypes, photographs and negatives housed in the *Bertha Wehnert-Beckmann Sammlung* at the *Stadtgeschichtliches Museum Leipzig*.

Figure 5: Bertha Wehnert-Beckmann, glass negative of a child and a dog (c. 1870s?), glass negative, Bertha Wehnert-Beckmann Sammlung, Stadtgeschichtliches Museum Leipzig, Inventarnummer F/2012/349.

of the bird brings a liveliness to the child's face. The exchange between animal and child suggests many things about the human who is ultimately the subject of the image. The presence of the bird, comfortable on the child's finger, indicates that the latter is gentle, playful, and capable of empathy. Photographers worked hard to find material and visual means to represent their sitters' inner life – particularly their capability for contemplation and empathy. Books, settled bodies, and thoughtful expressions were one way to represent such qualities; interactions with animals were another.

John Berger's "Why Look at Animals?" speaks at length to the visual association between children and animals just as the species were increasingly estranged by industrialization. Stuffed animals, hobby horses, and visits to the zoo, he writes, populated Victorian childhoods at a historical moment marked by the privatization and isolation of both humans and animals. Judging from the bulk of mid nineteenth-century photographic portraits that show children with some kind of animal, Berger is certainly right to identify this change happening in

Figure 6: Bertha Wehnert-Beckmann, double portrait of a child and a bird (c. 1870s?), photograph, Bertha Wehnert-Beckmann Sammlung, Stadtgeschichtliches Museum Leipzig, Inventarnummer F/2012/1522.

European cultures of childhood. Yet it is possible to interpret the presence of animals differently. In the German states at mid-century, the ability to connect empathetically with another creature was important – not because humans were so very empathetic, but precisely because they were feared not to be. Thus, for the first two and a half decades of the medium, expression and emotion were important features of the formal portrait, even as these qualities were difficult to represent. This effort to represent interiority would change in the 1870s as photographs became more ubiquitous and public. But early photographs, which were spare in number and often came only in singular images, served important emotional ends – demonstrating connections between creatures, providing tools of remembrance, capturing the physical qualities of distinct human beings, and speaking to things past. As creatures who were also to be remembered, non-human animals played an important role in the co-creation of the early genre and its innumerable iterations.

Bibliography

Auslander, Leora. "Beyond Words," *American Historical Review* 110, no. 4 (October 2005): 1015–1045.

Barthes, Roland. *Camera Lucida: Reflections on Photography*. Trans. Richard Howard (New York: Hill and Wang, 1981).

Batchen, Geoffrey. *Forget Me Not: Photography and Remembrance* (New York: Princeton Architectural Press, 2004).

Berger, John. "Why Look at Animals?" in *About Looking* (New York: Vintage Books, 1980), 1–26.

Brower, Matthew. *Developing Animals: Wildlife and Early American Photography* (Minneapolis: U of Minnesota Press, 2011).

Burt, Jonathan. "John Berger's 'Why Look at Animals?': A Close Reading," *Worldviews* 9, no. 2 (2005): 203–218.

Fudge, Erica. "A Left-Handed Blow: Writing the History of Animals," in *Representing Animals*. Ed. Nigel Rothfels, Kindle Version, Location 165–436 of 3650 (Bloomington: Indiana UP, 2002).

Halttunen, Karen. "Humanitarianism and the Pornography of Pain in Anglo-American Culture," *American Historical Review* 100, no. 2 (April 1995): 303–334.

Haraway, Donna. *When Species Meet* (Minneapolis: U of Minnesota Press, 2008).

Kete, Kathleen. "Animals and Ideology: The Politics of Animal Protection in Europe," in *Representing Animals*. Ed. Nigel Rothfels, Kindle Version, Location 439–703 of 3650.

Leonard, Sarah L. *Fragile Minds and Vulnerable Souls: The Matter of Obscenity in Nineteenth-Century Germany* (Philadelphia: U of Pennsylvania Press, 2015).

Lipsett-Rivera, Sonya. "A New Challenge: Social History and Dogs in the Era of Post-Humanism," *Sociedad Indiana* (2015). https://socindiana.hypotheses.org/320.

Lulka, David. "Animals, Daguerreotypes and Movement: The Despair of Fading and the Emergence of Ontology," *Journal of Material Culture* 19, no. 1 (2014): 35–58.

Scheer, Monique. "Are Emotions a Kind of Practice (And Is That What Makes Them Have a History)? A Bourdieuian Approach to Understanding Emotion," *History and Theory* 51, no. 2 (2012): 193–220.

Voigt, Jochen. *A German Lady: Bertha Wehnert-Beckmann, Leben & Werk einer Fotografiepionierin* (Chemnitz: Edition Mobilis, 2014).

Voigt, Jochen, and Christoph Kaufmann. *Der gefrorene Augenblick: Daguerreotypie in Sachsen, 1839–1860: Inkunabeln der Photographie in sächsischen Sammlungen: gemeinsamer Bestandskatalog "Daguerreotypie"* (Chemnitz: Edition Mobilis, 2004).

Brett Martz
Between the Animal and the Reader

A Comparison of the Affective Possibilities in Musil's "Can a Horse Laugh?" (1936) and "The Lady from Portugal" (1923)

If you have ever struggled to understand how the inner lives of non-human animals can on the one hand be so seemingly inscrutable, and yet on the other hand still invite us to try to experience feelings beyond the human, then you will also find yourself at one of the points that inspires the writing of the early twentieth-century Austrian author, Robert Musil. Coming of age when the ideas of "scientific materialism and philosophical irrationalism in liberal Vienna" dominated, Musil's writing is marked by a tendency to combine intellect and feeling: to think ecstatically and feel cerebrally.[1] Central to this inclination are his attempts to understand and write "the Other." This essay examines the barriers to and possibilities for fiction's capacity to represent the affective relationships between humans and non-humans, in particular non-human animals in two of Musil's short works. Analyses of the essay, "Kann ein Pferd lachen?" ("Can a Horse Laugh?"), as well as the novella, "Die Portugiesin" ("The Lady from Portugal") will explain how Musil's texts deploy the non-human animal in order to probe the frameworks for narrating, understanding, and experiencing emotions. This essay also attempts to expand on the limited research dedicated to Musil's writing on the non-human animal by drawing particular attention to how his choices of presentation, style, and genre drive the critical inflection he places on the role of animal figures in works that probe human emotions.

The first text under analysis, "Can a Horse Laugh?" is a short essay suffused with irony that emphasizes the limits of how humans understand emotions, but it also criticizes the discourses that enforce those limits. Its satirical structure presents a subtle yet undeniably pessimistic picture about the viability – in fiction or life – of approaching any emotion beyond the boundaries circumscribed by strictly defined anthropocentric frameworks. Simultaneously, the essay exposes those frameworks through its criticism of discursive authority and thus leaves the door slightly open for more optimistic attempts to transgress fixed categories for emotional understanding. "The Lady from Portugal," the second work under discussion, is an image-rich novella that is far more generous than

---

1 David Luft, *Eros and Inwardness in Vienna: Weininger, Musil, Doderer* (Chicago: U of Chicago Press, 2003), 35.

https://doi.org/10.1515/9783110753677-006

Musil's biting essay in terms of its portrayal of emotional possibilities. It, too, scrutinizes the objectifying structures such as authority and masculinity that are presented in "Can a Horse Laugh?". Through the introduction of a dying cat, it invites readers to imagine and possibly even feel the kind of ephemeral and ineffable emotions that elude objectifying gestures. Although the novella is more optimistic than the satirical essay, it too contains a disenchanted and somewhat negative perspective on the manner in which martial attitudes and the demands of regime administration prop up – typically male – identities and feelings. As David Luft explains, Musil "employed the metaphor of gender to describe two different kinds of knowledge, two different relations to experience, and the balance between thinking and feeling in the personality and in the culture."[2] Herr von Ketten, the novella's protagonist, is above all, a warlord, and yet through interactions with his wife, the titular lady from Portugal, and then eventually a stray cat, he develops a yearning for non-instrumentalized, vulnerable, and tender kinds of emotions at odds with his daily dealings. Ultimately, both texts confront the reader with the "absolute problem of alterity" that Kari Weil claims non-human animals present to their human counterparts.[3] This problem raises the question of how well one can understand the emotional lives of any other being, which in turn can call the status of one's own emotional self-understanding into question, particularly if the same conceptual or observational methods are used to interpret both other and self.[4]

Who's laughing? Discursive authority and the limits of emotions

Musil's short essay "Can a Horse Laugh?" appears in the 1936 collection *Nachlass zu Lebzeiten* (*Posthumous Papers of a Living Author*), and contains, among other culturally critical observations that Musil calls "little satires," numerous sketches containing non-human animals that Musil had written and published individually over two decades.[5] A diary entry from around 1918–19 lists a handful of these titles under the heading "Animal Book."[6] Through its ironic tone, "Can a Horse Laugh?" exhibits a subtle awareness of its own inadequacy that strategically destabilizes the

---

2 Luft, *Eros and Inwardness in Vienna*, 93.
3 Kari Weil, *Thinking Animals: Why Animal Studies Now?* (New York: Columbia UP, 2012), 32.
4 See Weil's chapter on "Seeing Animals," page 49 in particular.
5 Robert Musil, *Gesammelte Werke Band 7* (Reinbek: Rowohlt, 1978), 474. Translation mine.
6 Robert Musil, *Tagebücher Band 1* (Reinbek: Rowohlt, 1976), 340. Translation mine.

prejudices and assumptions that the discourses of scientific expertise disseminate and assure. It thus aligns itself with the trend in animal studies scholarship to rebuke uncritical applications of human frameworks as if they were universal ways of experiencing the world (i.e., careless anthropocentrism).[7] Musil's short essay regards anthropocentric frameworks as subjectively situated but at the same time still conditioned by structures of authority. While it is as much an examination of our own inner lives as it is that of a horse's ability to exhibit qualities suggesting such a life, it just as importantly calls attention to the precariousness of privileged ways of knowing, performed in the text via the voices of the psychologist, the learned skeptic, and ultimately the narrator too. Mindful of his training in physics, mathematics, and experimental psychology, Musil, who privileges the capacity of fiction for exploring emotions, nevertheless does not seek to have literature ultimately overtake science in any race towards ultimate representational legitimacy in the realm of feelings or any qualities.[8] Such an attitude would commit the same error of guaranteeing the prescriptive authority satirically attributed to the psychologist and the skeptic. Moreover, it would reinforce traditional dualisms, such as rationality and feeling, that he spent his life contesting, dualisms that also strictly separate human and non-human. Instead, his essay primarily interrogates the forces that establish and patrol the limits for understanding the emotional lives of others. As the introduction to this volume notes, the important role that emotions play in communication, moral reasoning, and decision making is now widely recognized. Musil was way ahead of the curve in coming to this conclusion. In his essay "Helpless Europe," he famously writes, "We do not have too much intellect and too little soul, but too little intellect in matters of the soul."[9] "Soul," according to Musil's essay "Profile of a Program" is "a complex interpenetration of feeling

---

7 See John Simons, *Animal Rights and the Politics of Literary Representation* (New York: Palgrave, 2002), 119–120. Simons criticizes certain representations of animals with human qualities in fables as "trivial anthropomorphism," because they do not deal with "the boundary of the human and non-human," whereas "strong" anthropomorphisms make such an attempt. The anthropocentric hue of "sentimentality" is also undesirable where it stands for a vulgar or superficial idealism towards animals or "bourgeois bad faith" as Tobias Menely describes it. Tobias Menely, *The Animal Claim: Sensibility and the Creaturely Voice* (Chicago: U of Chicago Press, 2015), 184–185. Alice Kuzniar exhorts readers to "resist" sentimentality so that one might encounter the "arduousness of breaching the gap between the species." In short, "sentimentality" is seen as negative when it is unreflective or uncritical. Alice Kuzniar, *Melancholia's Dog: Reflections on our Animal Kinship* (Chicago: U of Chicago Press, 2005), 6 and 134.
8 See Musil's essay "The Mathematical Man," in *Robert Musil: Precision and Soul: Essays and Addresses*, eds. Burton Pike and David Luft (Chicago: U of Chicago Press, 1990), 39–43. In it Musil asserts the need for intellect *and* feeling.
9 Robert Musil, "Helpless Europe," trans. Philip Beard, in *Precision and Soul*, 131.

and intellect," and essays such as this, as well as "Mind and Experience," deal with the interplay of thinking and feeling.[10]

"Can a Horse Laugh?" begins with the narrator's proud assertion that he has in fact seen a horse laugh despite the pronouncement of a respected psychologist to the contrary. The narrator admits that his motivation to proceed with his story stems from the opportunity to challenge such an esteemed opinion. The introduction of the psychologist's claim in the very first line establishes the authority of science to circumscribe the capacity for horses to behave like humans, while also arousing a curiosity about how the narrator might possibly refute such expertise. Even the essay's title suggests such a contest, because it is posed as a question that likely assumes most readers are skeptical (or at least curious) about the narrator's claim.

The reader soon discovers that the narrator possesses his own, possibly flawed assumptions, which are contained in the remark, "Now a horse has, so to speak, four shoulders and is therefore twice as ticklish as a person."[11] The narrator shows just how difficult it is to avoid projecting an anthropocentric manner of understanding onto the creature, imagining that the horse must be ticklish under its arms and legs, because that is typical for humans. If you as a reader suddenly relate to yourself or someone you know as an exception to this general observation, then you may have already anticipated one point of this essay, namely that these exceptions imply that it is questionable to apply general patterns of experiences universally.

The next few sentences describe how the stable boy combs the horse, and they remain free of any postulation about the horse's temperament, reading as if they were an objective report of observed reactions. For example, the agent behind the brush, namely the stable boy, disappears behind the impersonal actions of the brush itself:

> Already when the comb approached from a distance the horse laid back its ears, became restless, reached for it with its mouth, and when it couldn't get to it bared its teeth. But the comb marched merrily on, stroke for stroke, and the lips exposed more and more of the teeth [. . .][12]

---

10 Robert Musil, "Profile of a Program," in *Precision and Soul*, 10. For similar remarks from "Mind and Experience," see in particular pages 141–149 in *Precision and Soul*.
11 Robert Musil, "Can a Horse Laugh?" trans. Burton Pike, in *Selected Writings*, ed. Burton Pike (New York: Continuum Publishing, 1986), 317. The original text tempers the narrator's observation with a a non-committal "maybe" ("vielleicht"). Musil, *Gesammelte Werke Band 7*, 482.
12 Musil, "Can a Horse Laugh?," 317.

Whereas the reader might wonder if this treatment annoys the horse, such a thought never even occurs to the narrator. The candid style nevertheless invites such second guessing, which can perform on the level of the reader the same type of challenge that the narrator issues against the renowned psychologist. Perhaps the narrator refrains from interjecting any opinion, because he likely has never been confined to a stall and combed by a stable boy.

Eventually the text reaches its supposed payoff with the line, "And suddenly it began to laugh. It bared its teeth."[13] The narrator decides that the horse must be laughing, because the stable boy's stimulations have finally caused it to bare its teeth. The narrator's conclusion is reasonable; after all, it is not unusual for people to have similar physical reactions when they laugh. Yet readers anticipating a monumental or definitive piece of evidence in support of the narrator's seemingly extraordinary claim must be satisfied with only this scant proof that they themselves may have observed in their own interactions with horses and yet never considered to be a sign of horse humor. The narrator is certain the pair is having fun. "[. . .] the two of them played in obvious agreement," he maintains, judging by what he sees.[14] Yet it does not occur to him that maybe the horse is annoyed, and indeed an earlier version of the text suggests that the horse might be screaming rather than laughing.[15] Ultimately, the narrator simply draws a conclusion by relating his own experiences to his observations. The difficulty involved in applying the frameworks of amusement or annoyance to a horse draws attention to the general instability of such categories based on how we perceive them in others at large. Depending upon how one defined laughter, one could certainly argue, as the narrator does, that the horse and the stable boy are having a great time. On the other hand, one must remain cognizant of who defines and in what context. Paul Patton's contribution to *Zoontologies*, entitled "Language, Power, and the Training of Horses," explores the ethical dimensions of the power relationships between horses, their trainers, and human conceptions of beauty, arguing that horses exhibit trained reactions that "satisfy the culturally acquired desires of their trainers and riders."[16] In the context of Musil's essay, Patton reminds us to take care in projecting human values onto observed horse reactions.

---

13 Musil, "Can a Horse Laugh?," 317.
14 Musil, "Can a Horse Laugh?," 318. The translator chose the word "obvious," but Musil's term, "sichtlich" underscores the subjective nature of the observation. Musil, *Gesammelte Werke Band 7*, 483.
15 See "The Laughing Horse" ("Das lachende Pferd"). Musil, *Tagebücher Band 1*, 345.
16 Paul Patton, "Language, Power, and the Training of Horses," in *Zoontologies: The Question of the Animal*, ed. Cary Wolfe (Minnesota: U of Minnesota Press, 2003), 83–100, here 95.

Musil's next two comparisons highlight how any supposed insight into the inner states of others always contains a trace of unreliability. As the horse maneuvers to push the boy away with its face while refraining from biting him, it does so "like a farm girl would have with her hand."[17] The narrator's attempt to provide insight into the horse's disposition betrays somewhat masculine assumptions about the nature of human interactions, which is one reason why my chapter genders all pronouns referring to the narrator as masculine. What does one actually suppose when one sees a farm girl gently push away a teasing stable boy, and does point of view matter? Such a farm girl could be having fun, teasing, and playing, but it could just as easily be that she is annoyed but refrains from adamantly pushing the boy away out of fear of violent reprisal from which she, like the horse in a stall, cannot escape. Perhaps if the narrator declared herself to be a woman, she would present a different interpretation of the horse-farm girl comparison. Shortly thereafter the narrator reports, "[. . .] it acted exactly like a person who is being tickled so hard he can't laugh any more."[18] Again, the narrator applies no other understanding beyond that which he has seen in other humans or himself, but he still insists, despite evidence that the horse may be annoyed, that the horse laughs. Musil has his narrator make subtly problematic comparisons to reflect on the inadequacy of any framework for understanding others, expert or otherwise. For this reason, I am somewhat skeptical of Marie-Louise Roth's claim that the narrator somehow understands the horse via an act of empathy ("*Einfühlung*"). Her article correctly suggests that Musil's essay uses a "constructive irony" to awaken a critical perspective in the reader that can be used to question the prejudices of the psychologist's universal generalizations, but this irony can be constructively applied to the narrator as well.[19]

The text grants the discourse of expertise another rebuttal, albeit with an ironic twist. "The scholarly doubter will object that this shows that it could not really laugh. [. . .] this is insofar correct as of the two it was the stable-boy who every time whinnied with laughter. To be able to whinny with laughter seems in fact to be an ability possessed only by humans."[20] Here the narrator concedes to the scholarly doubter the privilege of being able to define what "laughter" is, and his concession forecloses the horse's ability to laugh and by extension any emotional dimension that one might associate with such an ability. On the

---

17 Musil, "Can a Horse Laugh?," 317.

18 Musil, "Can a Horse Laugh?," 318.

19 Marie-Louise Roth, "'Kann ein Pferd lachen?' Musils Ironie, eine perspektivische Verschiebung?" in *Robert Musils "Nachlaß zu Lebzeiten*," ed. Gudrun Brokoph-Mauch (New York: Peter Lang, 1985), 123–135, here 133.

20 Musil, "Can a Horse Laugh?," 318.

other hand, Musil's substitution of whinnying for the stable boy's laughter performs like an offbeat catachresis that calls the whole ability-defining theme of the essay into question.[21] Whinnying exists foremost in the domain of horses and thus is not strictly the capacity of humans, but apparently *only* humans can whinny with laughter solely because experts and skeptics agree that horses cannot laugh. However, if whinnying can be considered an expression of laughter, at least in humans, then by what authority could one preclude the capacity to laugh in horses when they whinny? The narrator's anthropomorphic move in the early part of the text, which granted horses the ability to laugh based on a supposed smile, here gets turned on its head. If one sees a stable boy whinnying, one cannot be sure that he is laughing. On a broader scale, one must come to terms with the notion that discursive power structures enforce and delimit emotional capacities, all thanks to the essay's random encounter with a supposedly smiling horse. In her article, "Literary Animal Agents," Susan McHugh concerns herself with the representation of animal agency and how non-human figures function in fiction. Such "agents," she concludes, "are never separable from human presences," and her claim that "species forms, approached as ways of knowing, indicate the limits of comparable human ways of being as well as insist on more open-ended potentials [. . .]" relates to the two texts under discussion here: "Can a Horse Laugh" probes limits. "The Lady from Portugal" explores potentials.[22]

In the midst of this uncertainty, the learned skeptic retrenches and redefines his position in the text's penultimate sentence, "So the scholarly doubt about the ability of animals limits itself to this, that an animal cannot laugh at jokes."[23] Denying the horse the ability to laugh at jokes would be easier to defend, but it evades the problem posed by the text. Just as the narrator could not really prove that the horse can laugh, neither can the skeptic categorically refute the narrator's claim. This impasse cannot be blamed on the horse, as the narrator finally remarks on the horse's inability to laugh at jokes, "But that can't always be held against the horse."[24] In all fairness, the horse cannot be blamed for lacking a faculty that by definition excludes it, because this is the

---

21 See Robert Musil, *The Man Without Qualities*, trans. Sophie Wilkins and Burton Pike (New York: Vintage Books, 1995), 41–44. In particular on page 42, Ulrich expresses dismay that the trend towards measured optimization and ultimately mechanization, which is the core of "Psychotechnik," would obviate other values that defy instrumentalization.

22 Susan McHugh, "Literary Animal Agents," *PMLA* 124, no. 2 (2009): 487–495, here 491 and 488.

23 Musil, "Can a Horse Laugh?," 318.

24 Musil, "Can a Horse Laugh?," 318.

fault of the skeptic, the psychologist, and their discursive authorities. With this final twist, the narrator underscores the capricious, and in this case anthropocentric, nature of categorizing and assigning qualities. The concluding quip punctuates a text that along the way deploys questionable comparisons ironically against the self-assured narrator's frank understanding of them as proof of his claim. In doing so, it expands the initial doubt about the ability to apply such categorical frameworks for the purposes of understanding non-human animals into a doubt about the adequacy of those frameworks themselves for doing anything more than making guesses about what others are doing and by extension how they may be feeling.

Ineffable vulnerability in "The Lady from Portugal"

Whereas the horse analyzed above is a device to criticize the strictures of commonly accepted emotional frameworks, the mysterious and frail cat in Robert Musil's 1923 novella, "The Lady from Portugal," performs a more optimistic function. Musil's novella probes the categories of interpersonal vulnerability and extrapersonal love as they press against social demands and individual expectations. The titles of the preliminary drafts for the story, "The little spirit-cat in Bozen" and "The little spirit-cat from beyond," both indicate that Musil's fascination with the emotional bearing of a strange, sick cat on its bystanders served as a primary germ for the story's development.[25] To say quite simply that the cat brings the two main figures in the story, Herr von Ketten and his Portuguese wife, closer together might sound like the hackneyed plot of yet another sentimental animal tale. While this basic summary is fundamentally accurate, it overlooks the novella's experimental density and complexity. Musil's abstruse style, which abounds with figurative language and vague imagery,[26] demands emotional work on behalf of the reader in order to comprehend the cat's significance for the figures within the

---

25 See *Robert Musils Tagebücher Band* 2 (Reinbek: Rowohlt, 1976), 1055–1060. The Frisé edition reorganizes these notes into a streamlined narrative form in volume seven of the collected works, pp. 762–765. The diary version has more references to key figures from Musil's life as well as textual edits. Certain portions of both texts are nearly identical, and multiple motifs from these "cat" sketches also appear in "The Lady from Portugal," such as: a soldier returning to his wife after war; the soldier's sickness; another rival man, and of course the sick cat.
26 On the prevalence and density of images in "The Lady from Portugal" see Karl Eibl, *Robert Musil, drei Frauen: Text, Materialien, Kommentar* (Munich: Hanser, 1978), 140–141.

novella as well as the text's wider exploration of tenderness and mystical intersubjectivity, by which I mean the capacity for two figures to overcome the alterity of a significant other. Musil's novella crystallizes this challenge in the following passage: "When [von Ketten] gazed into his wife's eyes, they were like new-cut glass, and although what the surface showed him was his own reflection, he could not penetrate further. It seemed to him that only a miracle could change this situation."[27] The lady from Portugal is quite foreign to von Ketten in many ways, most obviously on the basis of her culture and gender; nevertheless, he seeks to realize a love that will bring them so close together as to be almost one, a miraculous overcoming of his self reflected in her eyes. Because a key feature of this experience is its gossamer elusiveness, it is difficult to describe for both Musil and me; nevertheless, I would argue that the emotions under discussion orbit around the themes of empathy and self-dissolution. In her entry on "Empathy," Lori Gruen distinguishes between an "affective" empathy that "involves an imaginative resonance across differences," and a "cognitive" empathy that entails an "intention to shift perspectives or simulate/embody the perspective of another."[28] Musil's text seeks to fold these two categories into each other, and it thematically portrays the challenge of this task via von Ketten, his wife, and the cat. It simultaneously attempts to provide the reader with an aesthetic opportunity to experience the other in both affective and cognitive modalities.

My interpretation of the emotions Musil attempts to describe also shares the attitude of Cora Diamond's remark in her essay, "The Difficulty of Reality and the Difficulty of Philosophy," that "[t]he awareness we each have of being a living body, being 'alive to the world,' carries with it exposure to the bodily sense of vulnerability to death, sheer animal vulnerability, the vulnerability we share with them."[29] I stress *animal* vulnerability above all, because it is the cat that finally allows von Ketten more access to the feelings of interpersonal connection that elude him. To put this into more personal, colloquial, and possibly helpful terms: if one has ever collectively witnessed animal suffering, not in a violent, shocking manner as one might observe at a slaughterhouse, but in a somewhat pitiful way, as might be presented in a show about animal rescue, *and* at the same time, one has felt an inexplicable bond or heightened sense of

---

27 Robert Musil, "The Lady from Portugal," trans. Eithne Wilkins and Ernst Kaiser, in *Selected Writings*, ed. Burton Pike (New York: Continuum Publishing, 1986), 260.
28 Lori Gruen, "Empathy," in *Critical Terms for Animal Studies*, ed. Lori Gruen (Chicago: U of Chicago Press, 2018), 142–153, p. 146.
29 Cora Diamond, "The Difficulty of Reality and the Difficulty of Philosophy," in *Philosophy and Animal Life* (New York: Columbia UP, 2008), 43–89, here 74.

connection to a fellow spectator, be they a loved one or even a stranger, then one has gotten a sense of the phenomenon that Musil labors to portray in "The Lady from Portugal." It is beyond pity and yet related to an empathy that is radically open, selfless, but still also embodied. For this reason, this essay's deployment of the term "empathy" aligns itself closely with the insights provided by Derek Hillard's contribution to this volume. It does not simply suggest sympathy or cognitive perspective-taking as a basis for ethical action; instead, it points here towards a deeply affective and aesthetic experience prompted by the other that is incredibly difficult to describe. The following analysis will first attempt to explain the nature of this experience, because it appears in the novella before the cat shows up to facilitate it.

"The Lady from Portugal" takes place in the Middle Ages and contains some fairy tale tropes. It depicts not only castles, royalty, and warfare, but it also mentions nearby demons, a dragon, and a unicorn.[30] While von Ketten, born into and expected to uphold an intergenerational feud with the Bishops of Trent, has deep ties to his place of birth, his wife abandons her homeland to live with him in – what is to her – an exotic and portentous cliffside castle nestled into an almost supernatural forest landscape. "The Lady from Portugal" is, however, no fairy tale in a traditional sense in which one might expect to find fantastic elements performing preternatural acts in the service of allegory. Even the cat, whose appearance is so consequential for the narrative, neither speaks nor wears boots; it is just a sick cat, but its presence is perceived as somehow otherworldly. For example, its onlookers perceive it to have a halo. The fairy tale elements in Musil's novella, while nominally there, are phantoms of the imagination, which renders it difficult to discern any concrete connections to shared systems of belief in the service of allegory.[31]

Amid his fairy tale surroundings, von Ketten has a problem. He secretly loves tenderness and openness more than the violent and aloof warrior ethos that has shaped him and his family for generations. They have been perpetually unsuccessful in their conflicts against the Bishops, and this failure guarantees his continued participation in a set of circumstances that maintains his sense of self, namely that of a noble soldier in the mold of his forefathers.[32] In a section about the evening upon which Herr von Ketten's second son is conceived, the text starkly juxtaposes his private passion and public persona.

---

30 Musil, "The Lady from Portugal," 248.
31 See Eibl, *Drei Frauen*, 104, and Boa, "Austrian Ironies," 121.
32 Musil, "The Lady from Portugal," 247.

> What intimate, familiar things, by contrast [to the tender emotion he secretly desires], did the strategies of war, and political cunning and anger and killing seem to him! An act is performed because some other act has preceded it. The Bishop relies on his gold pieces, and the captain on the nobility's powers of endurance. To command is a thing of clarity; such a life is day-bright, solid to the touch, and the thrust of a spear under an iron collar that has slipped is as simple as pointing one's finger at something and being able to say: This is *this*. But the other thing is as alien as the moon.[33]

Warfare provides Herr von Ketten a dependable life and stable identity. Violence, here in the shape of a spear thrust, is simple by comparison to the aforementioned "tender," "alien" emotion he secretly loves. Despite his private wishes, von Ketten's name, which translates as "of chains" or "of fetters," quite literally binds him to the iron-clad reality of his courtly and military obligations. Thus, von Ketten feels compelled to love the "other," tender, inscrutable pangs in secret. The gender norms of Musil's time heavily influenced how he tries to resolve von Ketten's conflict between his hardened, warrior life and the secret emotion that the lady from Portugal's presence makes available to him. David Luft refers to these realms as "dream and reality" and notes that "[t]his split in modern consciousness was often associated with prejudices about the nature of masculinity and femininity, and the goal of Musil's reflections on gender was to achieve a more balanced understanding of these human qualities."[34] Additionally, one could argue that the text itself is as subtle and circumspect in divulging this secret as von Ketten himself, because von Ketten's vague admission lies tucked within a sober, almost aggressive inventory of certainties and thus might be easy to disregard.

Though my analysis is primarily concerned with the cat's role at the end of "The Lady from Portugal," the focus of my contribution on non-human animals in general necessitates a brief explanation of the appearance of another non-human animal, namely a wolf. First, Herr von Ketten's tactical acumen is compared to the hunting prowess of a wolf.[35] When von Ketten becomes ill and half incapacitated in the middle of the story, his wife develops a bond with a wild wolf that reminds her of her husband's virility, and it nobly commands respect from the other dogs in the castle.[36] Von Ketten is jealous of the devotion between the wife and the wolf but cannot reclaim his place by her side in his weakened state. He therefore has the wolf killed. In return she sneaks into his room and tells him, "I shall have a hood made of the pelt, and come by night

33 Musil, "The Lady from Portugal," 253.
34 Luft, *Eros and Inwardness*, 123.
35 Musil, "The Lady from Portugal," 251.
36 Musil, "The Lady from Portugal," 254.

and suck the blood from your veins."[37] In the context of this essay's argument, the wolf stands for an aggressive and possessive sort of desire that, as the lady from Portugal's response demonstrates, is not limited to von Ketten.

Scholars tend to view the wolf as a vehicle for exploring notions of the self, and in particular the masculine assumptions that underlie von Ketten's identity. For example, Karl Eibl deems the wolf's killing a "symbolic suicide" required for von Ketten to break free from his old life.[38] Susan Erickson arrives at a different conclusion in noting that Musil's comparisons actually destabilize themselves as referents, and it may be "wrong to think 'in terms of' a self at all."[39] Because ample evidence indicates that von Ketten is interested in an almost sublime state of selflessness that nevertheless returns to itself, I am sympathetic to Erickson's interpretation of the wolf as a poetic device in this manner; however, enough evidence exists to claim that the wolf represents precisely the opposite, namely the solidification of the self, and thus her argument might have been better served by pivoting to the cat. Wolfgang Müller-Funk's understanding of the wolf and cat as "proxy in the fight between man and woman" with the former corresponding to the male and the latter female maps too rigidly onto an external battle-of-the-sexes narrative.[40] Gender differences do figure prominently in the story, and other analyses make similar moves. For example, Paul Requadt associates the male and female with the text's alternating "factual" vs. "image" styles respectively, while Thomas Pekar argues similarly with the motifs of (male) vision and (female) sound.[41] Müller-Funk's reading of the cat and wolf figures is too systematic for my argument. The cat especially will be important not because it stands for the feminine, but because it could be anything, even "God." Musil wants to overcome the "otherness" underpinning the gender divide, not use it as a symbolic key for understanding the animals in the text.

Those familiar with Musil's oeuvre knows that he spent considerable effort trying to reconcile the categories of experience that comprise similar competing compulsions in von Ketten's life. It is therefore worth expounding upon how the terms "moon" and "tenderness" recur throughout "The Lady from Portugal"

---

37 Musil, "The Lady from Portugal," 257.
38 Eibl, *Drei Frauen*, 119.
39 Susan Erickson, "The Psychopoetics of Narrative in Robert Musil's 'Die Portugiesin'," *Monatshefte* 78, no. 2 (1986): 167–181, here 172.
40 Wolfgang Müller-Funk, *Komplex Österreich. Fragmente zu einer Geschichte der modernen österreichischen Literatur* (Vienna: Sonderzahl, 2009), 203.
41 Paul Requadt, "Zu Musils 'Portugiesin,'" in *Robert Musil*, ed. Renate von Heydebrand (Darmstadt: Wissenschaftliche Buchgesellschaft, 1982), 321–332, here 324; Thomas Pekar, *Die Sprache der Liebe bei Robert Musil* (Munich: Fink, 1989), 125.

and pertain to the secret realm of feeling that von Ketten cherishes. Moreover, these words appear in other texts by Musil on similar themes.[42] In the novella, the Portuguese woman, herself a "moon-lady / nocturnal enchantress" is connected to themes of tenderness, love, and Otherness.[43] Directly preceding the passage regarding von Ketten's dissatisfaction with public or tangible assets such as order, status, and riches, one reads:

> Tranquilly the woman sat there [. . .] a figure rising out of itself and falling back into itself, like the water of a fountain. And is the water of a fountain anything that can be ransomed and redeemed, can it be set free by anything but magic or some miracle, and thus issue forth wholly out of its self-borne, swaying existence? Embracing the woman, might he not suddenly be brought up short by the force of some magical resistance? This was not so – but is tenderness not even more uncanny?[44]

It is telling that the translation uses both "redeem" and "set free" to account for the verb "erlösen," because it indicates how von Ketten fancies the notion that ultimate redemption might lie within the possibility of his wife breaking free from the social and experiential forces that shape the self. If such release were possible, then they would be able to mingle together beyond the contours enforcing their alterity, like two streams of water released from the containers shaping them.[45] When the text presents the possibility to overcome the powers that keep the couple split, the words "zärtlich" or "Zärtlichkeit" ("tender/-ness") often appear. They are key terms for signifying the mysterious, "other" type of love that exists

---

42 Leaving aside the vast quantity of Musil scholarship on the "other condition / der andere Zustand" in general, it is still worth noting that studies devoted to analyzing "Die Portugiesin" compare von Ketten's two states of being with Musil's neologisms, "ratioïd" and "nicht-ratioïd" found in his 1918 essay, "Sketch of What the Writer Knows." Examples referenced in this chapter include Karl Eibl on p. 137 and Ronald Paulson on p. 116. Ronald Paulson, "A Re-examination and Re-interpretation of Some of the Symbols in Robert Musil's Die Portugiesin," *Modern Austrian Literature* 13.2 (1980): 111–121. In summary, the ratioïd zone deals with facts, rules, and repetition. It is important to understand these terms as existing on a continuum rather than as binary poles of rationality and irrationality. Birgit Nübel explains these terms concisely yet thoroughly in the *Robert Musil Handbuch*, eds. Birgit Nübel and Norbert Christian Wolf (Berlin: De Gruyter, 2016), 347–349.

43 Robert Musil, "The Lady from Portugal," 256. Both "moon" and "tenderness" reappear in a chapter sketch for *The Man Without Qualities* called "Mondrausch" ("Lunar Rapture"), one of Musil's later attempts to come to terms with the kind of experience that von Ketten secretly craves. Cf. Robert Musil, *Gesammelte Werke Band 5* (Reinbek: Rowohlt, 1978), 2034–2035.

44 Musil, "The Lady from Portugal," 252–253.

45 Compare the fountain with Erickson's discussion of "self as mollusk." "The Psychopoetics of Narrative," 169.

beyond von Ketten's typical war-driven sphere of causality and rationality.[46] "Tenderness" is not objectively localizable but instead surrounds its participants, making them one with their environment and each other.

This heightened sense of "tenderness" sheds the constraints of the ego.[47] A similar sentiment comes over von Ketten as he lies gravely sickened after having been stung by a fly. At this point in the narrative the war has concluded because the Bishop of Trent succumbed to a fatal illness, but instead of triumph, vulnerability reigns. In addition to a heretofore inconceivable state of peace during this moment of weakness, he also imagines a retreat away from his body and sense of self.

> Herr von Ketten and his moon-lady, his nocturnal enchantress, had issued forth from him and softly withdrawn to a distance: he could still see them, he knew that by taking a few great leaps he could still catch up with them, only he no longer knew whether he was already there with them or still here. Yet all this lay in some immense and kindly hand that was benign as a cradle and nevertheless weighed all things in scales, imperturbable, unconcerned as to the outcome. Doubtless that was God.[48]

The transcendence of the self's hard borders and perspective is a defining feature of von Ketten's bemused state. His near-death state dissolves his strictly situated subjectivity and lets him finally acquiesce to his preference for the tender "other" condition of submission. Even his body is no longer his own but rather "warm and helpless as an infant's" which relates to the sense of surrender suggested by the cradle imagery above.[49] The preliminary versions of the text ("The little spirit-cat in Bozen" and "The little spirit-cat from beyond") are even clearer about the manner in which this condition relinquishes an ego-directed experience of the world.[50] It is as if Musil suggests that one way to deal with the rigid reality of the other is to (dis)solve the problem of the self.

Both the preliminary sketches and the novella claim that these near-death and out-of-body experiences could represent God, which is an appropriate introduction to the cat's role in the story, because at its conclusion, the lady from

---

46 Eibl argues that these forces constitute the raison d'être of the entire von Ketten lineage. Eibl, *Drei Frauen*, 146.

47 Compare with Rosi Braidotti, "Animals, Anomalies, and Inorganic Others," *PMLA* 124, no. 2 (2009): 526–532, in particular 530. Her emphasis on ego-decentered interconnectedness and affective factors (alongside, not subordinate to, cognitive faculties) corresponds with similar ideas Musil raises in his "Lunar Rapture" passages.

48 Musil, "The Lady from Portugal," 256.

49 Musil, "The Lady from Portugal," 256.

50 See Robert Musil, *Gesammelte Werke Band 7* (Reinbek: Rowohlt, 1978), 763.

Portugal states, "If God could become man ("Mensch"), then He can also become a kitten."[51] These last spoken words of the novella, heard only by the couple, lend it a degree of hope for the kind of transcendent, tender state of love at its core. This experience of God stands in contradistinction to the established, statutory religion that the Bishop represents and the chaplain at the castle preaches, a chaplain whom von Ketten finds insufferable.[52] In short, the cat causes its onlookers to discover a spirituality that is closer to God, as von Ketten understands it, than the humans who represent holy institutions. For this reason, it is fair to compare it to the phenomenon of "becoming animal" that Gilles Deleuze and Félix Guattari write about in *A Thousand Plateaus*:

> Becomings-animal are basically of another power, since their reality resides not in an animal one imitates or to which one corresponds but in themselves, in that which suddenly sweeps us up and makes us become – a proximity, an indiscernibility that extracts a shared element from the animal far more effectively than any domestication, utilization, or imitation could: "the Beast."[53]

Unpacking this quotation reveals a number of connections to "The Lady from Portugal." The cat, an undomesticated wanderer, evokes a barely discernable, yet unnamable sense of affiliation among its onlookers that is at the same time deeply personal. No one attempts to reify this feeling and impose it upon another community member. The cat's role contrasts with that of the wolf in the story, which in Deleuze and Guattari's terms represents much more of a "correspondence" or "imitation." For many years von Ketten is locked into behaving like an archetypal, predatory wolf. Although this conduct begets tangible benefits, it hinders his escape from the compulsion towards convention and individuation that also enforces the personal distance between him and his wife – a distance he longs to surmount.

The novella describes the cat from its very arrival as out of the ordinary. In addition to ascribing a capacity for emotions and reflection to the cat, the text further expands upon its almost human endowments by comparing it to a guest and a small child.[54] The cat's status as a non-human animal elicits even more compassion than a sick human would under similar circumstances. Because von Ketten routinely slays foes in the name of conquest, human suffering seems an

---

51 Musil, "The Lady from Portugal," 266. Secondary sources contained in this chapter (e.g., Eibl, 120; Kuzniar,100; and Paulson, 120) mention the resemblance to a similar well-known utterance by Novalis. See also the *Robert Musil Handbuch*, 215.
52 Musil, "The Lady from Portugal," 259.
53 Gilles Deleuze and Félix Guattari, *A Thousand Plateaus: Capitalism and Schizophrenia* (London: Athlone Press, 1988), 279.
54 Musil, "The Lady from Portugal," 261.

unremarkable part of daily life to him. The sick cat and its association with his own illness leads him out of his previous dehumanizing mindset. As it begins to waste away and lose control of its bodily fluids, we are told, "In a human being this process of disembodiment ("Hinschwinden") would not have seemed so strange, but in the animal it was like a metamorphosis into a human being."[55] The cat takes on an almost messianic, sacred appearance that attracts attention because it is both extraordinary and yet somehow kindred. Its metamorphosis evokes a double sense of humanization on the one hand and divine incarnation on the other. For example, the text describes the cat's state as "luminously weak" and twice notes that it radiates a faintly perceptible "halo" ("Heilig-schein").[56] This motif of a holy glow radiating towards the participants is further enhanced by the text's reference to the cat's passage into death not just as simple suffering, but as a "martyrdom."[57] The text flattens any hierarchy that one might associate with anthropocentric, religious conceits. Thomas Pekar refers to this process as the cat's "apotheosis,"[58] but the cat does not turn into a human and then finally a god; it is all of these simultaneously.

The ascription of martyrdom is most important for how it unites many of its onlookers in a community of shared, yet also personal introspection. In particular the cat commands a sense of awe and connection from von Ketten, his wife, and her childhood friend; they cannot "escape the thought that it was his or her own destiny that was being vicariously accomplished in this little cat already half released from earthly bonds."[59] This reverence is more genuine than the servile deference that the religious figures in the story command. Each onlooker shares the sentiment that they are privately convinced that the cat's status affects their own individual fates, weaving them together in a mood that is somehow both shared yet distinct. For this reason, the cat's presence is not reducible to sympathy or a simple sense of pity against which Deleuze and Guattari warn.[60] Instead, it is fair to argue that Musil hints at Cora Diamond's aforementioned ideas of "being alive to the world" and "sheer animal vulnerability."[61] There is even a point where the childhood friend from Portugal, ostensibly von Ketten's rival, is seen bending over the cat in his lap, almost as a parent would to a child. This interaction reminds von Ketten of his own illness and malaise in the sense that

---

55 Musil, "The Lady from Portugal," 263.
56 Musil, "The Lady from Portugal," 262.
57 Musil, "The Lady from Portugal," 262.
58 Pekar, *Die Sprache der Liebe*, 132.
59 Musil, "The Lady from Portugal," 263.
60 Deleuze and Guattari, *A Thousand Plateaus,* 258.
61 Diamond, "The Difficulty of Reality and the Difficulty of Philosophy," 74.

"its deathly gentleness had been transformed into that little animal's body and so were no longer merely within him, but there in the midst of them all."[62] The cat facilitates, if only partially and subtly, the overcoming of a major problem in the novella, namely that of the Other. No one dares name this shared mood brought about by the cat's strange presence. Although the text blames this reticence on a lack of courage, it is also possible that the characters, like Musil himself, realize that codifying this vibe could rob it of its effect. It is also why it is problematic to label it simply "empathy." This may also be why von Ketten considers silencing his wife with his hand after she utters the supposed blasphemy of comparing the cat to God.[63] Von Ketten no longer cares about religious institutions by this point. The Bishop has been defeated and the chaplain has been embarrassed. Instead, could it be that he is wary of verbalizing the miracle he believes to have experienced, lest it be systematized like other constructs that had previously commanded his life?[64] The novella then promptly ends before Musil is stuck having to articulate any further.

Elizabeth Boa cynically asks, "How seriously are we to take salvation in the form of a cat?"[65] My answer is of course: very seriously. She sees the cat alternatingly as a "psychological truth," then an "intellectual postulate" before stating, somewhat pessimistically, that "the two halves of the Herr von Ketten's life, his own activity and his inner emotional life, his love for his wife and her inevitably separate existence, will never be completely united."[66] Her argument counterbalances some of the relatively more optimistic interpretations that others have drawn from the novella.[67] Yet even as she relies on the notion of "ironic reserve," which is more or less her way of respecting Musil's tendency to avoid committing to any systematized school of thought (e.g., psychology), she still remarks that he remains "committed to a critical realism based on a renewed postulation of

---

62 Musil, "The Lady from Portugal," 261.
63 Musil, "The Lady from Portugal," 266.
64 See Paul Requadt's distinction between public and private religion in this scene. Paul Requadt, "Zu Musils 'Portugiesin,'" 331.
65 Boa, "Austrian Ironies," 124.
66 Boa, "Austrian Ironies," 124.
67 See Requadt, "Zu Musils 'Portugiesin'," 331–332; Marja Rauch, *Vereinigungen: Frauenfiguren und Identität in Robert Musils Prosawerk* (Würzburg: Königshausen & Neumann, 2000), 101–102; Pekar, *Die Sprache der Liebe*, 123. Alice Kuzniar's conclusion is guardedly optimistic. "Musil acknowledges the self's extremity from the other, the abyss in between, but as an intimately known space. The Portuguese lady is a familiar 'Du,' yet she is also absolutely, unsolvably other. "Die Portugiesin" rejects, through the logic of its images, all false attributes of the self, only to find the key to oneself in the mysterious beloved." Kuzniar, "Inside Out," 105.

humane values."[68] Musil's trick in "The Lady from Portugal" is to infuse such realism with the spirit of possibility. The novella is a fantasy that could become reality. The cat functions like an angel in that it engenders hope and benevolence, but it is not really an angel. Any so-called "humane values" would have to acknowledge a flux that demands a radical openness beyond human selfishness. To quote Deleuze and Guattari again about "becoming animal" as it pertains to Kafka's work, "To become animal is to participate in movement, to stake out a path of escape in all its positivity, to cross a threshold, to reach a continuum of intensities that are valuable only in themselves, to find a world of pure intensities where all forms come undone [. . .]."[69] Hardened forms shape von Ketten's life up until the cat opens a door towards a fleeting sense of interconnectedness, "tenderness," and intense self-dissolution.

Presentation matters

In one of the most comprehensive investigations of Musil's engagement with non-human animals written to date, Florentine Biere clearly identifies crucial differences between Musil's critical position vis-à-vis such animals depending upon the genre in which he writes. In summary, whereas the theoretical positions found in his diary entries and essays tend to disparage "the false enthusiasm for the instinctual ("das Ungeistige"), bodily, and animal aspects of man," his literary projects offer a more hospitable space for using non-human animals to probe novel or ecstatic states of being.[70] Biere is right to suggest that Musil condemns cultural misappropriations of evolutionary theory or animal biology that wind up as philosophies of overzealous vitalism or crude racism; these lead to a "glorification of the animal in man" and "humanization of the animal" which constitute a failure to recognize differences between human and non-human animals, as well as a disavowal of the human as an animal with a mind/

---

68 Boa, "Austrian Ironies," 119, 131.
69 Giles Deleuze and Félix Guattari, *Kafka: Toward a Minor Literature* (Minneapolis: U of Minnesota Press, 1986), 13.
70 Biere returns to this theme repeatedly. Florentine Biere, "Unter Beobachtung: Robert Musils Tierleben," in *Medien, Technik, Wissenschaft: Wissensübertragung bei Robert Musil und in seiner Zeit*, eds. Michael Gamper, Ulrich Johannes Beil, and Karl Wagner (Zurich: Chronos Verlag, 2011), 219–237, here 222, 224. At times she argues only apprehensively about what seems to be a conflict between Musil's theoretical and literary positions; see 227. All translations of Biere's essay are mine.

conscience ("*Geisttier*").[71] I recommend a finer distinction: perhaps a more accurate object of criticism would simply be the overappraisal of mechanistic reflex training and/or instincts in general. Thus, Biere understandably associates
these trends with the lives of non-human animals as such; however, these are
always found in contexts in which Musil repudiates scientific frameworks that
stress instrumentalism, training, and measuring. She asks how one can reconcile Musil's theoretical repudiation of trends in animal psychology during his
time with his attendant recognition of animal lives as a precursor to radically
altered emotional states of being found in his literary works – states that Musil
clearly esteems; however, the problem lies not within the faculties and capacities of non-human animals in and of themselves, but rather in a cultural care-
lessness that encourages humans to live more instinctually or regimented on
the one hand, and fatuously praises ideas such as the "Racehorse of Genius" on
the other. As the narrator at the end of "Can a Horse Laugh?" rightfully notes of
similar comparative moves: this is not the horse's (or any non-human animal's)
fault!

In a sense, Musil was way ahead of his time in affirming proto anti-sentimental
and anti-anthropocentric stances akin to those that later developed in the field of
animal studies, and moreover, he might have possessed a higher appraisal about
the inner lives of non-human animals than Biere seems to allow. Could it not be
that he simply considered many of the Darwinists, behaviorists, and ethologists to
be misguided? When their mistakes or embellishments call for direct confrontation,
Musil undertakes such critique in his essays and diary entries, but even his fiction
demonstrates granularity between critical and experimental perspectives on humanity's relationship to non-human animals. "Can a Horse Laugh?" and its satire
of psychological expertise is critical. It invokes limits. Musil's novella, "The Lady
from Portugal," on the other hand, probes limits and therefore exhibits, relatively
speaking, a positive capacity for emotional potentialities. This capacity is not a fundamental property of the genre of the novella itself, but the novella, and fiction in
general, offers a discursive space for Musil to experiment with representations of
non-human animals and their relationships with humans.

In *Narratology beyond the Human: Storytelling and Animal Life*, David Herman theorizes "a continuum of strategies for presenting nonhuman experiences" that relies more on a matter of design or "discourse domains" than genre.[72]
In short, the continuum shifts from "presenting animal experiences in relatively

71 Biere, "Unter Beobachtung: Robert Musils Tierleben," 223.
72 David Herman, *Narratology beyond the Human: Storytelling and Animal Life* (Oxford: Oxford
UP, 2018), 139 and 202.

summative, globalizing terms – as refracted through human-centered practices and values" and moves towards attempts to render in greater detail what it might be like to experience the world from the point of view of an animal.[73] A brief glance at Musil's oeuvre finds some texts featuring non-human animals that are human-centered and others that are animal-centered. For example, "Die Affeninsel" ("Monkey Island"), like "Can a Horse Laugh?" also found in *Posthumous Papers of a Living Author*, shows how monkeys can mimic unfair and violent human hierarchal institutions, and thus in typical allegorical fashion, non-human animals, stand in for humanity's problems. It is "human-centered." On the other hand, richer explorations of the phenomenological dimensions of animal worlds, appear in other works by Musil, most notably in the two short stories that comprise the novella dyad, *Vereinigungen* (*Unions*, 1911). These novellas are far more symbolic and complex than "Monkey Island," and they are also more "animal-centered."

The narrative in "The Lady from Portugal" is never focalized through the cat, but it also does not rely on common feline tropes to portray societal structures. Despite this relatively anthropocentric hue, the text still performs what Herman considers to be "the upshot of modernist experimentation," namely to "spread the mind abroad" and show how "intelligent behavior is interwoven with worldly circumstances."[74] "The Lady from Portugal," through its performances and representations of vulnerability, empathy, and openness, attempts to counterbalance, with regard to non-human animals, the implied pessimistic observations found in "Can a Horse Laugh?" regarding the capability and difficulty in apprehending the emotional lives of others. The satirical essay ridicules uncritical models of projection not just in fiction but in the world at large and therefore deploys similar descriptive strategies as the novella, albeit in far more negative manner. Even as it claims to know the truth behind a horse's reaction, it subtly criticizes this certainty and therefore reinforces the frustrations inherent in a strictly binary (i.e., inner vs. outer) understanding of others' emotions. Any liberating possibilities for engaging others, cross-species or otherwise, depend upon how faithfully or sincerely storytellers deploy narrative strategies to challenge such binaries. Again, "Can a Horse Laugh?" uses a type of "human source – animal target" strategy for dealing with the horse, but only to spoof it. To be sure, advantages and opportunities for cross-species engagement inhere more strongly in strategies that consider non-human animals' perspectives, but if a similar narrative strategy can produce on the one hand a critical work about

---

73 Herman, *Narratology beyond the Human*, 139.
74 Herman, *Narratology beyond the Human*, 163.

a horse and on the other hand an experimental work about a cat, then readers must be on the lookout for other stylistic markers (e.g., tone) in favor of or against Herman's idea that "minds of all sorts [in fiction or externally] can be more or less directly encountered or experienced, depending on the circumstances."[75] For example, Roth's essay on "Can a Horse Laugh?" notes that irony is far less prevalent in Musil's texts that explore "mystical questions."[76] "The Lady from Portugal" is such a text, and consequently I would argue that is why it is more compatible with Herman's observations.

Conclusion

It might be cynically suggested that the cat's onlookers in "The Lady from Portugal" fall prey to similar anthropocentric gestures criticized in "Can a Horse Laugh?" First, I would argue that if one could somehow measure a proportion of irony, the essay contains far more than the novella and thus demands more discerning judgment from the reader. As discussed, genre matters, but certainly tone does too. Despite this difference, both texts work towards a reckoning of what it means to be human vis-à-vis our relationships with non-human animals, particularly as it pertains to emotional dimensions and potentialities. Whereas the essay harnesses the critical capacity of satire to work towards this goal, the novella flirts with the possibilities via a genre that resembles a realistic fairy tale. Second, it is impossible to nail down entirely what the cat represents for its onlookers, which is why, in some way, it can also be "God." This is precisely the opposite move occurring with the horse, the narrating onlooker, and his contest with the learned psychologist. They want scientific proof, a solid conclusion, regarding whether a horse can laugh. Here it is worth mentioning Matthew Calarco's interpretation of Jacques Derrida's emphasis on the "more difficult disruptive dimensions of human-animal relations, especially the finitude and embodied exposure that human beings share with animals" as opposed to "rationality in one's moral reasoning" as it pertains to "norms and policy."[77] Non-human animals concern us beyond any laws, debates, or habits we might cultivate concerning them and the possibility of their suffering. To repeat, it is important not to reduce empathy to sympathy when discussing the representation of human and

---

75 Herman, *Narratology beyond the Human*, 163.
76 Boa, "Austrian Ironies," 123.
77 Matthew Calarco, *Zoographies: The Question of the Animal from Heidegger to Derrida* (New York: Columbia UP, 2008), 118–119.

non-human animal interactions in Musil's texts. Our interactions with them have the capacity to affect us fundamentally, although such encounters are not necessarily a given. Again, Calarco writes, "[. . .] Derrida has insisted that there is a certain disruptive force in animal suffering, one that affects and challenges us prior to any reflection or debates we might have on the ethical status of animals."[78] "Can a Horse Laugh?" represents the framework of rational debates; the sick and mysterious cat in "The Lady from Portugal" represents a "disruptive force" beyond mere pity or cognizance. It is a force that moves von Ketten towards feelings that resemble vulnerability, self-effacement, and mystical interconnectedness, and Musil's attempt to set it in writing is a gesture towards overcoming, as best one might, the hard problem of alterity – a problem surfaced by the non-human animal in Musil's texts. The two texts under analysis in this chapter have the potential to contribute generously to current discussions in the field of animal studies as well as emotion studies, but Musil scholarship has always resonated strongly with the latter category while only dipping its toes in the former. It is my hope that the efforts here will help fuse future work on all three combined, namely animal studies, emotion studies, and Robert Musil, because there appears to be a need for more work precisely where these three intersect.

Bibliography

Biere, Florentine. "Unter Beobachtung. Robert Musils Tierleben," in *Medien, Technik, Wissenschaft. Wissensübertragung bei Robert Musil und in seiner Zeit*. Eds. Michael Gamper, Ulrich Johannes Beil, and Karl Wagner (Zurich: Chronos Verlag, 2011), 219–237.

Boa, Elizabeth. "Austrian Ironies in Musil's 'Drei Frauen,'" *Modern Language Review* 63, no. 1 (1968): 119–131.

Braidotti, Rosi. "Animals, Anomalies, and Inorganic Others," *PMLA* 124, no. 2 (2009): 526–532.

Calarco, Matthew. *Zoographies: The Question of the Animal from Heidegger to Derrida* (New York: Columbia UP, 2008).

Deleuze, Gilles, and Félix Guattari. *A Thousand Plateaus: Capitalism and Schizophrenia* (London: Athlone Press, 1988).

Deleuze, Gilles, and Félix Guattari. *Kafka: Toward a Minor Literature* (Minneapolis: U of Minnesota Press, 1986).

Diamond, Cora. "The Difficulty of Reality and the Difficulty of Philosophy," *Philosophy and Animal Life* (New York: Columbia UP, 2008), 43–89.

Eibl, Karl. *Robert Musil, drei Frauen: Text, Materialien, Kommentar* (Munich: Hanser, 1978).

---

[78] Calarco, *Zoographies*, 120.

Erickson, Susan. "The Psychopoetics of Narrative in Robert Musil's 'Die Portugiesin,'"
  Monatshefte 78, no. 2 (1986): 167–181.
Herman, David. *Narratology beyond the Human: Storytelling and Animal Life* (Oxford: Oxford
  UP, 2018).
Kuzniar, Alice. *Melancholia's Dog: Reflections on Our Animal Kinship* (Chicago: U of Chicago
  Press, 2005).
Kuzniar, Alice. "Inside Out: Robert Musil's 'Die Portugiesin,'" *Modern Austrian Literature* 26,
  no. 2 (1993): 91–106.
Menely, Tobias. *The Animal Claim: Sensibility and the Creaturely Voice* (Chicago: U of Chicago
  Press, 2015).
Müller-Funk, Wolfgang. *Komplex Österreich. Fragmente zu einer Geschichte der modernen
  österreichischen Literatur* (Vienna: Sonderzahl, 2009).
Musil, Robert. *Gesammelte Werke in neun Bänden*. Ed. Adolf Frisé (Reinbek: Rowohlt, 1978).
Musil, Robert. *Precisions and Soul: Essays and Addresses*. Eds. Burton Pike and David Luft
  (Chicago: U of Chicago Press, 1990).
Musil, Robert. *Selected Writings*. Ed. Burton Pike (New York: Continuum Publishing, 1986).
Musil, Robert. *The Man Without Qualities*. Trans. Sophie Wilkins and Burton Pike (New York:
  Vintage Books, 1995).
Musil, Robert. *Tagebücher in zwei Bänden*. Ed. Adolf Frisé (Reinbek: Rowohlt, 1976).
Nübel, Birgit. "Essays," in *Robert Musil Handbuch*. Eds. Birgit Nübel and Norbert Christian
  Wolf (Berlin: De Gruyter, 2016), 341–382.
Patton, Paul. "Language, Power, and the Training of Horses," in *Zoontologies: The Question of
  the Animal*. Ed. Cary Wolfe (Minneapolis: U of Minnesota Press, 2003), 83–100.
Paulson, Ronald. "A Re-examination and Re-interpretation of Some of the Symbols in Robert
  Musil's *Die Portugiesin*," *Modern Austrian Literature* 13, no. 2 (1980): 111–121.
Pekar, Thomas. *Die Sprache der Liebe bei Robert Musil* (Munich: Fink, 1989).
Rauch, Marja. *Vereinigungen: Frauenfiguren und Identität in Robert Musils Prosawerk*
  (Würzburg: Königshausen & Neumann, 2000).
Requadt, Paul. "Zu Musils 'Portugiesin,'" in *Robert Musil (Wege der Forschung)*. Ed. Renate
  von Heydebrand (Darmstadt: Wissenschaftliche Buchgesellschaft, 1982): 321–332.
Roth, Marie-Louise. "'Kann ein Pferd lachen?' Musils Ironie, eine perspektivische
  Verschiebung?" in *Robert Musils "Nachlaß zu Lebzeiten."* Ed. Gudrun Brokoph-Mauch
  (New York: Peter Lang, 1985), 123–135.
Simons, John. *Animal Rights and the Politics of Literary Representation* (New York: Palgrave,
  2002).
Weil, Kari. *Thinking Animals: Why Animal Studies Now?* (New York: Columbia UP, 2012).

Erika Quinn
Robots, Machines, and Humanity

The Affective World of *Metropolis* (1925)

"Since head and hands no longer understand each other, that will come to destroy the new Tower of Babel. Head and hands need a mediator. The heart must
be the mediator between head and hands."[1] So pronounces Thea von Harbou's
narrator in her 1925 novel *Metropolis*.[2] The idea that emotions can resolve tensions between labor and an increasingly "rational" management is personified
through the figures of Maria and Freder, the deeply feeling and caring young
people; the workers; and Joh Fredersen, the factory owner. Surprisingly, this
sentimental, even melodramatic story has attracted little notice in regard to its
emotional sensibility. It contains a love story, revenge, injustice, and oppression, yet emotions and their role in the narrative have not yet been interrogated.
The relationships between the workers and the machines, the robot Maria and
her creator Rotwang and the man who commissioned her, Joh Fredersen, and
the robot's relationship with the workers all hinge on key emotional moments
or impulses.

Additionally, the Weimar era itself is known as one of tumultuous change,
violence, and accordingly extreme emotions. However, until recently, emotions
have not been a topic of Weimar scholarship either; Kathleen Canning observes
a "deficit" in the historiography of the period in that it lacks sustained attention
to "lived experience, both everyday practices and most notably the mentalities,

---

1 Thea von Harbou, *Metropolis* (Vienna: Milena Verlag, 2002), 78; All translations mine unless
otherwise noted. Many thanks to Russell Spinney for his helpful comments on an early draft of
this essay.
2 The publication and release dates of both the novel and the film are inconsistent in the literature. R. L. Rutsky, "The Mediation of Technology and Gender: Metropolis, Nazism, Modernism," *New German Critique* no. 60 (Autumn 1993): 3–32, J. P. Telotte, "The Seductive Text of
'Metropolis,'" *South Atlantic Review* 55, no. 4 (Nov. 1990): 49–60, and Anton Kaes, *Shell Shock
Cinema: Weimar Culture and the Wounds of War* (Princeton, NJ: Princeton UP, 2011) all give
1926 as the film's release date. Andreas Huyssen, "The Vamp and the Machine: Technology
and Sexuality in Fritz Lang's *Metropolis*," *New German Critique* no. 24/25 (Autumn 1981–Winter
1982): 221–237, and Julie Wosk, "Metropolis," *Technology and Culture* 51, no. 2 (April 2010):
403–408 give 1927 as the release date for the film. The novel was serialized by the *Illustriertes
Blatt* ("*Illustrated Page*") before it was published in 1925.

https://doi.org/10.1515/9783110753677-007

consciousness, and emotions of actors and subjects" of the era.[3] This essay seeks to extend that investigation further.

The fact that humans in the story interact with machines and robots particularly heightens the question of human agency and sensibility. Since the nineteenth century, artificial humans such as automata have been figures of both inspiration and dread in the cultural imagination. The fact of the robot's centrality to the plot also helps clarify why the story has been read so differently over time by scholars: robots "can critique socialism, ideological totalitarianism, or the loss of humanist values in the workplace."[4] In particular, this last point about values in the workplace is central to *Metropolis*; the story suggests that humans are becoming mechanical creatures whose only experiences are stress and suffering. In this dystopian future, humans lack a full range of emotions and expression. This concern about dehumanization focuses on the mechanical reproduction of all kinds of objects; in *Metropolis* machines seem to possess an occult power to alter humanity. Harbou's fears were very much of her lifetime, shared with other writers from many points on the political spectrum. Turning to the non-human allows us to map a historically specific "emotional repertoire of humans" and therefore reveal the "limits of the human emotional imagination."[5]

The film *Metropolis* (1926), created by Thea von Harbou and Fritz Lang has long been a subject of literary, historical, and cultural investigation. Previous work has focused on Lang's vision of technology as seen in flying automobiles, skyscrapers, and industrial machines.[6] Other scholars have turned to examining gender through the form of Maria, the working-class savior and her evil double, the robot designed to wreak the workers' destruction.[7] The psychology of the film has also garnered attention from early on with Siegfried Kracauer's canonical analysis.[8]

---

3 Kathleen Canning, "The Politics of Symbols, Semantics, and Sentiments in the Weimar Republic," *Central European History* 43 (2010): 567–580, here 572. See also Russell Spinney, "A Skin of Hatred: How Bodies are Involved in the Memory of Emotions and Anti-Semitic Practice of the Weimar Republic," in *Feelings Materialized: Emotions, Bodies, and Things in Germany, 1500–1950*, eds. Derek Hillard, Heikki Lempa, and Russell Spinney (New York: Berghahn Books, 2020), 95–114; Sabine Hake, *The Proletarian Dream: Socialism, Culture, and Emotion in Germany, 1863–1933* (Berlin: De Gruyter, 2017), especially chapters 13–14.
4 Despina Kakoudaki, *Anatomy of a Robot: Literature, Cinema, and the Cultural Work of Artificial People* (New Brunswick, NJ: Rutgers UP, 2014), 143.
5 Rob Boddice, *The History of Emotions* (Manchester: Manchester UP, 2018), 104.
6 See Rutsky and Telotte.
7 Barbara Hales, "Taming the Technological Shrew: Woman as Machine in Weimar Culture," *Neophilologus* 94 (2010): 301–316; Huyssen; Wosk.
8 Siegfried Kracauer, *From Caligari to Hitler: A Psychological History of the German Film* (Princeton, NJ: Princeton UP, 1947).

While Harbou wrote the novel and screenplay almost simultaneously,[9] illustrating the closeness of the novel to the film, the novel's text provides much more explicit exposition of Harbou's attitudes about emotions. The original version of the film had much material from the novel removed from it because of the film's already long duration. The newly restored film version from 2002 returns much of the expurgated material from the novel to the film. For purposes of clarity, I am working primarily with the novel and will signal when the film is the artwork under examination.

Beginning with Kracauer's now-notorious analysis of *Metropolis* as a reactionary work that heralds the coming of Nazism, historians and film scholars have seen in it a political message. Kracauer's critique of the work lay in the manipulation of the workers by the "heart" Freder, the rebellious son, who unwittingly acts in his father's calculating interests.[10] Kracauer's analysis of this intergenerational psychodrama does not, in fact, address the emotional tenor or motivations of any of the characters. Without such grounding, Freder's and the workers' rebellion does seem historically specific to the interwar generation. The emotional tenor of the work, however, reveals important continuities with past emotional styles. Within the last decade, the political history of Weimar has started to take an "emotional turn." Scholars like the philosopher Martha Nussbaum raised attention to political emotions. Historians have followed her lead, investigating the emotions that drive social movements, revolutions, and political reconstruction, providing a foundation from which to look more closely at the emotions at play in Harbou's novel, and to challenge Kracauer's hypothesis.[11]

Historians interested in power dynamics who work in the realm of emotions often investigate collective agreements and constraints on members to adhere to

---

9 Reinhold Keiner, *Thea von Harbou und der deutsche Film bis 1933* (Hildesheim: Georg Olms Verlag, 1984), 95. The novel seems to have been a vehicle to get Lang's ideas onto paper rather than a stand-alone project. The book did not sell a significant number of copies. See Paul M. Jensen, "Metropolis: The Film and the Book, " in Fritz Lang, *Metropolis* (New York: Simon and Schuster, 1973), 6, and Donald Ray Richards, *The German Bestseller in the 20th Century: A Complete Bibliography and Analysis 1915–1940* (New York: Herbert Lang, 1968).
10 Kracauer, *From Caligari to Hitler*, 163.
11 Martha C. Nussbaum, *Political Emotions: Why Love Matters for Justice* (Cambridge, MA: Harvard UP, 2013); Martha C. Nussbaum, *Hiding from Humanity: Disgust, Shame, and the Law* (Princeton, NJ: Princeton UP, 2006); see, for example, Joachim C. Häberlen and Russell A. Spinney, "Introduction," (Emotions in Protest Movements in Europe since 1917) *Contemporary European History* 23, no. 4 (November 2014): 489–503; Anna Parkinson, *An Emotional State: The Politics of Emotion in Postwar West German Culture* (Ann Arbor: U of Michigan Press, 2015).

certain emotional norms. They began to coin terminology to describe those intra-personal dynamics, such as "emotional regimes" or "emotional communities."[12] While some actors, groups, and movements in interwar Germany may have sought to establish such cohesive regimes in particular milieux, I contend that the decentralized and deeply contested nature of Weimar politics, culture, and society hampered their creation. Perhaps, though, the existence of so many disparate groups gave rise to the "plurality of diverging styles, [. . .] conflictual, competitive, or otherwise mutually interdependent" evident in the era; they generated a creative potential despite their lack of dominance.[13] These myriad emotional styles included the "experience, fostering, and display of emotions, and oscillate[d] between discursive patterns and embodied practices."[14]

By bringing concepts from emotion studies to bear on Harbou and Lang's creation, one can further add to the discussion about the film's ambiguous form, aesthetic, and content. Despite its setting in a technological future, its authors were unable to see beyond their own society's culture to imagine a futuristic one: *Metropolis* captures early twentieth-century attitudes regarding emotions generally and particularly with regard to machines and animals. While *Metropolis* is often treated as a modernist vision of technology either to be admired or feared, its emotional sensibility is not futuristic in the least, drawing on nineteenth-century emotional tropes about the power and irrationality of the crowd, the promise and threat of mechanization, the affectionate relationship people had with domestic animals, and the frightening, "irrational," inscrutable, emotional motivations of the Other, woman. The Weimar era was one of political contestation in the streets: "the crowd" was often Othered as socialist, communist, or female by the dominant culture.[15] Industrial capitalism was undergoing important changes in the Weimar

12 Peter N. Stearns and Carol Z. Stearns, "Clarifying the History of Emotions and Emotional Standards," *American Historical Review* 90, no. 4 (October 1985): 813–836; Barbara H. Rosenwein, "Worrying about Emotions in History," *American Historical Review* 107, no. 3 (June 2002): 821–845.
13 Benno Gammerl, "Emotional Styles – Concepts and Challenges," *Rethinking History* 15, no. 2 (June 2012): 161–175, here 162. For examples of contested and conflicting emotional styles, see Kathleen Canning, "The Order and Disorder of Gender in the History of the Weimar Republic," in *Weimar Publics/Weimar Subjects*, eds. Kathleen Canning, Kerstin Brandt, and Kirstin McGuire (New York: Berghahn, 2010), 365; Eric Bryden, "Heroes and Martyrs of the Republic: Reichsbanner Geschichtspolitik in Weimar Germany," *Central European History* 43, no. 4 (December 2010): 639–665; Moritz Föllmer, *Individuality and Modernity in Berlin: Self and Society from Weimar to the Wall* (Cambridge: Cambridge UP: 2013), 33.
14 Gammerl, "Emotional Styles," 163.
15 For continuity from the previous century, see Susanna Barrows, *Distorting Mirrors: Visions of the Crowd in Late Nineteenth-Century France* (New Haven, CT: Yale UP, 1981). Barrows highlights

era, heightening older fears about labor exploitation and worker suffering and agitation, and many feared the emergence of a newly empowered woman in the 1920s in the absence of "male authority." Weimar emotional politics, then, while freshly energized by the experience of war and open expression, exhibited important continuities with past eras rather than presenting an emotional rupture entirely. This essay will trace these interactions through three main sections of the novel, starting with the opening scenes that explore the characters' emotional relationship with machines, followed by the creation of the robot Maria and the strong feelings it evokes; and lastly the famous ending of the narrative in which the robot incites the crowd of workers to riot in a frenzy of panic and rage.

Metropolis was the result of an established collaboration between Harbou and Lang. The couple had worked together on *Dr. Mabuse der Spieler* (*Dr. Mabuse the Gambler*, 1922), *Die Nibelungen* (*The Nibelungen*, 1924), and other films. Lang and Harbou were both in their mid-thirties when they created *Metropolis*. They had lived through the First World War as young adults and experienced the rapid industrialization of German society. They belonged to a generation experiencing massive change and upheaval, and their film reflects their own responses and attempts to cope with that change and tumult. Harbou's career as a bestselling author began in the prewar years; her oeuvre included fairy tales, what would now be considered young adult offerings, and nationalistic "blood and soil" novels. Most of these could be classified as *Unterhaltungsliteratur*, that is, popular fiction that did not seek to experiment with form or style. These were sentimental stories that upheld bourgeois and patriarchal norms for the sake of entertainment.[16] *Metropolis*, then, was not Harbou's first foray into speculative literature, but it was her first work that explored the role of technology in society. While the novel presents a technologically and scientifically plausible future, it does not "produce cognitive estrangement,"[17] unlike science fiction, since it does not envision any changes in social, cultural, or political relations per se. The problems it explores and the answers it provides had been articulated since the mid-nineteenth century, a point recognized by H. G. Wells when he reviewed the film.[18] Unlike Harbou's fiction, Lang's film did embark on formal

the political instability of Third Republic France in the 1890s, which, like Weimar, was an era of widespread strikes, assassinations, and violent demonstrations.

16 See Erika Quinn, "At War: Thea von Harbou, Women, and the Nation," *Women in German Yearbook* 33 (2017): 52–76.

17 M. Keith Booker and Anne-Marie Thomas, *The Science Fiction Handbook* (West Sussex: Wiley-Blackwell, 2009), 4.

18 H. G. Wells, "Mr. Wells Reviews a Current Film," [1927] in *The Science Fiction Film Reader*, ed. Gregg Rickman (New York: Limelight Editions, 2004), 5–12.

innovation and experimentation. Lang himself addressed the mash-up that was the film: "The main thesis was Mrs. Lang's, but I am at least fifty percent responsible because I made the film."[19]

The variety and polarization of the interpretations regarding the film are due in part, as mentioned above, to its origins with a director and screenwriter with quite different aesthetic and political sensibilities; when Fritz Lang fled to the United States in 1933 after the Nazi dictatorship was established, Harbou notoriously chose to remain in Germany. These tensions have long been understood by scholars and reviewers as a clash between two aesthetic and emotional approaches, those of Expressionism and *Neue Sachlichkeit* (New Objectivity). While Expressionism's roots lay in the pre-war era, its adoption in film was a Weimar innovation. Scholars of the style trace its emergence to "widespread disenchantment" with Weimar by 1920.[20] The initial nationalist elation of going to war in 1914 had transformed after the defeat in 1918 into "cynicism and detachment" – as well as "guilt and shame."[21] In Peter Gay's psychohistory, Expressionism arose from the revolt of the son against the father – in this case, the state.[22] Sons could belong to either the revolutionary left or right: both the *Reichsbanner Schwarz-Rot-Gold* (the Black-Red-Gold Imperial Banner, a veterans' group committed to defending the Republic) and the *Stahlhelm* (the Steel Helmet, a right-wing paramilitary group) marched in the streets and challenged the state's monopoly on violence. In standard Weimar periodization, this "Expressionist" era ended by 1925 and was followed by the stable rule of the *Vernunftrepublikaner* (rational republicans) who supported the Republic from political necessity rather than ideological conviction. Gustav Stresemann embodied the sturdy father figure and signaled the end of experimentation and a cooler political temperature.[23] The aesthetic movement that corresponded to this political moderation was New Objectivity, which sought to observe the world with matter-of-factness, sobriety, realism, and accuracy.[24]

Metropolis's political and aesthetic blurring is accompanied by stylistic ambiguity as well. Many have seen the film's compositional principles indebted to Expressionist style. *Metropolis* uses narrative and visual tropes from Expressionist

19 Peter Bogdanovich, *Fritz Lang in America* (New York: Praeger, 1967), 124, quoted in Kaes, *Shell Shock Cinema*, 173.

20 Peter Gay, *Weimar Culture: The Outsider as Insider* (New York: Harper & Row, 1968), 10.

21 Gay, *Weimar Culture*, 10.

22 Gay, *Weimar Culture*, 105. Anton Kaes notes that Freder is an "oedipal stock figure" drawn from Expressionist theater; *Shell Shock Cinema*, 177.

23 Gay, *Weimar Culture*, 118.

24 Gay, *Weimar Culture*, 119–120; Helmut Lethen, *Cool Conduct: The Culture of Distance in Weimar Germany*, trans. Don Reneau (Berkeley: UC Press, 2002).

theater[25] like the melodramatic "recognition of pain and suffering,"[26] exaggerated facial expression, bodily gestures, and the portrayal of trance-like states.[27] However, the film in particular also reveals affinities with New Objectivity through its embrace of "gleaming beautiful" machines and mundane objects.[28]

Machines as beasts, humans as machines

Metropolis places the relationship between humans and the machines they anthropomorphize at the center of its narrative. Readers are introduced to the physical and social structure of Metropolis, with its elite pleasure gardens in the penthouse, where joy radiates from the gardens in which Freder Fredersen frolics, and his father Joh Fredersen, the rational, cool-headed industrial magnate, has his office. Below are the machine works, hot, loud, and crowded, in the subterranean levels. The suffering workers are bound to the machines, which need constant attention. Their gauges, dials and indicators must be attended to for the sake of efficient and safe production. In the film, workers use precise, crisp, economical movements to align their bodies with the machines' functions and pace. Despite the fact that machines don't have bodies per se, but rather are constructed around frames or other structures,[29] Harbou projects sentience and bodily awareness onto them. The anthropomorphizing (the attribution of "human qualities to non-human animals"[30] and objects) of non-human animals has a long history, and observers of the phenomenon suggest that it, like empathy, helps humans render other living beings intelligible.[31] Feminist philosopher Kelly Oliver suggests that animal figures in texts reveal "the dependence of man, human, humanity, and subjectivity on animal, animals, and animality."[32] Because animals have long been understood as inferior to humans, they have represented, among other characteristics, humanity's sinful, especially lustful and voracious, nature,

---

25 Kaes, *Shell Shock Cinema*, 187.

26 Hake, *Proletarian Dream*, 21. This is evident in the novel's many exclamation points.

27 Gay, *Weimar Culture*, 106.

28 Kaes, *Shell Shock Cinema*, 171.

29 Stuart Hampshire, "Biology, Machines, and Humanity," in *The Boundaries of Humanity: Humans, Animals, Machines*, eds. James J. Sheehan and Morton Sosna (Berkeley: UC Press, 1991), 253–258, here 253.

30 Derek Ryan, *Animal Theory: A Critical Introduction* (Edinburgh: Edinburgh UP, 2015), 17.

31 Kari Weil, *Thinking Animals: Why Animal Studies Now?* (New York: Columbia UP, 2012), 19.

32 Kelly Oliver, *Animal Lessons: How They Teach Us to Be Human* (New York: Columbia UP, 2009), 5.

humans' ability to adapt to group pressures, and humans' species-level impera-
tives to eat and to reproduce. To be animal is to have a bodily nature. Oliver continues, "As animals make their way into [. . .] texts, they cross through fences erected
to keep them out [. . .]. It is telling that the violence toward animals in these philosophies of otherness – [. . .] correlates with how vehemently they reject the proximity between the animal and the human."[33] The more humans disavow their
connection to and similarity with animals, the more it reveals animals as a human
Shadow, that which Jungian psychotherapy suggests we exile in ourselves. In *Metropolis*, Freder and the workers relate to various machines as if they were animals – pets, beasts of burden, or predators. For example, the machines on the
factory floor are said to "want living humans for their food (*Futter*)."[34] The machines' aesthetics and function often form the basis of the humans' emotional relationships with them, evoking either desire or disgust.[35] In this way, the
machines exercise agency, albeit without intentionality.

In Freder's case, he enters his atelier and peers through a telescope at the
heavens. He approaches his machine, a rocket, which is of his own design and
manufacture. His emotional relationship to it is almost fatherly – he feels protective and proud of it and exercises his authority over a subordinate being.
Harbou describes the machine:

> the creation [*Geschöpf*] was not large and appeared even more delicate in the huge space
> and the flood of sunlight in which it stood. But the soft shine of its metal and the noble
> movement with which it set its upper body into motion [. . .] gave it something of the
> bright godliness of a perfectly beautiful animal that is without fear because it knows itself
> to be untamable.[36]

In his 1923 essay "The Machine," cultural critic Oswald Spengler claimed that
metal exercised "an uncanny mystical tug" on primitive humans, and that those
who worked with metal were seen as a magic workers.[37] Freder's atelier – a site
of resources, privilege, and esoteric knowledge – allows him to shape objects
that could seem to possess magical powers, i.e., the ability of flight. His status

---

33 Oliver, *Animal Lessons*, 4.

34 Harbou, *Metropolis*, 21.

35 Stephanie Downes, Sally Holloway, and Sarah Randles, "A Feeling for Things, Past and
Present," in *Feeling Things: Objects and Emotions through History*, eds. Stephanie Downes,
Sally Holloway, and Sarah Randles (Oxford: Oxford UP, 2018), 16. See also Katie Barclay, "New
Materialism and the New History of Emotions," *Emotions: History, Culture, Society* 1, no. 1
(2017): 161–183, especially 179.

36 Harbou, *Metropolis*, 19–20.

37 Oswald Spengler, *Der Untergang des Abendlandes: Umrisse einer Morphologie der Weltgeschichte* Bd. II Welthistorische Perspektiven (Munich: C. H. Beck, 1923), 621.

and knowledge allow him to wield power over machines in ways that the workers below cannot. In fact, the technological future of *Metropolis* does not boast any other new machines (except the robot). Innovation belongs to the elite, as does the comfortable emotional relationship with machines.

Freder strokes the machine's head and speaks to it, using the familiar "du" form. Here, he enacts a familiar relationship: it is as if he were speaking to a horse, especially after he mounts it. Pascal Eitler has observed an emerging discourse regarding love of animals in the nineteenth century German lands as urban middle-class families started to keep pets, as a practice of childrearing intended to inculcate responsibility and empathy. The idea that animals can love humans in return also developed, but these notions of animals' emotions and the sympathetic responses they evoked in humans were restricted largely to pets and domesticated livestock.[38] In *Metropolis*, Freder trusts the machine to bear his body weight and feels an emotional connection to it, created by the contact of his skin on its metal form, as well as his role in creating it, which gives him a sense of mastery over it. The physical connection between them evokes that of a horse and rider, which speaks to Freder's class standing as the master's son. Riding horses in this context was an elite pursuit, one that most common people did not have access to. Freder's easy sense of authority and confidence speak to his privilege. As he might relate to a domestic animal (or human child), Freder feels responsible to or beholden to it as he says, "nothing in the world seeks revenge more than a jealous machine that believes itself neglected."[39] Here, human emotions – jealousy, possessiveness, resentment, the longing for revenge – are ascribed to the machine, after it has evoked emotion in the human speaking to it. This connection that Freder experiences with his creation is "a projection" onto the machine in order "match" their experiences.[40] Perhaps when dreaming about reaching the stars, having a steadfast companion who noted your absence was very comforting.

Pausing in his one-sided conversation with the rocket, Freder hears a massive sound in the city below: "the machines of Metropolis roared: they wanted

38 Pascal Eitler, "Tierliebe und Menschenführung: Eine genealogische Perspektive auf das 19. und 20. Jahrhundert," in *Tierstudien 3: Tierliebe*, eds. Jessica Ullrich and Friedrich Weltzien (Berlin: Neofelis Verlag, 2013), 40–48, here 41; see also Boddice, *History of Emotions*, 101; Yi-Fu Tuan, "Animal Pets: Cruelty and Affection," in *The Animals Reader: The Essential Classic and Contemporary Writings*, eds. Linda Kalof and Amy Fitzgerald (Oxford: Berg, 2007), 141–153.
39 Harbou, *Metropolis*, 20.
40 Boddice, *History of Emotions*, 102–103.

to be fed."[41] The food the machines need is living humans. In a following scene, Freder confronts his father about the ravenous machines, and Joh Fredersen states they are necessary because of a labor shortage, perhaps echoing the real-life demographic trough Germany confronted after the First World War with millions of dead or disabled men. Freder continues to question him: "Aren't you afraid, Father, [. . .]. that one fine day there will be no more people to feed the human-devouring God-Machines and that the Moloch of glass, rubber, and steel, and the Durga of aluminum with platinum veins will die painfully of starvation?"[42] Joh replies that's why he must create a replacement labor supply. Harbou's mention of gods associated with war from the Hebrew Bible (Moloch was a Canaanite god associated with child sacrifice) and Hinduism (Durga is a warrior goddess who combats evils and demons that undermine peace) suggests the machines' omnipotence or their threatening Otherness, given the centrality of Christianity as a religion of salvation in the narrative.

Here Harbou's nineteenth-century sentimental viewpoint regarding industrial machinery and its effect on workers becomes clear. Using a language of submission, slavery and loss of agency to portray the workers' relationship to the voracious, anthropomorphized *Maschinentiere* (machine animals),[43] Harbou focuses on the workers' pain and suffering in a melodramatic way that could be read as either socialist or conservative paternalism.[44] Beginning in the 1840s and 1850s, German materialist thinkers like Hermann von Helmholz and Karl Marx began to celebrate the potential of the machine age as well as to warn about its dangers, particularly the threat of dehumanization machines posed.[45] Marx, in fact, observed that the industrial worker "does not feel content but unhappy" and the alienation from his own creative energies creates a situation in which the worker "no longer feels himself [. . .] in any but his animal functions – [. . .] and in his animal functions he no longer feels himself to be anything but an animal."[46] In participating in alienated labor, humans become abject creatures, no longer possessing subjectivity, but serving as the prey the machines hunger for in the novel.

41 Harbou, *Metropolis*, 21.
42 Harbou, *Metropolis*, 35.
43 Harbou, *Metropolis*, 22.
44 Hake, *Proletarian Dream*, 13.
45 Minsoo Kang, *Sublime Dreams of Living Machines: The Automaton in the European Imagination* (Cambridge, MA: Harvard UP, 2011), 229.
46 Karl Marx, "Estranged Labor," in *Economic and Philosophic Manuscripts of 1844*, trans. Martin Milligan (New York: Prometheus Books, 1988), 69–84, here 74.

In later decades, others like Ernst Kapp admired what they perceived as the vitalism of machines powered by steam, or later, electricity; their apparent animation revealed a kind of vital energy or life force. However, many in Europe sensed that "machines had taken on a life of their own, transcending their original purpose of serving humanity."[47] This life force had the potential to assert its own power, as the machines in the factory seem to do. They have stopped serving humans and started to devour them instead. The fear of being devoured is a deep, primal one: as Despina Kakoudaki observes, "nothing evokes the state of abjection better than absorption [being eaten]."[48] Kelly Oliver points out that Enlightenment thinkers believed humans were superior to other animals because of their omnivorousness – that lesser animals were so because they could eat only limited diets (as in the case of the factory machines).[49] In this way machines reveal their inferiority to humanity, yet render humanity like them as it becomes their food. This illustrates Oliver's point about disavowing humans' kinship with animals: in the novel, the machines represent the voracious appetite of Joh Fredersen's company and by extension, industrial capitalism in such a way as to distance readers from that uncomfortable similarity. Readers focus on the machines themselves rather than the man responsible for their creation, maintenance, and appetites.

In a continuation of the scene discussed above in which Freder challenges his father on the working conditions in the factory, Harbou's story further develops the idea of how humans lose their humanity through overwork and emphasizes the importance of distinguishing man from machine. Freder delivers an impassioned speech once his father unveils his plan to create artificial human workers: "Then let me say one thing, Father. Make sure that the robots don't have heads, or at least no faces. Or give them faces that always smile [. . .]. or closed visors, so that one isn't disgusted when one looks at them!"[50] Freder explains that as he walked across the factory floor, none of the workers, who all knew him, returned his greeting: "The machines [they were watching over] were too eager to wind up their nerves."[51] He sees himself in the workers and does not want to make that mistake should they ever be non-humans. Machines that look like or emote like humans would continue to evoke sympathy and pity while being undeserving of it since they cannot suffer. His sense of disgust at seeing

47 Kang, *Sublime Dreams*, 10.
48 Kakoudaki, *Anatomy of a Robot*, 154.
49 Oliver, *Animal Lessons*, 2.
50 Harbou, *Metropolis*, 36.
51 Harbou, *Metropolis*, 36.

robots foreshadows the sense of the uncanny that the actual robot the inventor Rotwang later creates evokes in the humans who interact with it.

In the novel, the workers' lack of emotional response as shown above is emphasized as key to their dehumanization. The workers themselves do not verbally express their emotions or articulate their relationship to the machines. They are described in short, incomplete sentences as having the "same faces."[52] They are no longer individuals, and Harbou, perhaps unwittingly, robs them of agency and subjectivity.[53] Embodying fears of "massification" among cultural critics like Siegfried Kracauer, they are voiceless and faceless, interchangeable, with only the narrator to describe their plight, and Freder and Maria to take note of it.[54]

Harbou's fearful perception of industrial machines was shared by her contemporaries. In his pessimistic assessment of the modern world, *Der Mensch und die Technik* (*Man and Technics*, 1933) Oswald Spengler bemoans, "The master of the world becomes the slave of the machines. They force him, us, and everyone, without exception, whether we know and wish it or not, in the direction of their course."[55] Indeed, in his better-known work written a decade earlier, *The Decline of the West*, Spengler warns that "Faustian Man has become the slave of his creation."[56] He explains that the machine works and forces humans to work along with it at its pace. With the advent of Fordist and Taylorist production techniques, and their tentative adoption by some German firms in the 1920s,[57] it seemed that a dark future of suffering humanity could be foreseen in the greed of

---

52 Harbou, *Metropolis*, 22.

53 "Affects and emotions subjectify us;" B. Gammerl et. al., "Feeling Differently: Approaches and their Politics," *Emotion, Space, and Society* (2017) https://doi.org/10.1016/j.emospa.2017.07.007.

54 Siegfried Kracauer, "Über Arbeitsnachweise," *Frankfurter Zeitung*, 17 June 1930, quoted in Föllmer, *Individuality and Modernity in Berlin*, 85. Cultural sociologist Eva Illouz observes that managerial capitalism, which was emerging in the 1920s and 30s, introduced a new emotional regime to the workplace, one that emphasized "professionalism", in other words, an emotionless affect. In order to achieve this goal, managers learned to perform emotional labor, taking care of their employees in order to prevent disruptive emotional outbursts. *Saving the Modern Soul: Therapy, Emotions, and the Culture of Self-Help* (Berkeley: UC Press, 2008), 59–73.

55 Oswald Spengler, *Der Mensch und die Technik: Beitrag zu einer Philosophie des Lebens* (Munich: C. H. Beck, 1933), 75. Our current awareness of the power digital technology wields in our own lives, and the automatic habituation that enables that, show that these concerns are still very present. See Yuval Noah Harari, *Homo Deus: A Brief History of Tomorrow* (New York: Harper Collins, 2017), 283–402.

56 Oswald Spengler, *Der Untergang des Abendlandes*, 625.

57 See Mary Nolan, *Visions of Modernity: American Business and the Modernization of Germany* (Oxford: Oxford UP, 1994).

the machines' human owners. Spengler's fear of being a tool is different than the workers' fear of being treated as a power source (food) in *Metropolis*. The logics of objectification and ingestion present different kinds of threats – a loss of individuality vis-à-vis the law or the social contract, versus possessing a non-negotiable lack of individuality.[58]

Although the factory machines (*Maschinentiere*) are portrayed as voracious beasts demanding constant human attention, the creator-engineer Freder gains satisfaction, meaning, and fulfillment from his relationship to the machine. He sees the rocket as a creative extension of himself and as an entity that elevates him. The workers, on the other hand, are dehumanized and subjugated by their relationships to the machines. It's about power – Freder has power over his rocket, the machines have power over the workers.[59] When directly depicting humans' relationship to machines, those machines bolster the privilege of the elite and further subjugate and exploit the underclass. Machines, then, are tools of capitalist polarization and simply amplify existing social relations and emotional affects; suffering and pleasure align with the hierarchical status quo.

The robot

The scene with Freder and his rocket illustrates the importance of objects – things – for human emotional lives, and even for our identities. The psychologist Mihaly Csikszentmihalyi observes that things have the ability to mediate human experience as they can "'embody goals, make [. . .] skills manifest, and shape the identities of their users.'" Indeed, they can define our sense of self by shaping our status, profession, or purpose, as in Freder's case.[60]

In the case of artificial humans, the relationship between humans and objects is more complex and multifaceted. Humans have long distinguished animate subjects from inanimate objects by the former's ability to feel, in both sensory and emotional meanings. Ute Frevert observes that emotions connect human beings to one another, but also to nature and to objects. Between humans, this emotional connection is founded on reciprocity; between humans

58 Kakoudaki, *Anatomy of a Robot*, 148.

59 Kang, *Sublime Dreams*, 40.

60 Mihaly Csikszentmihalyi and Eugene Rochberg-Halton, *The Meaning of Things: Domestic Symbols and the Self* (Cambridge: Cambridge UP, 1981, 1), quoted in Downes, Holloway, and Randles, "A Feeling for Things," 16.

and objects, the connection flows in one direction.[61] Theorists of Object-Oriented Ontology and alien phenomenologists seek to challenge the perceived inertness of objects: for them, inanimate and non-human objects can exert agency in the immediate environment and on history.[62] Objects have a capacity to "act" on people's feelings and alter their affective states; objects are actors that do not emote, but do produce and transmit feeling.[63] Harbou's word choice for the robot – *Maschinenmensch* – "machine person" – gets at the ambiguity between human/object that artificial humans represent and echoes the other hybrid creatures of the factory floor, the *Machinentiere*. In the novel, "the robot was never imagined as a pure machine or a pure human [. . .]. the robot is human and non-human, machine and non-machine, real and non-real. Just as they are never pure machines, humanoid robots can never be fully human."[64]

The famous scene in *Metropolis* in which the scientist-inventor Rotwang creates the *Maschinenmensch* Maria, complete with electrical stimulation and high-tech laboratory, evokes Mary Shelley's *Frankenstein*.[65] Closer examination of Harbou's novel, however, reveals other influences in regard to how human-like machines were imagined in the 1920s. Hanns Heinz Ewers published a best-selling German translation of Villiers de l'Isle-Adam's 1886 *L'Eve Future* (*The Eve of the Future Eden*) in 1920.[66] Adam's misogynistic novel sought to create an artificial woman who would correct for the perceived flaws in real women: their inconstancy and mortality. Harbou's scene of the robot Maria's creation echoes Adams': she wears "feminine armature in burnished silver leaf, radiant yet mat [te] white, [a] collar [and] gorget of metal. [She was a] mysterious creature of disturbing beauty."[67]

Other visions of humanlike machines appeared in Karel Čapek's 1920 play *R.U.R.* (*Rossum's Universal Robots*) in which robots serve as industrial laborers who

---

61 Ute Frevert, "Defining Emotions: Concepts and Debates over Three Centuries," in *Emotional Lexicons: Continuity and Change in the Vocabulary of Feeling 1700–2000*, eds. Ute Frevert et al. (Oxford: Oxford UP, 2014), 1–31, here 5.
62 Downes, Holloway, and Randles, "A Feeling for Things," 8.
63 Downes, Holloway, and Randles, "A Feeling for Things," 11.
64 Kathleen Richardson, "Technological Animism: The Uncanny Personhood of Humanoid Machines," *Social Analysis* 60, no. 1 (Spring 2016): 110–128, here 123.
65 Harbou uses neuter gender nouns – *Geschöpf, Wesen, Maschinenmensch* – for the robot. I will use "it" when it is relatively ungendered, i.e., without Maria's appearance, and the feminine pronoun when it becomes an imitation of Maria.
66 Villiers de l'Isle-Adam, *Eve of the Future Eden*, trans. Marilyn Gaddis Rose (Lawrence, KS: Coronado Press, 1981); Kaes, *Shell Shock Cinema*, 199.
67 De l'Isle-Adam, *Eve of the Future Eden*, 65.

look human enough to "pass."[68] Two kinds of stories dominate robot narratives: those that feature artificial-looking robots and those that feature human-looking "artificial people." *Metropolis* combines these two types, as the reader encounters the robot Maria before its skin is applied.[69] Skin is a very important component in terms of performing humanness and individuality – skin is a boundary, a sensory organ, and is a key vehicle of expression.[70] Before it receives its skin in the film, the robot's hard, shiny surface[71] and fixed facial expression signal its alien and threatening nature. In stories featuring artificial humans, metal skin is an aesthetic "obsession."[72] The blank, reflective quality of the robot's metal exterior marks it as a "site for projecting numerous kinds of difference."[73] The "metalface" also conceals the inner workings (and thus the vulnerability, if it exists) of the robot.[74] Klaus Theweleit described the "collective male fantasy" articulated during and after the First World War of armored women, which he argued was rooted in a deep reluctance, even an aversion, to blend with women.[75]

In Čapek's play, the first prototypes of the robots lack emotions, despite their human appearance: their inventor, Rossum, sought to create workers with the smallest number of needs. Therefore, his robots do not laugh, smile, or have a sense of taste. They have no "will, no passion, no history, no soul."[76] It was only after seeing the robots perform tasks that Rossum saw fit to give them a pain-sensing capability, to protect them as capital investments. According to the social anthropologist Kathleen Richardson, Čapek hoped that their human appearances would lead audiences to discuss the question of what it means to be human.[77]

Čapek's robots were exceptional in their human appearance: later models of robots from the 1920s (including the robot Maria in her "true" form) feature

---

68 Karel Čapek, *R.U.R.* (*Rossum's Universal Robots*), trans. Claudia Novack (New York: Penguin, 2004). Čapek coined the word "robot" from the Czech verb "to work." It had entered the vernacular by the time of Harbou's writing. Kakoudaki, *Anatomy of a Robot*, 141.

69 Kakoudaki, *Anatomy of a Robot*, 175.

70 Claudia Benthien, *Skin: On the Cultural Border Between Self and the World*, trans. Thomas Dunlap (New York: Columbia UP, 2002), vii; Nina G. Jablonski, *Skin: A Natural History* (Berkeley: UC Press, 2006), 3.

71 The skin is translucent in the novel.

72 Kathleen Richardson, "Mechanical People," *New Scientist* 190, no. 2557 (24 June 2006): 56–57.

73 Kakoudaki, *Anatomy of a Robot*, 117.

74 Kakoudaki, *Anatomy of a Robot*, 117.

75 Klaus Theweleit, *Männerphantasien* vol. 1 (Reinbek: Rowohlt, 1993), 211, quoted in Benthien, *Skin*, 117.

76 Čapek, *R.U.R.*, 9, 19.

77 Richardson, "Mechanical People," 56.

metallic surfaces – Harbou's *Maschinenmensch* is one in a line of forebears, a "skin job" who passes for human, in this case, in order to lead the workers astray.[78] In Harbou's novel, the robot is created to bring back a lost love, Hel, who left Rotwang for Fredersen. Rotwang sees its creation not only as recapturing the love he lost, but also to spitefully remind Fredersen, who ultimately also lost her through death, of his own pain. The robot, when it is created, is therefore a tool – first created to fulfill an emotional desire – which Fredersen decides to use for his own political gain – to suppress the workers' insurgency. After its initial introduction to Fredersen, who encourages Rotwang to continue with its construction, Rotwang kidnaps Maria, the template for the robot. At first, he intended to model the robot on Hel herself, but then chooses to use Maria instead. He seeks to imbue the machine with her human essence.

While Rotwang is depicted as overly emotional, with his use of many exclamation points in the text and rolling eyes, large gestures, and unkempt hair in the film,[79] Fredersen is pure "head" – ruthless, cold, and "rational." Similar to a machine himself, he even eats and drinks "mechanically."[80] Both men stand to gain emotionally from the construction of the robot in various ways. Kakoudaki points out that "mechanical bodies are designed to be immune to emotional or psychological torment, unaffected by grief or pain, and resistant to suffering."[81] In this, the *Maschinenmensch* may be a projection of both men's pain and grief, indeed, "fictions of unemotional robots may express the need to avoid affect, to respond to affect with logic, to represent affect as logic."[82]

The robot Maria lacks innate emotions (Rotwang has to program them in, highlighting their performative nature) as well as volition; she is a simulacrum without a soul. Rotwang is well aware of the being's limitations, given that he wants her to pass for human. He pleads with her, "Won't you smile? Won't you cry? I need both your smile and your crying."[83] If she lacks the ability to express emotion, he fears he will be no more than a "bumbler." Angrily he says to her, "Can I give you the smile of the angels who happily fall into Hell? Can I give you the tears that release Satan and speak to him in holy tones? Parody is your name and Idiot mine!"[84] Rotwang seems to appreciate the complexity of human

---

78 J. P. Telotte, *Robot Ecology and the Science Fiction Film* (New York: Routledge, 2016), 61.

79 Some have read this as an antisemitic caricature.

80 Harbou, *Metropolis*, 22.

81 Kakoudaki, *Anatomy of a Robot*, 69.

82 Kakoudaki, *Anatomy of a Robot*, 75.

83 Harbou, *Metropolis*, 120.

84 Harbou, *Metropolis*, 122.

emotional expression and experience and is humbled by his attempt to approximate them, unlike Victor Frankenstein.

Harbou's scene in which the robot is initially created depicts the experience of the uncanny. In Rotwang's laboratory, Joh Fredersen encounters a creature (*Wesen*) lacking a face; it possesses transparent skin and delicate, skeletal hands. It speaks in a voice of disgusting (*entsetzlich*) delicacy and tenderness and regards Fredersen with "crazed eyes" (*wahnsinnige Augen*).[85] All of these attributes seem to fascinate Fredersen. Following Rotwang's instruction, the *Maschinenmensch* approaches Fredersen and curtsies to him. It extends its hand to Fredersen, and "in that moment of contact he felt burned by an unendurable coldness. He wanted to shove the being away from him."[86] The contact with its cold body evokes anger and disgust in Fredersen. Yet Fredersen's fascination becomes aversion only when he comes into direct tactile contact, unlike in the film when the sight of the metallic robot causes Fredersen to draw back from it. Like Joh Fredersen's first encounter with the robot, the inventor's patron Ewald in de l'Isle-Adam's novel examines a prototypical robotic arm laid on a cushion and asks, "Isn't it really flesh I'm touching right now? It makes my own crawl, I give you my word!"[87] The uncanny experience of eyes contradicting what the brain knows to be true creates an affective response of fear or possibly disgust in Ewald as his own skin – which provides his boundaries and integrity as a human – crawls, indicating his vulnerability and malleability. Here, the reason for the close semantic kinship between the almost disentanglable connection between physical contact – touch – and psychic feeling (emotion) is clear. *Gefühl* (feeling) originally meant the former sense of feeling – of touching with one's skin – and first in 1826 the *Grimms' Dictionary* made the distinction from emotional feeling.[88] The uncanniness of the robot is based in its life-like appearance which is betrayed by its inhuman voice, its eyes, and ultimately, its cold skin. While Rotwang sought to create a perfect imitation of a human, he is himself aware of its shortcomings as he names it "Parody."[89] It's unclear whether he knows he can never bring Hel back to life and the artificial person is far inferior to her, or whether Rotwang recognizes the limits to engineering an artificial human in general. Is she a parody of the woman he loved and is mourning, or a parody of humanity itself?

Although the being lacks emotions, it evokes them powerfully in others. Sara Ahmed suggests that emotions are relational in that they can be exchanged,

---

85 Harbou, *Metropolis*, 63.

86 Harbou, *Metropolis*, 71.

87 De l'Isle-Adam, *Eve of the Future Eden*, 68.

88 Benthien, *Skin*, 187.

89 Harbou, *Metropolis*, 63.

particularly through the human body's most powerful and largest sensory organ, the skin. Skin both contains us and separates us from others, but skin also bears the impressions of contact by others.[90] For primates (including humans), touch reinforces social bonds and reassures because it communicates a lack of hostility and an impression of friendship.[91] This very important form of communication and expression is subverted by the touch of the non-human machine. Disgust, the emotion that overwhelms Fredersen when he encounters the *Maschinenmensch*'s touch, bears important similarities to Freud's conception of the uncanny. Ahmed points out disgust is the ambivalent desire and attraction toward objects felt to be repellent and is dependent on bodily contact.[92]

In his work "Das Unheimliche" ("The Uncanny," 1919), Sigmund Freud emphasizes the word's German etymology: *unheimlich* literally means "un-homelike," in opposition to *heimlich* – homelike, homely, comfortable. *Unheimlich* came to mean strange, uncanny, or creepy. In Freud's thought, uncanniness occurs when that which was once known, homely, and comfortable becomes alien. Freud concludes his essay with a claim that became a central tenet of psychoanalysis: "every affect arising from an emotional impulse – of whatever kind – is converted into fear by being repressed."[93] Indeed, for Freud, it seems emotions themselves – in any guise or valence – present a perceived threat to the unconscious. He elaborates on this point with his statement that the uncanny element is in itself nothing new or strange, that in fact, the uncanny had long been familiar to the psyche and was later repressed. In this reading, the robot is not only uncanny because of its similarity to a human, causing uncertainty about how to relate to it, but, I'd suggest, a Freudian reading could also signal a fear of death, indicated by the robot's cold body. Indeed, Fredersen's need for robot workers is rooted in his desire to provide a legacy for his son, thereby transcending death. This generational legacy was disrupted by the 1.8 million battlefield deaths of the First World War in which fathers buried sons. Germany's failure to mourn those dead is notorious, and many have seen the cultural productions of 1920s as exhibits of repressed grief.[94] Later theorists of "technological animism," in which humanlike qualities of personhood are ascribed to robots suggest that a disconnection between a robot's appearance and behavior can evoke discomfort and fear in an experience of the uncanny. The more

---

90 Sara Ahmed, *The Cultural Politics of Emotion* (New York: Routledge, 2015), 25.
91 Jablonski, *Skin*, 103.
92 Ahmed, *Cultural Politics of Emotion*, 84.
93 Sigmund Freud, *The Uncanny*, trans. David McClintock (New York: Penguin Books, 2003 [1919]), 148.
94 Kaes, *Shell Shock Cinema*, 179.

humanlike the robot appears, the more humanly it needs to behave to keep humans at ease with it.

In imagining the robot Maria, Harbou draws upon old misogynistic tropes: the workers' nurturing advocate, the human, modest, "good Maria" is opposed by the mechanical, brazen, "evil Maria," who seeks their destruction, conflating sexual and political morality. Despite the Weimar era's association with progressive, experimental gender roles and sexual expression, plenty of Germans adhered to "conventional, gendered standards of behavior" and expectations.[95] The robot's licentiousness displayed at the Yoshiwara Club, which is coded decadent, Eastern, corrupt, and modern, is another expression of her irrational emotionality. Here the status of the robot and her emotions are complicated: the non-human machine is meant to pass as a human, in particular the Others – women – "Orientals" – that represent emotionality in Western modern culture. For Harbou, emotionality is central to being human and also to femininity.

Judith Butler asserts that sex and gender are necessary components of subjectivity – of being seen and counted in society. For her, sex is a performative process in which actors reiterate scripts and behaviors. In doing so they create a discourse and materiality of sexedness. Sex is "one of the norms by which the 'one' becomes viable at all – that which qualifies a body for life within the domain of cultural intelligibility."[96] Here, "sex" is a cultural norm that governs the materialization of bodies, rather than a bodily given.[97] This is helpful to think about the robot's frame or body, if we like – it possesses the indication of hips and breasts, built intentionally by Rotwang in order to approximate Hel's body and those of other human women. Gender is a defining component of humanity.[98] Indeed, Kakoudaki observes that "artificial bodies" often betray "stereotypical gendering," and the "phallic and dangerous" type of female is a stock character in depictions of artificial humans.[99]

For Harbou as for the feminist scholars, gender is a key component of performing humanness; without it, the robot cannot possibly "pass" as human. In this case, while the sexual evil/chaste virtue dichotomy is centuries old, the robot Maria is an incarnation firmly seated in modernity. Both left- and right-wing authors and politicians sexualized violence during and after the First World

---

95 Föllmer, *Individuality and Modernity in Berlin*, 35.

96 Judith Butler, *Bodies that Matter: On the Discursive Limits of "Sex"* (New York: Routledge, 1993), 2.

97 Butler, *Bodies that Matter*, 5.

98 Kakoudaki, *Anatomy of a Robot*, 3, 188.

99 Kakoudaki, *Anatomy of a Robot*, 82.

War, due in part to their battlefield experiences as well as the widespread, sometimes violent protests on the home front.[100] Barbara Hales sees the conflation of robot and woman into the ultimate Other as an expression of fears both of technology and of the new emancipation possible for women in the 1920s.[101] At the end of *Metropolis*, the robot becomes the agitator, the protestor, the "red revolver bride"[102] who threatens stability, morality, and truth.

In the case of *Metropolis*, the robot fails to appear fully human with its transparent "skin" and lack of a face when it first encounters Joh Fredersen. In the later stage of development, which has captured Maria's own facial expressions, the robot looks and behaves like a human, although her lewd and volatile behavior is radically opposed to the human Maria's saintly comportment. Despite its convincing skin and physical appearance overall, the robot Maria is the "inverted form of the familiar," the uncanny.[103] Harbou is drawing on a long tradition of gendering automata, machines, and robots female, an act which conflates threatening Others.[104] The robot violates bourgeois feminine norms and her own modest and humble appearance in a simulacrum of Maria's skin and clothes with her sexual performance at the club. As it is programmed (one assumes) to "perform" humanity, she over-exaggerates gender at the Yoshiwara club – to grotesque and mesmerizing effect on the male viewers. Yet it's at this moment that it "passes" for human;[105] she is able to evoke sexual desire and pleasure from its audience in a way a human woman could.

Mechanical humans were a topic that captured the imagination of military and medical personnel as well as conservative and right-wing intellectuals in the 1920s and 30s. Some have read fascist or New Objectivitist dynamics or sensibilities into *Metropolis*; following Kracauer's lead, R. L. Rutsky sees the ultimate capitulation of the workers to Fredersen as "foreshadowing" the Nazi rise to power, with Freder playing the mediator role in place of Adolf Hitler.[106] While I agree that the ending does not signal the workers' emancipation, the Nazi reading is not plausible, since Harbou's workers and other characters do not adhere to a fascist emotional style; nor do Freder or Joh Fredersen. The experiences of the First World War, in particular Germany's defeat, led some

100 Klaus Theweleit, *Männerphantasien*; Belinda Davis, *Homefires Burning: Food, Politics, and Everyday Life in World War I Berlin* (Chapel Hill: UNC Press, 2003).
101 Hales, "Taming the Technological Shrew," 301.
102 Hake, *Proletarian Dream*, 189.
103 Freud, *The Uncanny*, 18.
104 Huyssen, "The Vamp and the Machine," 226.
105 Kaes, *Shell Shock Cinema*, 201.
106 Kracauer, *From Caligari to Hitler*, 163; Rutsky, "Technology and Gender," 10, 19–20.

veterans and thinkers to imagine a battlefield world that could do no harm to the humans fighting on it. This fantasy of invulnerability inspired the creation of a new human sensibility. Writers like Ernst Jünger imagined a new man encased in a "steel form" with a body so mechanized and tough so as to be beyond pain.[107] Jünger calls on men to view themselves as objects, to completely dissociate from their bodies and the experience of pain. The affective result is that the individual no longer exists, but worker-soldiers all represent a uniform type: their faces are "metallic [and] galvanized. The gaze is silent and fixed."[108] This "desire for emotional immunity" aligns robots with hypermasculinity[109] – a sensibility Harbou herself had expressed in earlier fiction in which her female protagonists embodied a "masculinist feminism."[110] This hypermasculinity and hardness can also be read as a fascist emotional style, whose other components include demonstrations of anger, pitilessness toward those seen as unfit, and conformity.[111] When they seized power, the National Socialists sought to spark a "revolution of feeling."[112] Even the rebellious and dangerous robot Maria does not adhere to this fascist sensibility, in part because neither Jünger nor Harbou could imagine a world with women who did not adhere to their own society's bourgeois gender norms or their opposite. Harbou's story is not revolutionary in terms of emotional affect nor in its portrayal of gender or social relations.

The robot and the masses

The 1920s saw the resurgence of powerful workers' organizations and challenges to state policy via strikes, legislation, and the growth of leftist political parties. The adoption of Taylorist and Fordist production practices – timed tasks, assembly line production, and a professional managerial class – renewed fears of

---

107 Jeffrey Herf, *Reactionary Modernism: Technology, Culture, and Politics in Weimar and the Third Reich* (Cambridge: Cambridge UP, 1984), 71–75.
108 Ernst Jünger, *On Pain* [Über den Schmerz, 1934], trans. David C. Durst (Candor, NY: Telos Press, 2008), 105.
109 Kakoudaki, *Anatomy of a Robot*, 81.
110 Conversation with William W. Hagen, November 26, 2019. See also Quinn, "At War: Thea von Harbou, Women, and the Nation."
111 Peter Fritzsche, *Life and Death in the Third Reich* (Cambridge, MA: Harvard UP, 2008), 3; Claudia Koonz, *The Nazi Conscience* (Cambridge, MA: Harvard UP, 2003), 154.
112 Nicholas Stargardt, *The German War: A Nation Under Arms, 1939–1945* (New York: Basic Books, 2015), 12.

dehumanization, exploitation, and alienation. Indeed, not only Taylorist production techniques viewed the worker as a machine capable of infinite productivity; so, too, did fascism and Bolshevism.[113] Another group of massed people, soldiers, were also highly visible during the Weimar era, through parades, street violence, veterans' organizations, and other institutions. Matthew Biro suggests that these men were often seen as "mass subject[s]"– that is, the soldier possessed an "immature or weak personality. [He] subordinated his individual will and desires to the goals and ideals of an organized group. Because he was less rational and less repressed than people who retained their independence from groups, the military subject was understood to be authoritarian: that is, favoring strict rules, established hierarchies, and rapid and unquestioning obedience."[114] While *Metropolis* presents concerns about mass behavior, it does not celebrate it, nor present those masses in the kind of aesthetic order so valued by National Socialism. Harbou's treatment of the massed workers aligns much more with nineteenth-century conceptions than fascist ones.

Although Harbou paints a sympathetic picture of workers' suffering, she does so through an overtly paternalistic lens. Workers cannot solve their own problems, but rather need an elite, rational mediator to bring about amelioration of their suffering. Harbou's patriarchal stance on gender replays familiar stereotypes about women. Maria, the nurturing maternal figure of the underground workers' world, and the "heart" of Freder's vision, is kind, generous, and personifies the bourgeois feminine ideal of the angel in the house. Her emotional labor soothes others' pain and lifts them up. Ironically, however, it could be her very caring that prevents workers from a revolt; she is also a pacifying force, using Christianity to soothe the troubled workers. It's the robot Maria, embodiment of "negative emotions" – anger, lust, and vengefulness – who presents a potential for the workers to change the exploitative system of Metropolis. Harbou's reliance on a traditional binary pair expresses her conservative emotional style as opposed to a fascist one, which well could embrace and celebrate the workers' violence. The robot's use by Rotwang and Joh Fredersen to incite a workers' revolt eventually leads workers to riot and destroy the lower city in which they live. Neither robot nor woman has agency: they both represent the ultimate Other of irrationality – either a warm, nurturing heart, or a callous, manipulative entity, and are therefore pawns to be used by those with more power.

---

113 Anson Rabinbach, *The Human Motor: Energy, Fatigue, and the Origins of Modernity* (New York: Basic Books, 1990), 2.
114 Matthew Biro, *The Dada Cyborg: Visions of the New Human in Weimar Berlin* (Minneapolis: U of Minnesota Press, 2009), 154.

When Rotwang's robot enters the cavern that holds the workers' underground meeting, Harbou's omniscient narrator describes the impact of her appearance. "All the women in the hall suddenly blushed in a violent (*heftige*) and sickly way, and the men paled."[115] These bodily responses may reveal emotions of discomfort, fear, aversion, or disgust. It's unclear precisely what about the robot Maria evokes this response; it seems that the workers sense something uncanny about the creature.

Elias Canetti's work on crowds echoes the work of affect theorists in regard to human tactile sensations. As Freud noted in "The Uncanny" about that which evades categorization, Canetti observes, "There is nothing man fears more than the touch of the unknown. He wants to *see* what is reaching toward him, and to be able to recognize or at least classify it. Man always tends to avoid physical contact with anything strange."[116] Humans' affect reaches beyond our bodies; skin is the boundary with which we distinguish ourselves from others. Canetti goes on to claim that only in the crowd does this fear of coming into physical contact with the unknown dissipate and in fact, become a comfort rather than a threat. In dense crowds, bodies touch, and the crowd's corresponding psychic constitution is dense as well. Those in the crowd share or experience one and the same body; boundaries dissolve and identities merge into one psychic-sensual entity.[117] Indeed, people often feel they are "transcending the limits" of their individual personhood.[118] Freud's observations about groups demonstrate that objects, in this case a robot, can exert agency: the workers identify with the robot Maria through a process of *Einfühlung*, of forging a "new perception of a common quality" between or among them despite their immediate response to her.[119] They are able to imagine a shared connection: Kakoudaki observes that the robot's allure rests on its "ability to stir others into action."[120] In that way, it exercises agency without feeling any emotions itself, but evokes them effectively (for its creator's purpose) in others.

The robot Maria instigates a classic "baiting crowd" as she calls on the workers to destroy the machines which enslave them. The crowd exhibits an "angry sensitivity and irritability toward those labeled enemies",[121] in this case,

---

115 Harbou, *Metropolis*, 155.

116 Elias Canetti, *Crowds and Power*, trans. Carol Stewart (New York: The Noonday Press, 1984), 15.

117 Canetti, *Crowds and Power*, 15.

118 Canetti, *Crowds and Power*, 20.

119 Sigmund Freud, *Group Psychology and the Analysis of the Ego*, trans. James Strachey (London: The International Psycho-Analytical Press, 1922), 71.

120 Kakoudaki, *Anatomy of a Robot*, 109.

121 Canetti, *Crowds and Power*, 22.

the machines, and by proxy, their owners and managers. She has given the crowd a goal and a direction, which strengthens individuals' experience of solidarity. According to Canetti, a "baited crowd" wants to kill, and its speed, elation, and conviction are "uncanny" because the individuals behave as one organism, like a hunting pack.[122] It's not all that surprising that once the disaster its violence has caused becomes clear, as floods threaten its homes and children, the baited crowd turns on the robot, a much more immediate and concrete figure on which to vent its fear and rage. In turning to fire as a tool of destruction, the crowd chooses a tool that represents the multitude.[123]

Metropolis ends with the *Maschinenmensch* celebrating the disaster of the flooded workers' underground. As they turn on her, building a pyre and she begins to burn, she seems to exult in the destruction. Much has been made of Harbou's conclusion – the agreement reached between head (Joh Fredersen), heart (Freder and Maria) and hands (the workers' foreman). It seems the work at the factory will go on as usual; no apparent change has emerged. The heart – the compassion for workers' suffering – seems to be subsumed into the romantic love between Maria and Freder. True to her nineteenth-century sensibility and previous fictional works, Harbou's science fiction story becomes a romance. The emotional relationships between humans and machines serve to bolster the status quo rather than upending it. This, just as much as the fascination with technology, may account for the film's popular success in a time of tumult.

Bibliography

Ahmed, Sara. *The Cultural Politics of Emotion* (London: Routledge, 2014).
Barclay, Katie. "New Materialism and the New History of Emotions," *Emotions: History, Culture, Society* 1, no. 1 (2017): 161–183.
Barrows, Susanna. *Distorting Mirrors: Visions of the Crowd in Late Nineteenth-Century France* (New Haven, CT: Yale UP, 1981).
Benthien, Claudia. *Skin: On the Cultural Border Between Self and the World*. Trans. Thomas Dunlap (New York: Columbia UP, 2002).
Biro, Matthew. *The Dada Cyborg: Visions of the New Human in Weimar Berlin* (Minneapolis: U of Minnesota Press, 2009).
Boddice, Rob. *The History of Emotions* (Manchester: Manchester UP, 2018).

---

122 Canetti, *Crowds and Power*, 49.
123 Canetti, *Crowds and Power*, 50.

Booker, M. Keith, and Anne-Marie Thomas. "Science Fiction in Western Culture," in *The Science Fiction Handbook* (Sussex: Wiley-Blackwell, 2009), 3–12.

Butler, Judith. *Bodies that Matter: On the Discursive Limits of "Sex"* (New York: Routledge, 1993).

Canetti, Elias. *Crowds and Power*. Trans. Carol Stewart (New York: The Noonday Press, 1984).

Canning, Kathleen. "The Politics of Symbols, Semantics, and Sentiments in the Weimar Republic," *Central European History* 43 (2010): 567–580.

Čapek, Karel. *R.U.R (Rossum's Universal Robots)*. Trans. Claudia Novack (New York: Penguin, 2004).

The Complete *Metropolis*, Dir. Fritz Lang [1927], (Kino Lorber, 2010 [1927]).

Daston, Lorraine, and Gregg Mitman, eds. *Thinking with Animals: New Perspectives on Anthropomorphism* (New York: Columbia UP, 2005).

Davis, Belinda J. *Home Fires Burning: Food, Politics, and Everyday Life in World War I Berlin* (Chapel Hill: UNC Press, 2000).

Downes, Stephanie, Sally Holloway and Sarah Randles, eds. *Feeling Things: Objects and Emotions through History* (Oxford: Oxford UP, 2018).

Eitler, Pascal. "Tierliebe und Menschenführung. Eine genealogische Perspektive auf das 19. und 20. Jahrhundert," in *Tierstudien 3: Tierliebe*. Eds. Jessica Ullrich and Friedrich Weltzien (Berlin: Neofelis Verlag, 2013), 40–48.

Föllmer, Moritz. *Individuality and Modernity in Berlin: Self and Society from Weimar to the Wall* (Cambridge: Cambridge UP, 2013).

Frevert, Ute. "Defining Emotions: Concepts and Debates over Three Centuries," in *Emotional Lexicons: Continuity and Change in the Vocabulary of Feeling 1700–2000*. Eds. Ute Frevert et al. (Oxford: Oxford UP, 2014), 1–31.

Fritzsche, Peter. *Life and Death in the Third Reich* (Cambridge, MA: Harvard UP, 2008).

Freud, Sigmund. *Group Psychology and the Analysis of the Ego*. Trans. James Strachey (London: The International Psycho-Analytical Press, 1922).

Freud, Sigmund. *The Uncanny*. Trans. David McClintock (New York: Penguin Books, 2003 [1919]).

Gammerl, Benno. "Emotional Styles – Concepts and Challenges," *Rethinking History* 15, no. 2 (June 2012): 161–175.

Gammerl, Benno. "Feeling Differently: Approaches and their Politics," *Emotion, Space, and Society* (2017) https://doi.org/10.1016/j.emospa.2017.07.007.

Gay, Peter. *Weimar Culture: The Outsider as Insider* (New York: Harper & Row, 1968).

Häberlen, Joachim C., and Russell A. Spinney, "Introduction," (Emotions in Protest Movements in Europe since 1917) *Contemporary European History* 23, no. 4 (November 2014): 489–503.

Hake, Sabine. *The Proletarian Dream: Socialism, Culture, and Emotion in Germany, 1863–1933* (Berlin: De Gruyter, 2017).

Hales, Barbara. "Taming the Technological Shrew: Woman as Machine in Weimar Culture," *Neophilologus* 94 (2010): 301–316.

Hampshire, Stuart. "Biology, Machines, and Humanity," in *The Boundaries of Humanity: Humans, Animals, Machines*. Eds. James J. Sheehan and Morton Sosna (Berkeley: UC Press, 1991), 253–258.

Haraway, Donna. "A Cyborg Manifesto," in *Simians, Cyborgs, and Women: The Reinvention of Nature* (Routledge, 1991), 149–182.

Harbou, Thea von. *Metropolis* (Vienna: Milena Verlag, 2014).

Herf, Jeffrey. *Reactionary Modernism: Technology, Culture, and Politics in Weimar and the Third Reich* (Cambridge: Cambridge UP, 1984).

Huyssen, Andreas. "The Vamp and the Machine: Technology and Sexuality in Fritz Lang's *Metropolis*," *New German Critique* no. 24/25 (Autumn 1981–Winter 1982): 221–237.

de l'Isle-Adam, Villiers. *Eve of the Future Eden*. Trans. Marilyn Gaddis Rose (Lawrence, KS: Coronado Press, 1981).

Jablonski, Nina G. *Skin: A Natural History* (Berkeley: UC Press, 2006).

Jensen, Paul M. "Metropolis: The Film and the Book," in Fritz Lang, *Metropolis* (New York: Simon and Schuster, 1973).

Jünger, Ernst. *On Pain*. Trans. David C. Durst (Candor, NY: Telos Press, 2008).

Kaes, Anton. *Shell Shock Cinema: Weimar Culture and the Wounds of War* (Princeton, NJ: Princeton UP, 2011).

Kakoudaki, Despina. *Anatomy of a Robot: Literature, Cinema, and the Cultural Work of Artificial People* (New Brunswick, NJ: Rutgers UP, 2014).

Kang, Minsoo. *Sublime Dreams of Living Machines: The Automaton in the European Imagination* (Cambridge, MA: Harvard UP, 2011).

Keiner, Reinhold. *Thea von Harbou und der deutsche Film bis 1933* (Hildesheim: Georg Olms Verlag, 1984).

Koonz, Claudia. *The Nazi Conscience* (Cambridge, MA: Harvard UP, 2003).

Kracauer, Siegfried. *From Caligari to Hitler: A Psychological History of the German Film* (Princeton, NJ: Princeton UP, 1947).

Marx, Karl. "Estranged Labor," in *Economic and Philosophic Manuscripts of 1844*. Trans. Martin Milligan (New York: Prometheus Books, 1988), 69–84.

Nolan, Mary. *Visions of Modernity: American Business and the Modernization of Germany* (Oxford: Oxford UP, 1994).

Oliver, Kelly. *Animal Lessons: How they Teach us to be Human* (New York: Columbia UP, 2009).

Quinn, Erika. "At War: Thea von Harbou, Women, and the Nation," *Women in German Yearbook* 33 (2017): 52–76.

Rabinbach, Anson. *The Human Motor: Energy, Fatigue, and the Origins of Modernity* (New York: Basic Books, 1990).

Richardson, Kathleen. "Mechanical People," *New Scientist* 190, no. 2557 (24 June 2006): 56–57.

Richardson, Kathleen. "Technological Animism: The Uncanny Personhood of Humanoid Machines," *Social Analysis* 60, no. 1 (Spring 2016): 110–128.

Rosenwein, Barbara H. "Worrying about Emotions in History," *American Historical Review* 107, no. 3 (June 2002): 821–45.

Rutsky, R. L. "The Mediation of Technology and Gender: Metropolis, Nazism, Modernism," *New German Critique* no. 60 (Autumn 1993): 3–32.

Ryan, Derek. *Animal Theory: A Critical Introduction* (Edinburgh: Edinburgh UP, 2015).

Spengler, Oswald. *Der Mensch und die Technik: Beitrag zu einer Philosophie des Lebens* (Munich: C. H. Beck, 1933).

Spengler, Oswald. *Der Untergang des Abendlandes: Umrisse einer Morphologie der Weltgeschichte* Bd. II Welthistorische Perspektiven (Munich: C. H. Beck, 1923).

Stargardt, Nicholas. *The German War: A Nation Under Arms, 1939–1945* (New York: Basic Books, 2015).

Stearns, Peter N. and Carol Z. Stearns. "Clarifying the History of Emotions and Emotional Standards," *American Historical Review* 90, no. 4 (October 1985): 813–36.

Telotte, J. P. *Robot Ecology and the Science Fiction Film* (New York: Routledge, 2016).

Telotte, J. P. "The Seductive Text of 'Metropolis,'" *South Atlantic Review* 55, no. 4 (Nov. 1990): 49–60.

Theweleit, Klaus. *Männerphantasien: Frauen, Fluten, Körper, Geschichte* (Frankfurt a. M.: Roter Stern, 1977).

Weil, Kari. *Thinking Animals: Why Animal Studies Now?* (New York: Columbia UP, 2012).

Wells, H. G. "Mr. Wells Reviews a Current Film," [1927] in *The Science Fiction Film Reader*. Ed. Gregg Rickman (New York: Limelight Editions, 2004), 5–12.

Wosk, Julie. "Metropolis," *Technology and Culture* 51, no. 2 (April 2010): 403–408.

Empathic Understanding between Humans and Non-Humans

Claudia Mueller-Greene

"Penetrating the Innermost Heart"

Emotion, Music, and the Psychical Power of Machines in E. T. A. Hoffmann's "The Automata" (1814)

In 2019, the news magazine *60 Minutes* presented an unsettling segment that discussed the use of fMRI scans to "reveal the physical makeup of our thoughts and feelings."[1] A cognitive neuroscientist explained the stunning advances in his field. The technique of functional magnetic resonance imaging of the brain has reached such a degree of sophistication that it enables scientists to recognize even "complex thoughts from spirituality to suicide."[2] Emotions appear as distinctive patterns of brain activation and can be detected with uncanny accuracy. One of the reporters was put into a scanner and asked to elicit certain emotions in herself. Afterwards, a computer program took the data gathered by the scanner and correctly identified her emotions as disgust and envy. The journalists were astounded.

This piece of news about a veritable mind-reading machine would have intrigued the Romantic writer Ernst Theodor Amadeus Hoffmann. It sounds like one of his own fantastic literary creations: a machine gains insight into our innermost thoughts and feelings by using a technology based on magnetism. This description indeed covers part of the plot of "Die Automate" ("The Automata"), Hoffmann's enigmatic tale about automata that was written and first published in 1814.[3] Five years later, it appeared in Hoffmann's collection of stories *Die Serapions-Brüder* (*The Serapion Brothers*, 1819–1821). This essay explores how Hoffmann's "The Automata" represents and reflects emotional human-machine interactions, with a particular focus on the role of music. It does so by paying special attention to emotions and to the "non-human" within the larger context of machines, which besides machines also encompasses the

---

1 Lesley Stahl, "Scientists Are Using MRI Scans to Reveal the Physical Makeup of Our Thoughts and Feelings," 18 June 2020, https://www.cbsnews.com/news/functional-magnetic-resonance-imaging-computer-analysis-read-thoughts-60-minutes-2019-11-24/.
2 Stahl, "Scientists."
3 E. T. A. Hoffmann, "Die Automate," in *Die Serapions-Brüder: E. T. A. Hoffmann Sämtliche Werke*, vol. 4, ed. Wulf Segebrecht (Frankfurt a. M.: Deutscher Klassiker Verlag, 2001), 396–429 [= *DKV4*]. All translations from German sources are mine unless otherwise indicated.

Dedication: In Erinnerung an Markus Forkl

https://doi.org/10.1515/9783110753677-008

realms of animate and inanimate non-human nature.[4] How does the non-human produce and transmit emotions in "The Automata"? How does it affect the protagonists' feelings and how do they react? How does the story depict the functions of human-made music, of machine music, and of the music of nature in interactions where music alters the affective states of humans? How might Hoffmann's literary evocation of the emotional and aesthetic "agency" of the non-human prompt readers to reassess their notions of human nature and of art?[5] The emotional and aesthetic interaction between the human and the non-human through music can be regarded as the thematic core of "The Automata."

The first part of this chapter outlines the cultural and aesthetic context of "The Automata." The second part discusses "The Automata" by focusing on the non-human elements and their emotional effects on the human characters. The third part specifically addresses music and its relationship to emotions, the human, and the non-human. The essay concludes by pondering how Hoffmann's "The Automata" can stimulate our twenty-first century imagination and provoke us to rethink and reclaim our ideas of art and of human nature.

The cultural and aesthetic context of "The Automata"

E. T. A. Hoffmann took a keen interest in the scientific and technological developments of his time, was fascinated with humanlike and musical machines, and in his diary he even expressed the wish to build an automaton himself.[6] At the same time, he was influenced by German Idealism and followed contemporary debates in natural philosophy, medicine, and psychology. In these disciplines, a popular topic was animal magnetism (mesmerism), physician Franz Anton Mesmer's concept of a natural force in all living beings – human and non-human animals – that can be tapped into for healing purposes. Mesmer's theory of an invisible physical force or magnetic fluid had gradually developed into the idea of a mainly psychical power that enables a Magnetiseur or mesmerizer to place patients

4 On the non-human, see Richard Grusin, "Introduction," in *The Nonhuman Turn*, ed. Richard Grusin (Minneapolis: U of Minnesota Press, 2015), vii–xxix.
5 On non-human agency, see Jeffrey Scott Marchand, "Non-Human Agency," in *Posthuman Glossary*, eds. Rosi Braidotti and Maria Hlavajova (London: Bloomsbury, 2018), 292–295.
6 See Claudia Liebrand, "Automaten/Künstliche Menschen," in *E. T. A. Hoffmann-Handbuch: Leben – Werk – Wirkung*, eds. Christine Lubkoll and Harald Neumeyer (Stuttgart: Metzler, 2015), 244.

in a somnambulistic state to cure them. Hoffmann was so captivated by it that "traces of magnetism are to be found in virtually all his works."[7] The more sinister aspects of magnetism, such as the dark empathic power of the Magnetiseur to invade and manipulate the psychic life of the magnetized person, particularly preoccupied his poetic imagination.[8]

The aesthetic principles of German Romanticism, such as irony, self-referentiality, and the importance of the reader's response, critically shaped "The Automata." Romanticism's emphasis on the *effect* of art is encapsulated in Novalis's definition of poetry: "Poésie = Gemütherregungskunst," which means "poetry = the art of stirring the heart."[9] The word "Gemüt" means "soul" or "heart" and figures prominently in "The Automata," where it serves as a term for subjective interiority, imagination, and emotion. Romantic literature appreciates those aspects of life that had been held in rather low esteem by the Enlightenment: the realm of feeling and the power of imagination. It privileges the fantastic, the dreamlike, ambiguity, and uncertainty. As far as the realm of nature is concerned, Romanticism focuses on the mysterious, the enigmatic, and the sublime.

All these Romantic elements can be found in "The Automata." Moreover, Hoffmann came up with his own poetological concept, the "Serapiontic Principle." As a general aesthetic principle, it can be also applied to other forms of art like music. It originates from the frame narrative of *The Serapion Brothers*, where it is established by the fictitious group of writers whose readings and conversations make up the book. The name "Serapiontic" refers to the very first tale about a hermit who commands exceptional poetical gifts, rooted in his imaginative powers, but who is possessed by the delusion that he is Saint Serapion. Lothar, one of the writers, wants Serapion to serve as the model of the newly founded circle of poets, except for his delusion. According to Lothar, the hermit lacks the "ability to discern that duplexity which uniquely determines our earthly existence."[10] Lothar elaborates on this concept of "duplexity" in a key passage that is fundamental to the whole book: "There is an inner world and a spiritual ability to behold it with full clarity in the perfect splendor of the most vibrant life. But it is

---

7 Maximilian Bergengruen and Daniel Hilpert, "Magnetismus/Mesmerismus," in *E. T. A. Hoffmann-Handbuch: Leben – Werk – Wirkung*, eds. Christine Lubkoll and Harald Neumeyer (Stuttgart: Metzler, 2015), 293.

8 On the negative aspects of empathy, see Fritz Breithaupt, *The Dark Sides of Empathy* (Ithaca, NY: Cornell UP, 2019).

9 Novalis, *Das philosophisch-theoretische Werk: Werke, Tagebücher und Briefe Friedrich von Hardenbergs*, vol. 2, ed. Hans-Joachim Mähl (Darmstadt: WBG, 1999), 801.

10 *DKV4*, 68.

our earthly inheritance that it is the outer world, in which we are confined, which operates as the lever that sets this ability in motion."[11]

A poet capable of affecting his readers forcefully must be a genuine seer who truly inhabits the inner world his words are supposed to convey, just like Serapion. But unlike the insane hermit, the real poet does not lose sight of the outer world. Instead, he is aware of the material world as the outward "lever," which has set his own inward experience in motion. By putting his pen to paper, the poet wields this lever himself to move his readers in an analogous way.[12] To prevent his friends and himself from dull literary efforts, Lothar proclaims the "Serapiontic Principle,"[13] which they should follow as "true Serapion Brothers": "May each of us at least strive quite seriously to get a clear grasp of the picture he visualizes in his mind's eye, – in every one of its forms, colors, lights and shadows, and then, when he feels himself thoroughly permeated and kindled by it, bring it out into outer life."[14]

Hoffmann's "Serapiontic artist" practices a specific *Gemütherregungskunst* (Novalis), a specific "art of stirring the heart": by drawing on his *inner* visions he attempts to evoke a vivid and emotional experience in his audience.[15] But what happens when *soulless* machines come into play? What does it mean when automata are pulling the "lever" – a strikingly mechanical metaphor in itself – and affecting our psychic life? Is it conceivable that *inanimate* powers of a merely *mechanical* "Serapiontics" could be exerted to stir our hearts? Such mysterious occurrences involving machine music seem to transpire in "The Automata."

Hoffmann, also a composer and music critic, is renowned for his essays, which are considered a main source of Romantic music aesthetics.[16] "The Automata" itself contains remarkable passages about music, which were first published in the *Allgemeine Musikalische Zeitung* (General music journal).[17] In "Beethoven's

---

11 *DKV4*, 68.

12 On the historical and cultural context of emotional impression and expression, see Ute Frevert, *Vergängliche Gefühle* (Göttingen: Wallstein, 2013), 12–15. On *inside* and *outside*, see Monique Scheer, "Topographies of Emotions," in *Emotional Lexicons: Continuity and Change in the Vocabulary of Feeling 1700–2000*, eds. Ute Frevert et al. (Oxford: Oxford UP, 2014), 35–39.

13 *DKV4*, 70.

14 *DKV4*, 69.

15 Hoffmann's Serapiontic Principle corresponds to the "experience-aesthetic model" that evolved in the eighteenth century in opposition to the "rhetorical model" of emotional communication. See Thomas Anz, "Emotional Turn? Beobachtungen zur Gefühlsforschung," in *Literaturkritik.de*, 14 July 2020, https://literaturkritik.de/id/10267.

16 See Werner Keil, "Dissonanz und Verstimmung: E. T. A. Hoffmanns Beitrag zur Entstehung der musikalischen Romantik," *E. T. A. Hoffmann Jahrbuch* 1 (1992–1993): 119.

17 On "The Automata," see *DKV4*, 1377–1390.

Instrumental Music," Hoffmann emphasizes the unique power of music to reach and move people: "Music unlocks for man an uncharted realm, a world which has nothing in common with the outer sensual world surrounding him and in which he leaves behind all *definite* feelings to abandon himself to an inexpressible longing."[18] He characterizes Beethoven as "a purely Romantic composer," because his "music sets in motion the levers of fear, of awe, of horror, of pain, and arouses that infinite longing which is the essence of Romanticism."[19]

Yet the emotional impact of music is constantly challenged by the essentially mechanical nature of the technical demands in music. In Hoffmann's literary texts and especially in "The Automata," music is often represented as determined by a conflict between oppositions: between subjective interiority and objective exteriority, vocal and instrumental music, nature and mechanics. At times, the implicit literary staging of this inherent difference in music subverts the explicit formulations of Romantic ideas of music. Helmut Müller-Sievers views Hoffmann's acute awareness of the exterior, mathematical, and mechanical character of music as a sign that he actually leaned towards "unromantic music."[20] However, there is more evidence that Hoffmann precisely insisted on the inner conflict between the interior emotional and the exterior mechanical aspects of music without privileging one aspect. His staging of the conflicting nature of music is not unromantic, but indeed fully compatible with Romantic music aesthetics. After all, Romanticism is not about the fulfilment of unity, but about the longing for this fulfillment. And the longing is fueled by this inherent rift in music.

Encounters with the non-human in "The Automata"

After "The Poet and the Composer,"[21] "The Automata" is the second tale of the "Serapion Brother" Theodor about the poet Ferdinand and the composer Ludwig. In the following "turn toward the nonhuman,"[22] this essay explores elements

---

18 E. T. A. Hoffmann, "Beethovens Instrumental-Musik," in *Fantasiestücke in Callot's Manier: E. T. A. Hoffmann Sämtliche Werke*, vol. 2/1, ed. Hartmut Steinecke (Frankfurt a. M.: Deutscher Klassiker Verlag, 1993), 52 [= *DKV2/1*].
19 *DKV2/1*, 54.
20 Helmut Müller-Sievers, "Verstimmung. E. T. A. Hoffmann und die Trivialisierung der Musik," *Vierteljahrsschrift für Literaturwissenschaft und Geistesgeschichte* 63, no. 1 (1989): 118.
21 *DKV4*, 94–118.
22 Grusin, *Nonhuman Turn*, xx.

in "The Automata" relating to the non-human and their emotional effects on humans. What are the relevant forms in which the non-human – "variously conceived of as animals, plants, organisms, climatic systems, technologies, or ecosystems"[23] – appears in "The Automata"? From the beginning, the reader's attention is directed to the non-human in the form of *technologies*. The two friends experience three very different encounters with automata in the story, which have a profoundly unsettling effect on them, particularly on Ferdinand.

The first encounter involves the so-called "talking Turk," an android with "Oriental grandezza."[24] Unlike his real-life counterpart, the chess-playing Turk created by the inventor Wolfgang von Kempelen,[25] the "talking Turk" enjoys high popularity because of his performance as an oracle. People ask him questions, and his prophecies often reveal an inexplicable insight into their psyches and futures. He is a man-like machine with whirring wheels that remains an "odd living-dead figure,"[26] needs to be wound up from time to time and cannot seriously be mistaken for a real human. Apart from his appearance, the Turk has another humanlike quality: he is able to talk. Ferdinand is curious about the trick behind the seeming miracle and persuades Ludwig to accompany him and a group of friends to put the celebrated automaton to the test. Before their visit to the Turk, Ludwig stresses his inability to see such life-like figures "without being seized by a feeling of uncanniness and horror."[27] Contrary to his misgivings, Ludwig's first impression of the Turk turns out to be more benign. The android seems to him "extremely droll"[28] and does not fall into the "uncanny valley," the effect of uncanniness that robots have when they look too humanlike.[29] Prompted by the buzzing wheelwork of the automaton, which strikes him as "vulgar,"[30] Ludwig makes a joke that bizarrely illustrates the difference between a human organism and a merely mechanical android: "Well, gentlemen, listen! We

---

23 Grusin, *Nonhuman Turn*, x.

24 *DKV4*, 401.

25 See Claudia Lieb, "Der gestellte Türke: Wolfgang Kempelens Maschinen und E. T. A. Hoffmanns Erzählung *Die Automate*," *E. T. A. Hoffmann Jahrbuch* 16 (2008): 82–97.

26 *DKV4*, 396.

27 *DKV4*, 399. See Kathleen Richardson, "Technological Animism: The Uncanny Personhood of Humanoid Machines," *Social Analysis* 60, no. 1 (2016): 110–128.

28 *DKV4*, 401.

29 The robot specialist Masahiro Mori identified this effect and called it the "uncanny valley," since it appears as a deep minimum in a graph that shows the feeling of familiarity (canniness) as a function of human likeness of robots. See Jan Plamper, *The History of Emotions: An Introduction* (Oxford: Oxford UP, 2015), 27–28.

30 *DKV4*, 401.

might at best have some roasted meat in our stomachs, but this Turkish Excellency there has a roasting spit on top of it."[31] By caricaturing the Turk's purely mechanical nature, Ludwig not only reassures himself and his friends of their superior status as metabolizing, sentient living beings, but also reasserts the categorical boundary between humans and machines, which the Turk challenges. Initially, the "jovial mood"[32] of the irreverent young gentlemen is rewarded with a disappointing divinatory output by the Turk until Ferdinand asks him a question. The answer of the mechanical psychic, only audible to Ferdinand, shocks him so much that he cannot hide his dismay. It is when the humanoid not only displays *humanlike* abilities, like his historical chess-playing counterpart, but truly *superhuman* powers, that the fun ends.

Ferdinand confides in Ludwig that the Turk has reached into his innermost being[33] with his prophecy. He tells him a secret he has hitherto kept all to himself: the story of the emotionally most intense and momentous event of his life. Some years ago, he tried to sleep in a hotel, when suddenly, coming from the next room, the divine voice of a woman sang a song that went to his very heart and stirred it ineffably. An unnameable rapture and the "pain of an infinite longing" seized him, and he had the impression that his "whole being dissolved in nameless, heavenly delight."[34] Ferdinand recites the Italian text of the song "Mio ben ricordati" that engendered in him such feelings:

> Remember, beloved,
> if it should happen that I die,
> how this faithful soul
> loved you.
> And if cold ashes
> can love
> in the urn,
> I shall love you.[35]

A woman has a premonition of her death and transformation into non-human "cold ashes." She implores her beloved's remembrance of her faithful love for him and poignantly promises that her ashes in the urn will continue to love him, should this be possible. Ferdinand recounts that he fell asleep and had a

---

31 *DKV4*, 401.
32 *DKV4*, 402.
33 *DKV4*, 403: "in mein Innerstes gegriffen."
34 *DKV4*, 405.
35 Pietro Metastasio, "Mio ben ricordati," from his opera libretto *Alessandro nell' Indie*. Translated by Richard Wigmore. 18 June 2020. https://www.oxfordlieder.co.uk/song/3161.

dream in which the singer entered his room. The next morning, he watched the occupant of the adjacent room departing and recognized the singer of his dream: "it was the dream image."[36] Ferdinand admits that he abstained from making any inquiries about the lady. Instead, he has painted and framed a miniature portrait of her and secretly worn it ever since. He tells Ludwig that, thinking of his beloved, he asked the Turk whether he would live to experience another moment like the one when he was happiest. The Turk demanded him that he turn the hidden picture on his breast around. He obeyed, only to receive the oracle: "The moment you next see her again, you will have lost her!"[37]

Unfathomably, the Turk accomplishes the miracle of reading Ferdinand's innermost thoughts and feelings, far surpassing the most advanced brain imaging techniques of today. It is this fantastic turn of the encounter with the Turk which upsets Ferdinand and also disconcerts Ludwig and the whole group of friends. During the course of the event, the automaton elicits an unwholesome concoction of emotions in the young gentlemen, ranging from aversion and curiosity before the visit, to amusement, dissatisfaction, and finally shock and alarm. Any uncanniness of the Turk's humanlike appearance does *not* affect them very strongly.[38] Instead, it is the automaton's seemingly magic mind-reading capability that has this profoundly disturbing effect.

Ferdinand and Ludwig socialize again with the group of gentlemen and learn from an elderly member of the club that the mastermind behind the Turk is a certain Professor X, a specialist in physics and chemistry, who is known for his collection of "the most marvelous automata, primarily musical."[39] Driven by their need to unravel the mystery behind the Turk, the two friends visit Professor X. When the Professor unlocks his exhibition hall, they have their second encounter with automata, the only one without any incursion of the fantastic into the world of reality. The hall contains a collection of "the most well-known androids that had been constructed until Hoffmann's time."[40] Like the Turk, the musical androids and non-humanlike musical machines are at least partially based on historical models, among others, on Jacques de "Vaucanson's

---

36 *DKV4*, 406.

37 *DKV4*, 408.

38 Similarly, in his interpretation of Hoffmann's "The Sandman," Freud emphasizes that the humanlike automaton Olimpia is not the main source of uncanniness in the story. See Sigmund Freud, "The 'Uncanny'," in *The Standard Edition of the Complete Psychological Works of Sigmund Freud*, vol. XVII (1917–1919) (London: Hogarth Press, 1955), 227.

39 *DKV4*, 412.

40 Frank Wittig, *Maschinenmenschen: Zur Geschichte eines literarischen Motivs im Kontext von Philosophie, Naturwissenschaft und Technik* (Würzburg: Königshausen & Neumann, 1997), 74.

flute-player and the harmonica player,"[41] the famous female humanoid of the Geneva watchmakers Jaquet-Droz.[42] Unlike the Turk, these machines are not endowed with any magical powers. The earsplitting concert Professor X's machine orchestra performs proves to be an aesthetic disappointment. It is characterized by "utmost rhythmical precision,"[43] is blatantly mechanical and so noisy that Ferdinand and Ludwig cut their visit short to escape "the mechanic and his machines."[44] Emotionally, the machine music has not quite the same effect on the two friends. Ferdinand reacts with admiration for the mechanical feat, in spite of its aesthetic shortcomings. The musician Ludwig is outraged by the assault on his ears.

While they are walking, they immerse themselves in a discussion about machine music and other technological advances in music. Ludwig wonders why it needs a human performer to achieve the powerful emotional effect of music. Applying the Serapiontic Principle to music, Ludwig is speculating whether the reason for the deficiency of machine music lies in the absence of that human faculty which, unlike the body, cannot be replaced by automata: "Is it not rather the soul (*Gemüt*) which only uses those organs of the body to bring into the active life that which has sounded in its deepest depth; so that it can resound audibly for others and arouse the same resonances in them [. . .]?"[45] This theory of Ludwig's about the power of music to evoke human emotions explains why the mechanical precision of Professor X's machine music has, despite its technical perfection, such a counter-productive emotional effect and is unable to reach the hearts of the listeners.

But then their conversation takes an interesting turn from the human soul to nature and from soulless machine music to a "higher mechanics of music,"[46] whose purpose is "the discovery of the perfect sound."[47] According to Ludwig, a "musical sound is the nearer to perfection the more closely it resembles the mysterious tones of nature"[48] which have "a powerful effect on the human soul (*Gemüt*)."[49] He is convinced that echoes from a primeval music reverberate in

---

41 *DKV4*, 420.
42 See Rudolf Drux, "Der literarische Maschinenmensch und seine technologische Antiquiertheit: Wechselbeziehungen zwischen Literatur- und Technikgeschichte," *Dresdner Beiträge zur Geschichte der Technikwissenschaften* 29 (2004): 10.
43 *DKV4*, 417.
44 *DKV4*, 418.
45 *DKV4*, 419.
46 *DKV4*, 421.
47 *DKV4*, 421.
48 *DKV4*, 421.
49 *DKV4*, 422.

those moving sounds of nature which should be the object of a higher mechanics of music. As promising inventions of such an advanced approach to music, Ludwig mentions the harmonica, the harmonichord, and the storm harp.

Outside of the town, they experience their third encounter with automata, this time mainly auditory. Still immersed in their philosophical reflections about music and its mysterious dual origin in the human soul and in nature, they suddenly hear extraordinary tones arising from behind the hedges of a garden. The sounds, first resembling the tone of a harmonica, take the form of a female voice singing the song of Ferdinand's secret love. Through the open gate, the friends notice Professor X in the middle of the garden. Around him, "crystal sounds flickered up from the dark bushes and trees and streamed, united in a wondrous concert, like fire flames through the air, penetrating the innermost heart and igniting it to the highest rapture of heavenly anticipations."[50] This concert is "wondrous" in at least two ways. Firstly, it is an example of what seems to be a perfect achievement of a "higher mechanics of music." Secondly, the concert confirms that Professor X has somehow succeeded in "penetrating" Ferdinand's "innermost heart." The Professor is obviously not only the mastermind behind the Turk's shocking prophecy but also behind the haunting performance of the song "Mio ben ricordati." Ferdinand reacts in horror: "I feel, too clearly, that a strange power has penetrated my innermost being and seized all its hidden strings, making them resound at its pleasure [. . .]!"[51]

Ferdinand is summoned to another city, but Ludwig obtains some new information from the elderly gentleman about Professor X. He confides in Ludwig that the Professor's true calling consists of a relentless quest for a "deep penetration into all areas of natural science"[52] and that he uses a garden as his laboratory. The Professor's secret discoveries and inventions in music are especially praised by the man. Months later, Ludwig receives a letter from Ferdinand, in which he tells him that by a strange coincidence on his journey, he stumbled into the wedding of his beloved singer. When she saw him, she fainted into the arms of Professor X. Ferdinand cannot remember what happened afterwards, since he has been afflicted with amnesia. Ludwig realizes that his friend suffered a nervous breakdown. He is mystified when he learns that Professor X has been in town for the entire time. "The Automata" ends abruptly, with Ludwig's hope that the fulfillment of the Turk's prophecy might eventually prove salutary to his friend. Back in the frame narrative, the "Serapion Brother" Theodor defends the fragmentary character of

---

50 *DKV4*, 425.
51 *DKV4*, 425.
52 *DKV4*, 426.

his story: "the imagination of the reader or listener should only receive a couple of rather forceful impulses and then go on swinging freely by itself."[53]

In his garden laboratory, the physicist Professor X is dealing with the non-human in a way reminiscent of August Wilhelm Schlegel's dictum "poetry insists on magic from physics."[54] Hidden by the tall hedges of the garden, the Professor's science becomes indistinguishable from magic. The change of scenery is significant. Almost somnambulistically, the two friends have been walking from Professor X's official collection of automata in his "splendidly decorated hall"[55] to his "mysterious laboratory."[56] In his hall, the Professor acts like a "mechanic"[57] who steers his musical automata towards a deafening "fortissimo."[58] The mystery of nature is deliberately kept inaudible in this exoteric exhibition of lifeless musical mechanics. On the other hand, in his secluded garden, the Professor appears as a life-giving gardener: "everything around him became animated and lively."[59] Seemingly under the command of the magician Professor X, an initially non-human tone "became the deeply mournful melody of a female voice."[60] Synesthetic flamelike crystal tones are flickering up from the bushes and trees. The Professor is wielding an invisible technology that somehow allows him to transcend categorical boundaries and to merge the non-human with the human, the auditory with the visual.[61] The garden is depicted as a liminal zone in which the inner and the outer worlds are dynamically flowing into each other, temporarily suspending the condition of "duplexity." Contrary to the shrill machine music in the exhibition hall, the esoteric garden concert ends quietly, creating an atmosphere in which the receptive listener might catch some overtones of the mystery of nature: "the tones died away in pianissimo."[62] Its emotional effect on Ferdinand's *Gemüt*, though, is devastating. Just as after the Turk's prophecy, he feels that he has lost ownership over his inner life. But this time it is worse,

---

53 *DKV4*, 427–428.
54 August Wilhelm Schlegel, *A. W. Schlegels Vorlesungen über schöne Literatur und Kunst: Zweiter Teil (1802–1808)* (Stuttgart: Göschen'sche Verlagshandlung, 1884), 62.
55 *DKV4*, 417.
56 *DKV4*, 426.
57 *DKV4*, 418.
58 *DKV4*, 417.
59 *DKV4*, 425.
60 *DKV4*, 424.
61 On "transgressive science," see Paola Mayer, "Transgressive Science in E. T. A. Hoffmann's Fantastic Tales," in *E. T. A. Hoffmann: Transgressive Romanticism*, ed. Christopher R. Clason (Liverpool: Liverpool UP, 2018), 65–77.
62 *DKV4*, 425.

because he realizes that the inner sanctum of his soul with his ideal love for the singer has not only been invaded but manipulated all along. By stirring Ferdinand's heart in a detrimental manner, Professor X's non-human music of a "higher mechanics" proves to belong to the nightside of *Gemütherregungskunst* (art of stirring the heart; Novalis).

In these three incidents, the two protagonists encounter the non-human in a variety of different technologies: on the one hand, they explore realistic and partly historical androids and non-humanlike musical machines from the eighteenth century, among which the prophesying Turk is the only one endowed with fantastic powers; on the other hand, they are confronted with an inscrutable technology that exerts immense "psychical power,"[63] be it through the prophecies of the Turk or through the music of an apparently invisible "higher mechanics."

To many of Hoffmann's contemporary readers it must have been evident that this invisible technology in "The Automata" is presumably supposed to be an exceedingly sophisticated use of animal magnetism.[64] Mesmerism is not explicitly mentioned in "The Automata," but expressions such as "influence" and "rapport" that were strongly associated with mesmerism repeatedly pop up in the text. Another hint for mesmerism as a driving force in the plot is that Theodor calls Ferdinand's infatuation with the singer a "somnambulistic love-affair."[65] There is an interesting connection between the motifs of mesmerism and automata, which is discussed in the scholarly literature. The condition of the mesmerized person "is essentially that of a marionette, turning the magnetiseur into a sort of maker of automata."[66] Claudia Liebrand views Ferdinand as such a puppet: "Ferdinand is being remotely controlled and converted into an automaton by his phantasmagoric nocturnal experience with the singer."[67] This reading is supported by Ferdinand's descriptions of himself as acting "mechanically"[68] and "thoughtlessly"[69] in situations involving the singer. His obsessive love for the singer seems to be driven by unconscious emotional forces he cannot resist. Liebrand points out that Ferdinand, like other characters of Hoffmann, appears to be subjected to a program he has not given himself, but which has been uncannily imposed upon

---

63 *DKV4*, 414: "psychische Macht."
64 On mesmerism in "The Automata," see Claudia Liebrand, "Die Automate (1814)," in *E. T. A. Hoffmann-Handbuch: Leben – Werk – Wirkung*, eds. Christine Lubkoll and Harald Neumeyer (Stuttgart: Metzler, 2015), 107–110.
65 *DKV4*, 428.
66 Mayer, "Transgressive Science," 73.
67 Liebrand, "Automate," 110.
68 *DKV4*, 406 and 426.
69 *DKV4*, 426.

him in an obscure way.[70] To some extent, Ferdinand has become non-human himself, by metaphorically turning into another of Professor X's automata.

Which other relevant forms of the non-human, apart from technology as the conspicuous focus, can be discerned in "The Automata"? The other domain of the non-human that is highlighted is the realm of inanimate nature, in particular its ethereal aspects such as the sounds of nature. Attention to the non-human also reveals a striking absence in the story: despite the importance of natural music, no animals or their diverse enticing contributions to the music of nature are mentioned. The absence of animals and their sounds underlines that the moving "nature tones" Ludwig describes belong to the realm of inanimate nature and are, therefore, no emotional expression of any subjective interiority.

A consideration of gender completes this analysis of non-human elements in "The Automata." The central humanlike machine, the Turk, is a male android. Moreover, all the humans talking about machines and interacting with them are men: Ferdinand, Ludwig, the group of young men, the elderly gentleman who tells them about the Professor, and Professor X himself. This generates a conspicuously masculine atmosphere in the story. Ferdinand, being pushed into the role of the victim and automaton, suffers a gradual loss of his masculinity, whereas Professor X with his powerful control over other human beings, technologies, and nature itself appears especially patriarchal. His desire to "penetrate" other peoples' minds and hearts as well as the mystery of nature has a noticeably phallic quality, which also manifests itself in his "piercing"[71] look. Furthermore, his "highly repugnant"[72] voice contrasts sharply with the "divine voice"[73] of the singer, the only female character in "The Automata."[74] However, Professor X seems to have command over her voice or even to be the creator of it in the first place. After the garden concert, one wonders whether the singer is a secret "high tech" musical automaton of Professor X.[75] Her vocal and visual appearances might also be two separate phenomena synthesized by Professor X's mesmerizing technology. In any case, the singer's vague existence gives the impression of being mysteriously dependent on Professor X's manipulations. The question of whether she is human or non-

---

70 Liebrand, "Automate," 110.

71 *DKV4*, 416.

72 *DKV4*, 417.

73 *DKV4*, 405.

74 On voice, gender, and the "Verstimmung" of male characters in Hoffmann, see Müller-Sievers, "Verstimmung," 98–119.

75 On the suggestion the singer could be read as an automaton, see Monika Schmitz-Emans, "Die Poesie der Maschinen: Literarische Darstellungen von Automaten und Kunstmenschen im Zeichen ästhetischer Autoreflexion," *Neohelicon* XXIV, no. 2 (1997): 253.

human remains shrouded in uncertainty. Interestingly, it is not only Professor X who seems to prefer ideal female automata to women of flesh and blood. When Ferdinand falls in love with the singer after his fateful night at the hotel, he is obviously afraid of learning anything about the real woman. Instead of trying to find her, he is keen on keeping her just an idol. He paints a miniature portrait based on the "dream image"[76] he is harboring of her and gladly contents himself with wearing that non-human art object close to his heart. Finally, another result of a gender analysis of "The Automata" is that the natural non-human is explicitly marked as motherly. When Ludwig expounds his ideas about the origin of music and humanity, he is referring to nature as a nurturing "mother" who is enveloping her children with "holy music."[77] Ironically, it is the patriarchal figure of Professor X who manages to artificially recreate this music of Mother Nature in his laboratory.

Music, human feeling, and the non-human

Four types of music are distinguishable in "The Automata": emotionally expressive human music, expressionless machine music, sublime natural music, and the music produced by a "higher mechanics of music." Ludwig contrasts emotional human music with the lifeless attempts of machine music.[78] He characterizes emotive human music in line with the Serapiontic Principle: by expressing the emotions in his heart (*Gemüt*) through music, the musician communicates them to the listeners and stirs their hearts similarly. Human music is expression of *Gemüt* as well as *Gemütherregungskunst*; it expresses and arouses emotions. Due to the absence of *Gemüt*, the music of Professor X's conventional musical machines must result in an aesthetic failure, as Ludwig argues: "Trying to make effective music by means of valves, springs, levers, cylinders, or whatever other mechanical apparatus, is a pointless attempt to achieve the end solely by relying on the means, without realizing that the means can only accomplish that end when the inner force of the heart (*Gemüt*) animates them and regulates even their slightest movements."[79]

Human music has a privileged access to the inner life of emotions, feelings, and spirituality, and is, according to Ludwig, able to "arouse those unidentified, inexpressible feelings in us akin to nothing else on earth and to evoke the

---

76 *DKV4*, 406.
77 *DKV4*, 421.
78 *DKV4*, 419–420.
79 *DKV4*, 419.

anticipations of a distant spirit realm and our higher being therein."[80] Philosopher Susanne Langer's theory of art addresses this special relationship between music and emotions in an illuminating way that can deepen our understanding of the role of music in "The Automata." Her aesthetics focuses on feeling and constitutes a substantial contribution to emotion studies. According to Langer, art in general expresses human feeling.[81] Her definition of the word "feeling" is extremely broad and can be used to refer to everything which can be felt, from physical sensations to complex emotional and intellectual states of consciousness.[82] A defining quality of feelings is their inherent non-discursivity. Here the specific strength of music comes into play. For Langer, music has a structural affinity to feeling, which makes it an ideal medium to symbolize feeling: "there are certain aspects of the so-called 'inner life' – physical or mental – which have formal properties similar to those of music – patterns of motion and rest, of tension and release, of agreement and disagreement, preparation, fulfilment, excitation, sudden change, etc."[83] Forms of human feeling are more congruent with musical forms than with the forms of language. For this reason, music can reveal the nature of feelings more appropriately and effectively than language.[84] However, this revelation is no simple self-expression, but the result of an artistic and symbolic transformation. According to Langer, music "is not usually derived *from* affects nor intended *for* them; but we may say, with certain reservations, that it is *about* them."[85] Langer's concept of music as a symbolic expression of feeling is not incompatible with Ludwig's "Serapiontic" approach to music. It is definitely compatible with Hoffmann's own ideas about music, which are not to be confused with the statements of any of his fictional characters. In "Beethoven's Instrumental Music," Hoffmann distances himself from a naive theory of musical self-expression by appreciating "Besonnenheit" (temperance): "the master [Beethoven], fully the equal of Haydn and Mozart in temperance, disassociates himself from the inner realm of sounds and commands it as absolute ruler."[86] This temperance in composing bespeaks the composer's profound knowledge of emotions.[87] Music can articulate feelings without becoming

---

80 *DKV4*, 419.
81 See Susanne Langer, *Problems of Art: Ten Philosophical Lectures* (New York: Charles Scribner's Sons, 1957), 15.
82 See Langer, *Problems*, 15.
83 Susanne Langer, *Philosophy in a New Key: A Study in the Symbolism of Reason, Rite, and Art*. Third edition. (Cambridge, MA: Harvard UP, 1957), 228.
84 See Langer, *Philosophy*, 235.
85 Langer, *Philosophy*, 218.
86 *DKV2/1*, 55.
87 See Langer, *Philosophy*, 222.

one with them. It is capable of expressing a wealth of wordless "knowledge of emotional and organic experience, of vital impulse, balance, conflict, the *ways* of living and dying and feeling."[88] These thoughts will be revisited in the analysis of the hotel scene which features Ferdinand's first encounter with the singer.

The third type of music is the sublime music of non-human nature, which Ludwig also describes as the origin of human music. He is musing about a time "when the human mind did not apprehend nature, but nature apprehended the human mind."[89] Ludwig's theory generally implies that human interiority – expressed in human music – has its origin in the exteriority of non-human nature to which it ultimately returns: comparable to a Möbius strip, the bond between human and non-human nature neither has an inside nor outside nor end. They exist "in irreducible alterity and infinite connection."[90] There is no stable boundary between the two, nor is there between human and non-human music: "Can the music which dwells within us be any other than the music which is hidden in nature as a deep mystery [. . .]?"[91] Ludwig identifies this music of nature with the "holy mystery of nature."[92] When he depicts the primeval origins of the human, he mentions that Mother Nature enfolded the human being "with a holy music [. . .]; and wondrous sounds proclaimed the mysteries of her eternal activities."[93] At the heart of the mystery of nature and music is evidently the idea of *natura naturans*, the productive activity of nature. It is the working principle behind the eternal circle of being, that part of the "nonhuman" that affect theorist Brian Massumi describes as "nature as naturing, nature as having its own dynamism."[94] Just as human music expresses human feeling, natural music expresses the mystery of nature, *natura naturans*.

The fourth type of music is based on a "higher mechanics of music"[95] which Ludwig and Ferdinand are discussing when they stumble into Professor X's garden concert only to realize that the scientist has indeed invented such a technology.[96] Professor X not only succeeds in simulating perfect nature tones; he manages to transform them into the voice of Ferdinand's beloved singer. After the garden scene, the earlier hotel scene appears in a dubious light. Suddenly it seems possible that

---

88 Langer, *Philosophy*, 244.
89 *DKV4*, 421.
90 Brian Massumi, "The Autonomy of Affect," *Cultural Critique* 31 (Fall 1995): 83–109, here 100.
91 *DKV4*, 423.
92 *DKV4*, 424.
93 *DKV4*, 421.
94 Massumi, "Autonomy," 100.
95 *DKV4*, 421.
96 *DKV4*, 424–425.

the sublime music Ferdinand heard that night was artificially generated. This new perspective on his precious love constitutes the cruel turning point of the story that ends with Ferdinand's nervous breakdown.

The hotel scene contains the tale's most powerful description of the aesthetic and emotional effects of music.[97] Apparently dealing with the effects of *human* music, the hotel scene later – after the garden scene – appears to have been about technologically synthesized *non-human* music. It is worth taking another look at the scene. Ferdinand describes an experience that is marked by an ecstatic dissolution of boundaries: the melody *is* love, his *Gemüt is* ear. Temporarily, the "duplexity" of the outer and inner world is suspended. Besides the divine beauty of the music, Ferdinand experiences its sublimity.[98] The aesthetic effect of the sublime is characterized by its mixed nature, causing feelings of strangely enjoyable pathos, of pleasurable pain and fear. It is connected to what Friedrich Nietzsche referred to as our "metaphysical delight in the tragic."[99] In Susanne Langer's words, the song that enraptures Ferdinand so much conveys a tragic "knowledge" to him of "the *ways* of living and dying and feeling."[100] Langer emphasizes the fleeting transience of these emotional insights music elicits in us: "Because no assignment of meaning is conventional, none is permanent beyond the sound that passes; yet the brief association was a flash of understanding."[101] Ferdinand experiences such a flash of *anagnorisis*, a profoundly emotional recognition of the mystery of nature, of *natura naturans*, and the eternal circle of living, loving, and dying he is a part of. His experience of the sublime is also an experience of what Nietzsche called the Dionysian.[102] Nietzsche stresses the important role of music in the evocation of this specific aesthetic emotion: "only the spirit of music allows us to understand why we feel joy at the destruction of the individual."[103] Music as a Dionysian art does not hide the painful truth: "In Dionysiac art and its tragic symbolism [. . .] nature speaks to us in its true, undisguised voice: 'Be as I am! – the primal mother, eternally creative beneath the surface of incessantly changing

---

97 *DKV4*, 404–406.
98 On "aesthetic emotions," see Martin von Koppenfels and Cornelia Zumbusch, "Einleitung," in *Handbuch Literatur & Emotionen* (Berlin: De Gruyter, 2018), 1–36.
99 Friedrich Nietzsche, *The Birth of Tragedy and Other Writings*, eds. Raymond Geuss and Ronald Speirs, trans. Ronald Speirs (Cambridge: Cambridge UP, 1999), 80.
100 Langer, *Philosophy*, 244.
101 Langer, *Philosophy*, 244.
102 On Nietzsche's concept of the Dionysian, see Birgit Recki, "Gefühle in der philosophischen Ästhetik," in *Handbuch Literatur & Emotionen*, eds. Martin von Koppenfels and Cornelia Zumbusch (Berlin: De Gruyter, 2018), 75–78.
103 Nietzsche, *Birth of Tragedy*, 80.

appearances, eternally forcing life into existence, forever satisfying myself with these changing appearances!'"[104] Like Hoffmann's "holy music," Nietzsche's Dionysian music speaks to us of the mystery of *natura naturans*, our eternally creating and annihilating "mother."[105]

The human is integrated into this circle of life and death, coming from the non-human and returning to it, thereby "becoming imperceptible."[106] Feminist philosopher Rosi Braidotti delineates this liminal condition of the human and the blurring of the boundaries between the human and the non-human: "What we most truly desire is to surrender the self, preferably in the agony of ecstasy, thus choosing our own way of disappearing, our way of dying to and as our self. This can be described also as the moment of ascetic dissolution of the subject; the moment of its merging with the web of non-human forces that frame him/her, the cosmos as a whole."[107] Braidotti's "web of non-human forces" can be read as another expression for *natura naturans*. Her description of the pull of the non-human is reminiscent of the Freudian "instinct to return to the inanimate state."[108]

This dominance of the inanimate over the animate poses a permanent challenge to the human. Ferdinand's deeply emotional, Dionysian insight into the truth of the circle of life and death is not only elicited by the stirring music, but also by the haunting text of the Italian song.[109] Poignantly, the song emphasizes the two most important, eminently *human* attempts to overcome death: *remembrance* and *love*. It also implies the two different perspectives we have on death, when we face our own death and when we are confronted with the death of our beloveds. In the song, the woman expresses the hope that her "cold ashes" might still be able to love. It is striking that she does not invoke any transcendent life of her soul, but instead tries to think of her inanimate remains as still imbued with feeling. This creates an emotionally disturbing outlook for her beloved whom she implores to remember her. It is precisely this incongruous image of the loving "cold ashes" that brings home the fundamental incompatibility of the living human being and her non-human, inorganic state in the future. The death theme of the song contributes to the powerful Dionysian effect on the listener.

---

104 Nietzsche, *Birth of Tragedy*, 80.
105 On the affinity of *natura naturans* with the Dionysian, see Salomo Friedlaender, *Friedrich Nietzsche: Eine intellektuale Biographie* (Leipzig: Göschen'sche Verlagshandlung, 1911), 19.
106 Rosi Braidotti, *The Posthuman* (Cambridge: Polity, 2013), 136.
107 Braidotti, *The Posthuman*, 136.
108 Sigmund Freud, *Beyond the Pleasure Principle*, ed. and trans. by James Strachey (New York: Norton & Company, 1961), 32.
109 *DKV4*, 405.

What does it mean when the music that moved Ferdinand so deeply was not the emotional expression of a singer of flesh and blood, but generated by an unknown technology as inanimate as the "cold ashes" in the song? What does it mean when machines perfectly simulate sounds of nature and human music which have strong emotional, aesthetic, Dionysian effects on us? What does it mean when machines – which do not live, love, remember, or die – engender such profoundly human experiences? What does it mean when machines can read our minds and manipulate our innermost thoughts and feelings? "The Automata" evokes a world in which such technological miracles seem to happen. It does not come up with answers, but it ultimately implies that such machines and the masterminds behind them wield a potentially huge amount of power over us. What is more, by detecting and pressing the levers that stir our hearts and minds, these powerful technologies uncannily reveal that our innermost feelings and thoughts with their physiological foundations are themselves, at a fundamental level, automatic and mechanical in nature. Automata capable of playing deeply moving music with virtuosity also unveil the exterior, mathematical, and mechanical character of music. This emotional and aesthetic agency of machines casts doubt on the special status of the human. It exposes and exploits the fragility of our human qualities. Under the spell of such potent machines, our humanity, with its rich subjective interiority and artistic expressivity, is deprived of its uniqueness and self-determination.

"The Automata" demonstrates the problematic effects of such technologies. After his stay in the hotel, Ferdinand develops an unhealthy idolatry for the singer. The prophecy of the Turk gravely traumatizes him; shortly after witnessing the Professor's wondrous concert, he suffers a nervous breakdown and memory loss. The fact that later in life Ferdinand joins the army and goes into battle "sound of mind and body and with joyous desire to fight,"[110] as Theodor reassures his Serapion Brothers, might actually indicate that Ferdinand has not fully recovered and is driven by a death instinct.

Staying human in a technological world

The implicit underlying key to understanding these technological miracles in "The Automata" is likely to think of Professor X as an extraordinarily powerful mesmerizer who has developed a highly advanced use of animal magnetism. However,

---

110 *DKV4*, 428.

present-day readers will not usually make this connection. The "impulses" coming from Theodor's "fragment" have a different impact on our twenty-first century imaginations. Instead of animal magnetism, they might make us think of today's functional magnetic resonance imaging and the modern technological use of electromagnetic waves. We can imagine Professor X's mesmerizing concert as coming from apparently invisible musical devices. Intriguingly, in "A Cyborg Manifesto" (1985) Donna Haraway analyzes modern, practically invisible microelectronics in an illuminating way that can shed some light on the technological and "psychical" power of Professor X.[111] She refers to the phenomenon of *invisibility* in technology in the context of what she considers a third crucial boundary breakdown, namely the blurring of the boundary between the *physical* and the *nonphysical*:[112] "Modern machines are quintessentially microelectronic devices: they are everywhere and they are invisible."[113] It almost sounds like the description of a modern form of animal magnetism when she points out that "our best machines are made of sunshine; they are all light and clean because they are nothing but signals, electromagnetic waves [. . .]."[114] She highlights two important aspects of these invisible microelectronic devices, power and consciousness: "Miniaturization has turned out to be about power; small is not so much beautiful as preeminently dangerous [. . .]. They [microelectronic devices] are as hard to see politically as materially. They are about consciousness – or its simulation."[115] Interestingly, Haraway sees this power with its encroachment upon consciousness proportionally linked to its degree of transgressiveness and secrecy: "Ultimately the 'hardest' science is about the realm of greatest boundary confusion, the realm of pure number, pure spirit, C^3I, cryptography, and the preservation of potent secrets."[116] Professor X, secretly wielding the levers of an invisible technology to exert "psychical power"[117] through prophecies and music, can be viewed as an early epitome of such a "hard" scientist who transgresses the boundary between the physical and the nonphysical.

---

111 See Donna Haraway, "A Cyborg Manifesto: Science, Technology, and Socialist-Feminism in the Late Twentieth Century," in *Manifestly Haraway* (Minneapolis: U of Minnesota Press, 2016), 12–14.
112 On the other two boundary breakdowns between the distinctions human/animal and organism/machine, see Haraway, "Cyborg," 10–12.
113 Haraway, "Cyborg," 12–13.
114 Haraway, "Cyborg," 13.
115 Haraway, "Cyborg," 13.
116 Haraway, "Cyborg," 14.
117 *DKV4*, 414.

The Professor's dark powers of empathy and *Gemütherregungskunst* (art of stirring the heart) feel strangely familiar to us readers in the twenty-first century whose hearts and minds are constantly "penetrated," "stirred," and manipulated by powerful new technologies and media, often without us being aware of it. In this regard, Hoffmann's text is uncannily prescient in its evocation of potent technologies and their possible impacts on the human condition. This condition is always open to change, as philosopher Hannah Arendt, a key political thinker on the human and the non-human, explains: "Whatever enters the human world of its own accord or is drawn into it by human effort becomes part of the human condition."[118] New technologies, "the things that owe their existence exclusively to men nevertheless constantly condition their human makers."[119] Like any other "fabrication" of *homo faber*, every technological innovation starts new chains of events when it is incorporated into the human world, "a process whose outcome cannot be entirely foreseen and is therefore beyond the control of its author."[120] Since Hoffmann's time, the human condition has been changed pervasively by technological revolutions and we are confronted with the immense benefits and grave problems of this development. "The Automata" is a text that implies the high potential of technology and some of its problematic repercussions on the individual. It presages that technologies can be used by humans to influence, manipulate, and control other humans. Interactions between technologies and humans are complex, pervaded by power, and not the same for every individual, as the inscrutable and asymmetrical relationship between Professor X and Ferdinand illustrates.

Of particular interest is the depiction of the relation between machines and art in "The Automata." Monika Schmitz-Emans points out that the story's indication that the singer might be an android contributes to an "utterly ambivalent portrayal of the connection between art and mechanics," and suggests that "art must be considered to be a product of an enigmatic machinery."[121] "The Automata" demonstrates that the merging of human art and non-human technology, and especially the simulation of the human voice, touches on what makes us feel human. Even if the product appears to be the same, there is a fundamental difference to us if the poignant song "Mio ben ricordati" is sung by a woman or by an android. The song itself is about those experiences that make up the core

---

118 Hannah Arendt, *The Human Condition* (Chicago: U of Chicago Press, 1998), 9.
119 Arendt, *Human Condition*, 9.
120 Hannah Arendt, "The Concept of History: Ancient and Modern," in *Between Past and Future: Eight Exercises in Political Thought* (New York: Penguin, 2006), 60.
121 Schmitz-Emans, "Poesie der Maschinen," 253.

of human life and, consequently, of art: love, mortality, and remembrance. Interestingly, the Italian *"ricordare"* and the German *"erinnern"* ("to remember") refer to the heart, to subjective interiority, and thus to *Gemüt*. Mnemosyne, the goddess of memory, is the mother of the muses and therefore of art. The myth implies that art is always an act of remembrance. In remembering, we go inward to recollect the past; in art we go outward and express the recollection by means of an artistic transformation. This leads to a durable materialization of memory. Both acts we experience as profoundly human. For Arendt, "[w]orks of art are thought things, but this does not prevent their being things."[122] She elaborates that "[t]hought is related to feeling and transforms its mute and inarticulate despondency."[123] In the creative process, a second transformation must be achieved: "The reification which occurs in writing something down, painting an image, modeling a figure, or composing a melody is of course related to the thought which preceded it, but what actually makes the thought a reality and fabricates things of thought is the same workmanship which [. . .] builds the other durable things of the human artifice."[124] Memory, in turn, is sustained by works of art, "because remembrance and the gift of recollection, from which all desire for imperishability springs, need tangible things to remind them, lest they perish themselves."[125] The song "Mio ben ricordati," in which a woman desires her love to be remembered after her death, is itself a performative enactment of the human urge to preserve love in the face of death by remembering and creating art. As an expression of the heart and mind, it distinctly seems to belong to a "web of *human* forces."[126] The suspicion its performance might be the product of a purely mechanical "Serapiontics" and no true "thought thing" causes unease and deprives it of its emotional value. The humanity behind a work of art deeply matters to us.

"The Automata" is an ironic, evasive, and ambiguous text, but it cannot be considered altogether neutral regarding the powerful technologies it depicts. Ferdinand's narrative arc is alarming and can be read as a warning. Ideas of the human as endowed with a unique capacity for complex feelings, thoughts, and art are undermined by the potent "psychical power" of machines. The story exposes the vulnerability of these human qualities and at the same time shows that they are worth being protected. It is up to the individual to deal with new technologies critically and to avert technological intrusions and manipulations.

---

122 Arendt, *Human Condition*, 168–169.
123 Arendt, *Human Condition*, 168.
124 Arendt, *Human Condition*, 169.
125 Arendt, *Human Condition*, 170.
126 Cf. Braidotti's "web of non-human forces," *The Posthuman*, 136.

The fundamental anthropological question of what constitutes the human is understandably left open. Human nature is represented as inextricably linked to non-human nature and technologies, which is illustrated most clearly in the intricate connection between natural music, human music, and a "higher mechanics of music." "The Automata" somehow encourages us to question the human *and* to defend it. Human nature itself is not the same as the human condition and the problem of it seems ultimately unsolvable for humans. Defining the human would be, in Arendt's words, "like jumping over our own shadows."[127]

"Brains and cultures coevolve"[128] and so do human nature and technological development. The nature of the human is dynamic and must be evaluated in the context of this ongoing evolutionary process. More than two hundred years after the publication of "The Automata," music can be generated by AI algorithms, a development that increasingly blurs the boundary between human and machine creativity.[129] The brain-computer boundary is being transgressed via "brain implants that could change humanity,"[130] as Moises Velasquez-Manoff argues in a remarkable article. People suffering from neurological disabilities could benefit from such implants. At the same time, highly problematic consequences of such innovations are likely to ensue. The neurobiologist Rafael Yuste helped develop a non-surgical technology that can read and write to the brain. It enabled his team to "implant" perceptions of things into a mouse that it had not seen: "We manipulated the mouse like a puppet."[131] Considering these new technologies, Velasquez-Manoff wonders: "What happens if people are no longer sure if their emotions are theirs, or the effects of the machines they're connected to?"[132] Essentially the same question lies at the heart of "The Automata" and points to the main source of uncanniness in the story. Today, the potential to manipulate the "levers" of human emotions is growing rapidly. "The Automata" can be read as a reminder that we have to judge the desirability of our high-tech

---

127 Arendt, *Human Condition*, 10.

128 Robert Sapolsky, *Behave: The Biology of Humans at Our Best and Worst* (New York: Penguin, 2018), 672.

129 See Clive Thompson, "What Will Happen When Machines Write Songs Just as Well as Your Favorite Musician?" in *Mother Jones* (March/April 2019), accessed 16 September 2020, https://www.motherjones.com/media/2019/03/what-will-happen-when-machines-write-songs -just-as-well-as-your-favorite-musician/.

130 Moises Velasquez-Manoff, "The Brain Implants That Could Change Humanity," in *The New York Times* (Aug. 28, 2020), accessed 16 September 2020, https://www.nytimes.com/2020/ 08/28/opinion/sunday/brain-machine-artificial-intelligence.html.

131 Velasquez-Manoff, "Brain Implants."

132 Velasquez-Manoff, "Brain Implants."

environment critically. Only then do we have a chance to avoid falling prey to the Professor X's of our times and to help shape what it means to be human in the twenty-first century.

Bibliography

Anz, Thomas. "Emotional Turn? Beobachtungen zur Gefühlsforschung," in *Literaturkritik.de*. 14 July 2020. https://literaturkritik.de/id/10267.

Arendt, Hannah. "The Concept of History: Ancient and Modern," in Hannah Arendt, *Between Past and Future: Eight Exercises in Political Thought* (New York: Penguin, 2006), 41–90.

Arendt, Hannah. *The Human Condition*. (Chicago: U of Chicago Press, 1998 [1958]).

Bergengruen, Maximilian, and Daniel Hilpert. "Magnetismus/Mesmerismus," in *E. T. A. Hoffmann-Handbuch: Leben – Werk – Wirkung*. Eds. Christine Lubkoll and Harald Neumeyer (Stuttgart: Metzler, 2015), 292–297.

Braidotti, Rosi. *The Posthuman* (Cambridge: Polity, 2013).

Breithaupt, Fritz. *The Dark Sides of Empathy*. Trans. Andrew Hamilton (Ithaca, NY: Cornell UP, 2019).

Drux, Rudolf. "Der literarische Maschinenmensch und seine technologische Antiquiertheit. Wechselbeziehungen zwischen Literatur- und Technikgeschichte." *Dresdner Beiträge zur Geschichte der Technikwissenschaften* 29 (2004): 3–19.

Freud, Sigmund. *Beyond the Pleasure Principle*. Ed. and trans. James Strachey (New York: Norton & Company, 1961).

Freud, Sigmund. "The 'Uncanny,'" in *The Standard Edition of the Complete Psychological Works of Sigmund Freud*, vol. XVII (1917–1919). Trans. James Strachey (London: Hogarth Press, 1955), 218–252.

Frevert, Ute, et al., eds. *Emotional Lexicons: Continuity and Change in the Vocabulary of Feeling 1700–2000* (Oxford: Oxford UP, 2014).

Frevert, Ute. *Vergängliche Gefühle* (Göttingen: Wallstein, 2013).

Friedlaender, Salomo. *Friedrich Nietzsche: Eine intellektuale Biographie* (Leipzig: Göschen'sche Verlagshandlung, 1911).

Grusin, Richard, ed. *The Nonhuman Turn* (Minneapolis: U of Minnesota Press, 2015).

Grusin, Richard. "Introduction," in *The Nonhuman Turn*. Ed. Richard Grusin (Minneapolis: U of Minnesota Press, 2015), vii–xxix.

Haraway, Donna. "A Cyborg Manifesto: Science, Technology, and Socialist-Feminism in the Late Twentieth Century," in Donna Haraway, *Manifestly Haraway* (Minneapolis: U of Minnesota Press, 2016), 3–90.

Hoffmann, E. T. A. "Beethovens Instrumental-Musik," in *Fantasiestücke in Callo'ts Manier*. *E. T. A. Hoffmann Sämtliche Werke*, vol. 2/1. Ed. Hartmut Steinecke (Frankfurt a. M.: Deutscher Klassiker Verlag, 1993), 52–61.

Hoffmann, E. T. A. *Die Serapions-Brüder*. *E. T. A. Hoffmann Sämtliche Werke*, vol. 4. Eds. Wulf Segebrecht and Ursula Segebrecht (Frankfurt a. M.: Deutscher Klassiker Verlag, 2001).

Keil, Werner. "Dissonanz und Verstimmung: E. T. A. Hoffmanns Beitrag zur Entstehung der musikalischen Romantik." *E. T. A. Hoffmann Jahrbuch* 1 (1992–1993): 119–132.

Koppenfels, Martin von, and Cornelia Zumbusch, eds. *Handbuch Literatur & Emotionen* (Berlin: De Gruyter, 2018).

Koppenfels, Martin von, and Cornelia Zumbusch. "Einleitung," in *Handbuch Literatur & Emotionen*. Eds. Martin von Koppenfels and Cornelia Zumbusch (Berlin: De Gruyter, 2018), 1–36.

Langer, Susanne K. *Philosophy in a New Key: A Study in the Symbolism of Reason, Rite, and Art* (Cambridge, MA: Harvard UP, 1957).

Langer, Susanne K. *Problems of Art: Ten Philosophical Lectures* (New York: Charles Scribner's Sons, 1957).

Lieb, Claudia. "Der gestellte Türke. Wolfgang Kempelens Maschinen und E. T. A. Hoffmanns Erzählung *Die Automate*." *E. T. A. Hoffmann Jahrbuch* 16 (2008): 82–97.

Liebrand, Claudia. "Die Automate (1814)," in *E. T. A. Hoffmann-Handbuch: Leben – Werk – Wirkung*. Eds. Christine Lubkoll and Harald Neumeyer (Stuttgart: Metzler, 2015), 107–110.

Liebrand, Claudia. "Automaten/Künstliche Menschen," in *E. T. A. Hoffmann-Handbuch: Leben – Werk – Wirkung*. Eds. Christine Lubkoll and Harald Neumeyer (Stuttgart: Metzler, 2015), 242–246.

Lubkoll, Christine, and Harald Neumeyer, eds. *E. T. A. Hoffmann-Handbuch: Leben – Werk – Wirkung* (Stuttgart: Metzler, 2015).

Marchand, Jeffrey Scott. "Non-Human Agency," in *Posthuman Glossary*. Eds. Rosi Braidotti and Maria Hlavajova (London: Bloomsbury Academic, 2018), 292–295.

Massumi, Brian. "The Autonomy of Affect." *Cultural Critique* 31 (Fall 1995): 83–109.

Mayer, Paola. "Transgressive Science in E. T. A. Hoffmann's Fantastic Tales," in *E. T. A. Hoffmann: Transgressive Romanticism*. Ed. Christopher R. Clason (Liverpool: Liverpool UP, 2018), 65–77.

Müller-Sievers, Helmut. "Verstimmung. E. T. A. Hoffmann und die Trivialisierung der Musik." *Vierteljahrsschrift für Literaturwissenschaft und Geistesgeschichte* 63, no. 1 (1989): 98–119.

Nietzsche, Friedrich. *The Birth of Tragedy and Other Writings*. Eds. Raymond Geuss and Ronald Speirs. Trans. Ronald Speirs (Cambridge: Cambridge UP, 1999).

Novalis. *Das philosophisch-theoretische Werk. Werke, Tagebücher und Briefe Friedrich von Hardenbergs*, vol. 2. Ed. Hans-Joachim Mähl (Darmstadt: WBG, 1999).

Plamper, Jan. *The History of Emotions: An Introduction*. Trans. Keith Tribe (Oxford: Oxford UP, 2015).

Recki, Birgit. "Gefühle in der philosophischen Ästhetik," in *Handbuch Literatur & Emotionen*. Eds. Martin von Koppenfels and Cornelia Zumbusch (Berlin: De Gruyter, 2018), 62–82.

Richardson, Kathleen. "Technological Animism: The Uncanny Personhood of Humanoid Machines," *Social Analysis* 60, no. 1 (Spring 2016): 110–128.

Sapolsky, Robert. *Behave: The Biology of Humans at Our Best and Worst* (New York: Penguin, 2018).

Scheer, Monique. "Topographies of Emotions," in *Emotional Lexicons: Continuity and Change in the Vocabulary of Feeling 1700–2000*. Eds. Ute Frevert et al. (Oxford: Oxford UP, 2014), 32–61.

Schlegel, August Wilhelm. *A. W. Schlegels Vorlesungen über schöne Literatur und Kunst. Zweiter Teil (1802–1808)* (Stuttgart: Göschen'sche Verlagshandlung, 1884).

Schmitz-Emans, Monika. "Die Poesie der Maschinen: Literarische Darstellungen von Automaten und Kunstmenschen im Zeichen ästhetischer Autoreflexion." *Neohelicon* XXIV, no. 2 (1997): 237–279.

Stahl, Lesley. "Scientists Are Using MRI Scans to Reveal the Physical Makeup of Our Thoughts and Feelings." 18 June 2020. https://www.cbsnews.com/news/functional-magnetic-resonance-imaging-computer-analysis-read-thoughts-60-minutes-2019-11-24/.

Thompson, Clive. "What Will Happen When Machines Write Songs Just as Well as Your Favorite Musician?" in *Mother Jones* (March/April 2019). Accessed 16 September 2020. https://www.motherjones.com/media/2019/03/what-will-happen-when-machines-write-songs-just-as-well-as-your-favorite-musician/.

Velasquez-Manoff, Moises. "The Brain Implants That Could Change Humanity," in *The New York Times* (Aug. 28, 2020). Accessed 16 September 2020. https://www.nytimes.com/2020/08/28/opinion/sunday/brain-machine-artificial-intelligence.html.

Wittig, Frank. *Maschinenmenschen: Zur Geschichte eines literarischen Motivs im Kontext von Philosophie, Naturwissenschaft und Technik* (Würzburg: Königshausen & Neumann, 1997).

Andrea Meyertholen

I Know What the Caged Cat Feels

Feeling Empathy, Framing Animality, and Finding Humanity at the Zoo

For several months in 1901, the German impressionist artist Max Slevogt fre-
quented the Frankfurter Zoo to observe and paint its non-human residents, including the big cat species.[1] The resultant images of panthers, leopards, lions,
and tigers mark a pivotal departure from the art historical tradition of the animal picture for the simple fact that Slevogt painted the cats in their cages. Although his peers and predecessors also visited zoos and royal menageries, their
studies served as preparatory sketches for later works of animals roaming wild
or tamed. Even after Carl Hagenback's introduction of bar-less enclosures in
1907, artists did not typically paint animals at the zoo, as actually encountered.
Slevogt's phenomenal inclusion of the cage presents a rare, constructive moment for both animal pictures and the possibilities for posthumanist thought,
because his paintings provide a unique testing ground to explore the emotional
frontiers of the human/non-human divide. In literally and figuratively framing
the viewing experience, the cage signals a variety of meanings depending on
standpoint (inside/outside), inhabitant (human/animal), and cultural connotation (prison/zoo).[2] An imprisoned person could lead observers to make assumptions about the person's guilt, violence, and criminality, but a caged animal
might constitute an act of cruelty and elicit outrage or distress in visitors who
imagined zoo life from a human perspective.[3]

   Slevogt forces his audience into this visitor-perspective through unexpected
compositional and stylistic choices that elicit emotional involvement through

---

1 Ellen Spickernagel, *Der Fortgang der Tiere: Darstellungen in Menagerien und in der Kunst des
17.–19. Jahrhunderts* (Cologne: Böhlau, 2010), 53.
2 On prisons, see Stephen Eisenman, *The Abu Ghraib Effect* (London: Reaktion Books, 2007);
Michel Foucault, *Discipline and Punish: The Birth of the Prison* (New York: Vintage Books,
1995); *Foucault and Animals*, eds. Matthew Chrulew and Dinesh Wadiwel (Leiden: Brill, 2016);
and Christoph Jahr, *Lager vor Auschwitz: Gewalt und Integration im 20. Jahrhunderts* (Berlin:
Metropol, 2013).
3 On distressed zoo-goers, see Erich Unglaub, *Panther und Aschanti: Rilke-Gedichte in kulturwissenschaftlicher Sicht* (Frankfurt a. M.: Lang, 2005), 61–63, and fn 256, 258, 259. For a history
of animal pictures, see Kai Artinger, *Von der Tierbude zum Turm der blauen Pferde: Die künstlerische Wahrnehmung der wilden Tiere im Zeitalter der zoologischen Gärten* (Berlin: Reimer,
1995).

https://doi.org/10.1515/9783110753677-009

difference and distance. Rather than demand strong affective responses, his art-works offer an alternate model for emotional engagement that appeals to the spectator's intellect and prompts deeper reflection on the nature of humanity. Though not sentimentalized or anthropomorphized, Slevogt's cats are not en-tirely anti-anthropocentric, nor should they be. While on the surface, his zoo scenes might seem to assert human supremacy over animals, it will be shown through analysis of his paintings how Slevogt critiques anthropocentric assump-tions that only the human species matters. At the same time, his paintings rely on an anthropocentric perspective insofar as they encourage the spectator to in-terpret the cats in terms of human values, categories, and experiences. As I will argue, the potential for anti-anthropocentrism – for resisting premises of human centrality and supremacy – lies not in denying the limitations of our necessarily human viewpoint, but in acknowledging them and utilizing the very qualities which comprise our humanity to find paths around them that could effect radical change. Central to this posthumanist endeavor is understanding how humanist subjectivity constructs itself and its Others through the presence and absence of an inner emotional life (*Gefühle*). As a constitutive principle enabling the differ-entiation and production of an Other, the concept of *Gefühle* is relatively new de-spite, as Jan Plamper formulates, the tendency to "treat feelings as something common to all humans, inherent and intimate, the inner sanctum of autonomy, the site in which human subjectivity crystallizes in its purest form."[4] Though depth-surface discourses of a human interiority (*Innerlichkeit*) distinct from the outside world predate the Middle Ages, only during the eighteenth century did categories such as emotions, thinking, feeling, and sensation migrate inward to form the core of individual identity and Western subjectivity.[5]

---

4 Jan Plamper, *The History of Emotions: An Introduction* (Oxford: Oxford UP, 2015), 25–26. Ad-ditional histories of emotion include Rob Boddice, *The History of Emotions* (Manchester: Man-chester UP, 2018); Pascal Eitler, "Der 'Ursprung' der Gefühle: Reizbare Menschen und reizbare Tiere," in *Gefühlswissen: Eine lexikalische Spurensuche in der Moderne*, eds. Ute Frevert et al. (Frankfurt a. M.: Campus, 2009), 93–119 and "'Weil sie fühlen, was wir fühlen.' Menschen, Tiere und die Genealogie der Emotionen im 19. Jahrhundert," in *Historische Anthropologie* 19, no. 2 (2011): 211–228; Ute Frevert et al., eds., *Emotional Lexicons: Continuity and Change in the Vocabulary of Feeling 1700–2000* (Oxford: Oxford UP, 2014); Margit Pernau, "Zivilität und Bar-barei – Gefühle als Differenzkriterien," in *Gefühlswissen*: 233–262.
5 Compare to Jane K. Brown, *Goethe's Allegories of Identity* (Philadelphia: U of Pennsylvania Press, 2014); Frederick C. Beiser, *German Idealism: The Struggle against Subjectivism, 1781–1801* (Cambridge, MA: Harvard UP, 2008); Rüdiger Campe and Julia Weber, "Rethinking Emotion: Moving beyond Interiority," in *Rethinking Emotion: Interiority and Exteriority in Premodern, Mod-ern and Contemporary Thought*, eds. Rüdiger Campe and Julia Weber (Berlin: De Gruyter, 2014), 1–18; Jerrold Seigel, *The Idea of the Self: Thought and Experience in Western Europe since the*

Whether or what animals feel and the extent to which they have *Gefühle* or *Innerlichkeit* is not at issue per se.[6] Determinative is whether one believes or perceives animals to possess the inner emotional life which, until the mid-nineteenth century, was reserved for humans and defined humanity. If we believe that animals feel and have inner depth, then we could subsequently believe to know their feelings, penetrate their surface, and relate to their experiences. The perceived potential for shared emotional experience opens a conduit through which we can empathically "feel into" (*Einfühlung*) and sympathetically or compassionately "feel with" (*Mitgefühl*) beings other than ourselves. Slevogt's vision of feline Otherness does not preclude the possibility of inner emotional life. Rather, his cats appear as unknowable and emotionally inaccessible beings that human viewers could nonetheless imagine knowing and accessing emotionally. Key to achieving this paradox is the cage and the deprivation of freedom it signifies. By analyzing the pictorial strategies framing the relationship of Slevogt's zoo cats to the spectator and comparing them to concomitant German-language poetry on the same subject, I argue that *Einfühlung*, not *Mitgefühl*, proves decisive in escaping an anthropomorphic paradigm which defines subjectivity based on the presumption of human singularity. The difference between *Einfühlung* and *Mitgefühl* is crucial. The latter risks reinforcing anthropocentrism to dangerous consequences; the former opens avenues for radical politics.

My animal, my other: Why anthropocentrism matters

The field of animal studies has everything and nothing to do with its titular beings, as indicated by the expansive reach of this sprawling "super-interdiscipline," to

---

Seventeenth Century (Cambridge: Cambridge UP, 2005); and Charles Taylor, *Sources of the Self* (Cambridge: Cambridge UP, 1989).

6 On the animal's physiological or psychological ability to feel emotions, see Heike Baranzke, "Die Würde der Tiere. Zu den theologischen Wurzeln und dem ethischen Ort eines Topos der modernen Tierethik" in *Topos Tier. Neue Gestaltungen des Tier-Mensch-Verhältnisses*, eds. Annette Bühler-Dietrich and Michael Weingarten (Bielefeld: transcript, 2016), 41–64; Marc R. Fellenz, *The Moral Menagerie: Philosophy and Animal Rights* (Urbana: U of Illinois Press, 2007); Nastasja Klothmann, *Gefühlswelten im Zoo: Eine Emotionsgeschichte 1900–1945* (Bielefeld: transcript, 2015); Corinne Michelle Painter, *Phenomenology and the Non-Human Animal: At the Limits of Experience* (Dordrecht: Springer, 2007); and Michael Weingarten, "Das Tier in mir. Eine problematische anthropologische Fiktion des Liberalismus," in *Topos Tier*: 87–102.

use Cary Wolfe's tongue-in-cheek phrasing.[7] Whereas its philosophical questions specifically interrogate the human/animal distinction, its fundamental interest lies in determining how the human species constructs Otherness in general. Defining what is *not* human also reveals those characteristic features understood to be uniquely human along with the anxieties surrounding its destabilization as a category. At the heart of posthumanism is the liberal humanist tradition that invariably establishes subjectivity in terms of the human being.[8] Indeed, the very idea of Western subjectivity, Matthew Calarco emphasizes, is "never simply a neutral subject of experience but is almost always a *human* subject, and metaphysics is founded [. . .] on specifically *human* modes of subjectivity."[9] However, as Cary Wolfe notes, "just because we study nonhuman animals does not mean that we are not continuing to be humanist – and therefore, by definition, anthropocentric."[10] Such critiques inadvertently reproduce the same humanist frameworks and practices they seek to dismantle and so never reach a *post*humanist promised land for animals. Happening instead is a re-delineating of the human/ animal divide that fails to challenge the nature or existence of the divide itself. Instead, the animal is brought into the fold of personhood, most notably through the extension of legal protections. The animal's physiology has not altered; only the philosophical criteria by which its non-humanness is judged. That humanness is, in fact, a malleable construct speaks to the arbitrary nature of its borders.

The ethical and legal stakes of these categories are most urgently outlined by Jacques Derrida, who identifies Jeremy Bentham's classic question as the

7 Cary Wolfe, *What is Posthumanism?* (Minneapolis: U of Minnesota Press, 2010), 115. Foundational texts on animal studies include Tom Regan, *The Case for Animal Rights* (Berkeley: UC Press, 1983) and Peter Singer, *Animal Liberation: A New Ethics for Our Treatment of Animals* (New York: Avon, 1975).

8 Representative works on posthumanism include: Donna Haraway, "A Cyborg Manifesto: Science, Technology, and Socialist-Feminism in the Late Twentieth Century," in *Simians, Cyborgs, and Women: The Reinvention of Nature* (New York: Routledge, 1984), 149–181; and *The Companion Species Manifesto: Dogs, People, and Significant Otherness* (Chicago: Prickly Paradigm, 2003); N. Katherine Hayles, *How We Became Posthuman: Virtual Bodies in Cybernetics, Literature, and Informatics* (Chicago: U of Chicago Press, 1999); Ursula Heise, "The Android and the Animal," *PMLA* 124, no. 2 (2009): 503–510; and "From Extinction to Electronics: Dead Frogs, Live Dinosaurs, and Electric Sheep" in *Zoontologies: The Question of the Animal* (Minneapolis: U of Minnesota Press, 2003), 59–81; and Cary Wolfe, *Animal Rites: American Culture, the Discourse of Species, and Posthumanist Theory* (Chicago: U of Chicago Press, 2003); "Human, All Too Human: 'Animal Studies' and the Humanities," *PMLA* 124, no. 2 (2009): 564–575; *What is Posthumanism?*; and *Zoontologies*, editor.

9 Matthew Calarco, *Zoographies: The Question of the Animal from Heidegger to Derrida* (New York: Columbia UP, 2008), 12 (original emphasis).

10 Wolfe, "Human," 568.

critical turning point for reconfiguring how we think about animals and our ethical obligations to them.[11] Where Aristotle deprived animals of moral worth by using language as a marker and Descartes denied their rational faculties, likening them to machines, Bentham reformulates the line of inquiry: "The question is not, Can they *reason?* nor Can they *talk?* but Can they *suffer?*"[12] In reframing the question to focus on inability and passivity (vulnerability and suffering) as opposed to agency and ability (language and reason), Bentham shifts the ontological dimensions of the debate. For Derrida, the capacity to suffer pain – broadly defined as emotional, psychological, and/or physical – opens the door for ethical obligation and facilitates the move beyond anthropocentrism.

Derrida invokes the theory of alterity formulated by Emmanuel Levinas, who thematizes the face as the locus of Otherness that places moral demands upon those confronted by it: "The Other faces me and puts me in question and obliges me by his essence qua infinity."[13] This encounter is rupture and connection at once; in facing the Other, we see a face not unlike our own which, despite its similarity, represents ultimate separateness precisely because we *can* face it. Its solicitations are invasive and asymmetrical, calling us into ethical accountability for the Other without expecting the same regard in return. Yet because we are called, we are morally compelled to respond. As Levinas writes: "The being that expresses itself imposes itself, but does so precisely by appealing to me with its destitution and nudity – its hunger – without my being able to be deaf to that appeal."[14] While destitution and deprivation indicate the Other's passivity and vulnerability, that its appeal is verbal is made explicit and so explicitly human by Levinas who recognizes discourse as essential for experiencing alterity ("The face speaks. The manifestation of the face is already discourse").[15] While Derrida critiques Levinas for an anthropocentric reliance on language, he uses the opportunity to convert a humanist theory of

---

11 See Jacques Derrida, *The Animal That Therefore I Am*, trans. David Willis (New York: Fordham UP, 2008); *The Beast & The Sovereign*, Vol. 1, trans. Geoff Bennington (Chicago: U of Chicago Press, 2010); *The Beast & The Sovereign*, Vol. 2, trans. Geoff Bennington (Chicago: U of Chicago Press, 2011); "'Eating Well,' or The Calculation of the Subject: An Interview with Jacques Derrida," in *Who Comes after the Subject?* (New York: Routledge, 1991), 96–119; and *Of Spirit: Heidegger and the Question*, trans. Geoff Bennington and Rachel Bowlby (Chicago: U of Chicago Press, 1991).
12 Jeremy Bentham, *An Introduction to the Principles of Morals and Legislation* (Oxford: Oxford UP, 1996), 283, fn. 6 (original emphasis).
13 Emmanuel Levinas, *Totality and Infinity: An Essay on Exteriority*, trans. Alphonso Lingis (Pittsburgh: Duquesne UP, 1969), 207.
14 Levinas, *Totality*, 200.
15 Levinas, *Totality*, 66.

Otherness into a posthumanist moment. In his famous fascination with the gaze of the cat in *The Animal That Therefore I Am*, Derrida transcribes Levinas's immanently human face onto that of the animal Other.

Flipping the asymmetrical axis of the transaction, Derrida describes the sense of discomfort, helplessness, and shame at having his naked body gazed upon by his pet cat. The reversal of gaze prompts Derrida to reflect upon Levinas's exclusion of the non-human animal and the structural anthropocentrism of humanism in general. Tending to observe the animal from a privileged position empowered by language, philosophers and scientists interpret, name, and speak for animals without expecting the observed to observe the observers. When we, like Derrida, are the Other, confronting the animal with our human face, would it be ethically obliged to respond to our destitution, nakedness, and hunger? Unlike the calculable, relatively readable face of a human Other, the gaze of Derrida's cat is interminably inscrutable: "innocent and cruel perhaps, perhaps sensitive and impassive, good and bad, uninterpretable, unreadable, undecidable, abyssal and secret."[16] Like "every bottomless gaze, as with the eyes of the Other," he continues, "the gaze called 'animal' offers to my sight the abyssal limit of the human: the inhuman or the ahuman, the ends of man."[17] The cat addresses Derrida not with the shared "auto" of agency, able to exercise *auto*nomy or write *auto*biographies. This is the "abyss" separating animal from human. Rather, the cat addresses him with shared finitude, as a being vulnerable to extinguishment. The animal must not prove through agency, language, or reason its deservedness to live; its passive existence is enough to issue the ethical call regardless of whether the animal would feel obliged to us – or feel at all. Though unable to say definitively that it *can* suffer, we are nevertheless ethically obligated to respond as if it *could* when confronted by its passive face, however impassive its features. As Wolfe postulates, "Why should not the supremely moral act be that directed toward one such as the animal Other, from whom *there is no hope, ever, of reciprocity*?"[18] In this regard, the animal truly exists at the "ends of man" as the utmost Other.

Ultimately, every being is an Other whether history has regarded it as human or not. As with Derrida's cat, evidence of humanness from the "inhuman or the ahuman" cannot be expected and risking the reductivity of binary constructs of human/non-human could lead and has led to catastrophic atrocities. Derrida cites primal moments in the Bible condoning animal sacrifice to underscore the danger

---

16 Derrida, *The Animal*, 12.
17 Derrida, *The Animal*, 12.
18 Wolfe, *Animal Rites*, 199 (original emphasis).

of a culture willing to engage in the "noncriminal putting to death" of non-human beings like animals.[19] Organized around human subjectivity, the discourse of Western humanism has structured a hierarchal opposition between human and animal to excuse and justify the "noncriminal putting to death" of the non-human abject, be it for safety, food, or merely because one can. Derrida does not shy away from tying the "noncriminal" sacrifice of animals to the sort of mass killings of the Holocaust.[20] If it is all too easy to assimilate animals into humanity and extend to them human rights, it just as easy to take them away, casting them – or other humans – back into abject animals that must be separated from society through cages or eliminated from it altogether. Derrida moreover calls attention to the "many 'subjects' among mankind who are not recognized as subjects," as historically seen in the legal disenfranchisement of numerous minority groups, women, and children.[21] Not recognized as fully human "subjects" before the law, such individuals were often regarded and accordingly treated as animals. The radical incalculability and hence alterity represented by his house cat does not, for Derrida, rely on anthropocentric categories of human/non-human, nor does it assume reciprocity. At the end of every being is the beginning of an Other, and in our mutual finitude and shared inabilities, he and the cat are simply two beings co-existing in the world.[22]

The solution is not for humans to become non-human animals or animals to become human. We should not self-congratulatorily grant animals the right to be considered human or treat them as little humans, nor should we claim with false empathy to know the world as seen or felt by them.[23] Empathy need

---

19 Derrida, *Of Spirit*, 112.

20 For example, both J. M. Coetzee (*The Lives of Animals*) and Charles Patterson (*Eternal Treblinka*) connect mass killings of animals with the genocides of the twentieth century. As Wolfe synopsizes, genocide becomes a possible, even lawful, reality when "we take for granted the prior assumption that violence against the animal [i.e., nonhuman] is ethically permissible." Wolfe, "Human," 568.

21 Derrida, "Force of Law: The 'Mystical' Foundation of Authority," *Cardozo Law Review* II, nos. 5–6 (1990): 952–953, here 951.

22 On Derrida, philosophy, and the animal, see Peter Adamson, ed., *Animals: A History* (Oxford: Oxford UP, 2018); Peter Atterton and Tamra Wright, eds, *Face to Face with Animals: Levinas and the Animal Question* (Albany: SUNY Press, 2019); Anne Emmanuelle Berger and Marta Segarra, eds., *Demenageries: Thinking (of) Animals after Derrida* (Amsterdam: Rodopi, 2011); David Farrell Krell, *Derrida and Our Animal Others: Derrida's Final Seminar, the Beast and the Sovereign* (Bloomington: Indiana UP, 2013); Gary Steiner, *Animals and the Limits of Postmodernism* (New York: Columbia UP, 2013); and Judith Still, *Derrida and Other Animals: The Boundaries of the Human* (Edinburgh: Edinburgh UP, 2015).

23 Kathleen Kete's history on the topic calls the house pet as child "de-animalized animals" in Kete, *The Beast in the Boudoir: Petkeeping in Nineteenth-Century Paris* (Berkeley: UC Press, 1994).

not be discounted as a tool, only wielded judiciously and critically. Our human bodies cannot be escaped, but our faculties of reason and empathy can be utilized to think about the question of animals as statements contrary to fact; in other words, to act *as if* animals can suffer. As *Einfühlung* connects emotionally, the faculty of reason recognizes and respects the Other's Other-beingness without expecting hope of reciprocity. One imagines being and feeling like animals yet still recognizes the finitude of the human body. In other words, thinking non-anthropocentrically entails an empathic and self-consciously anthropocentric approach. Slevogt's zoo paintings present a model for empathy that allows viewers to feel with a non-anthropomorphized animal without abandoning the human perspective.

Trapped in paradise: Inside the concrete jungle of Slevogt's zoo cats

This human perspective is the only standpoint possible in Slevogt's paintings and not only because of his human viewership. In staging his paintings at the zoo, Slevogt places his cats at a physical location designed to display animals for human visual consumption. While its inhabitants are non-human, the zoo is a thoroughly human institution, conceived and constructed for human purposes such as education, entertainment, and socializing.[24] As an institution predicated on spectacle and spectatorship, the zoo became a popular site for artists who took advantage of the opportunity to observe the reality of otherwise inaccessible live exotica.[25] Demand was so great that zoos reserved weekly times to open just for artists, among whom Slevogt numbered when at the Frankfurter Zoo. Of the animals on display, the zoo's prized collection of big cats and a young orangutan named Seemann most piqued the artist's interest. Yet how Slevogt presents each animal type in relation to the human spectator differs considerably.

---

24 For the development of zoos and animal shows see Eric Ames, *Carl Hagenbeck's Empire of Entertainments* (Seattle: U of Washington Press, 2008); John Berger, "Why Look at Animals," in *About Looking* (New York: Vintage Books, 1991), 3–28; Robert J. Hoage and William A. Deiss, eds., *New Worlds, New Animals: From Menagerie to Zoological Park in the Nineteenth Century* (Baltimore: Johns Hopkins UP, 1996); Klothmann, *Gefühlswelten*, 67–183; Nigel Rothfels, *Savages and Beasts: The Birth of the Modern Zoo* (Baltimore: Johns Hopkins UP, 2002), esp. 13–43 and 143–188; and Patrick Wirtz, "Zoo City: Bourgeois Values and Scientific Culture in the Industrial Landscape," in *Journal of Urban Design*, 2, no. 1 (1997): 61–82.
25 See Artinger, *Tierbude*; Spickernagel, *Fortgang*, 51; Unglaub, *Panther*, 53–59.

While the paintings of Seemann in the arms of his keeper impress intrinsic linkages between man and ape through compositional and physiognomic parallels, Slevogt institutes structural difference between cat and audience to reinforce the fundamental dissimilarity of species. Dispensing with the anthropomorphized commonalities evident in his orangutan portrayals, Slevogt depicts his cats perched, pacing, and patently catlike, physically and symbolically estranged from each other as well as the spectator.

In *Die Schwarzen Panther* (The black panthers) and *Zwei Leoparden im Käfig* (Two caged leopards) from 1901, a latticework of iron bars running the length and width of the canvas divides us from the title felines.

Figure 1: Slevogt, *Zwei Leoparden im Käfig*, 1901. Niedersächsisches Landesmuseum, Hannover, made available under the Creative Commons Zero Public Domain Designation.

Each species is encountered as visitors would have experienced them at the Frankfurter Zoo, from the outside looking in. The long metal bars recall the Parisian cityscapes of two artistic influences for Slevogt, Édouard Manet and Gustave Caillebotte. Each incorporated the metal structures to great effect as symbols of modern urban industry and compositional devices for flattening the illusion of depth. For instance, the series of black bars in Manet's *The Railway* (1873) sever the steam-enswathed background from the painting's foreground where a woman and girl rest at the precipice of the picture plane. Whereas Manet's iron fence thrusts his figures into the spectator's space, Slevogt's zoo cage locks the spectator out of the entire painting, thereby conveying the message that humans neither belong in nor gain entry to the cats' world. We look but do not touch.

Even this view is partial, though, due to the radical placement of the bars at the surface of the canvas and the artist's characteristically Impressionist style. The top-to-bottom verticals obstruct our view, while the strong horizontals isolate each cat to its own half of the canvas. Loose brushwork and broad, quick strokes suggest the contours of blurred objects without allowing crystallized form to emerge. Although German Impressionism tended toward darker palettes than its French counterpart, the somberness of Slevogt's colors is especially extreme. In *Die Schwarzen Panther*, gradations of grays and heavy-handed browns enshroud the cage's content and serve to camouflage the cats' black bodies. We make out just enough of their obscured silhouettes to identify the shadow of one panther perched atop the wooden scaffold, and the restless profile of another pacing against the bars in the foreground. As in *Zwei Leoparden im Käfig*, the world inside the cage lacks the verdant vibrancy of a natural habitat. In contrast, the spectator is confronted with the stark reality of life in a zoo cage: industrial, drab, and monotonous. The animate brushwork breathes life into the cats only to arouse unutilized energy. Both leopards and one panther lie about their quarters, gazing idly outward. The sole panther in motion is captured mid-stride as it repeats the endless back-and-forth journey across the canvas. Even if time inside the cage stretches out eternally and unchangingly, the spectator's world outside the bars goes on. Attuned to temporality and fleetingness, the Impressionist approach heightens the transitory nature of the exchange. Like typical zoo-goers, we pass by, pause, stare, and then move on.

Before we do so, Slevogt invites the viewer to engage in deeper consideration of the cats' caged existence. For the cage to feature so prominently in a visual medium as an obstacle to vision indicates the artist's intent to provoke a reaction. The peculiar obstruction of the canvas so completely through bars finds precedence only in Adolph Menzel's 1868 painting *Drei Bären im Käfig* (Three caged bears). Despite the similar full-frontal view of the animal through a zoo cage, Menzel's composition differs considerably. Whereas Slevogt places us further away to take in the full height of the cage, Menzel crops the canvas closely around a barred window for an intimate encounter. Situated up against the heavy iron bars, the audience stands eye level with the trio of plaintive-looking bears close enough to touch. Their sizeable incisors and curved claws, clearly capable of maiming, do not threaten but grasp at the bars with a desperation communicated by the bears' piercing, pleading eyes. Their anthropomorphized features and projection of identifiable human emotion anticipate Charles Darwin's *The Expression of the Emotions in Man and Animals* (1872), which established interspecies equivalencies in non-verbal communicative forms by comparing human and animal facial expressions. Yet that Menzel imagines his bears to reach out and beg for understanding through shared emotional experience with their human audience indicates that he paints this work after *On the Origin of Species* (1859) united humans and animals within a common developmental framework through the theory of evolution, thus providing scientific validation for the reevaluation of animal emotions begun by eighteenth-century dialectics of Enlightenment and Sentimentalism.[26]

Although Slevogt post-dates both publications, he chooses not to give a face to his cats or their pain. The possibility of physical or emotional suffering is obliquely broached through insinuations of boredom and unutilized energy, rather than explicitly rendered through contorted bodies or facial features. The Impressionist brushstrokes obfuscate any facial expression, even if viewers were near enough to discern one. From this distanced standpoint, the cats' bodies and catlike behaviors are wholly on display, as are larger portions of the encompassing cages. We are compelled to process the cats as they outwardly appear, as non-human Others whose Otherness is absolute and unknowable, but perhaps not impenetrable. Slevogt's panthers and leopards are not the one-dimensional killing machines of the "snarling cat" scenes made famous by Eugène Delacroix or Peter Paul Rubens. A fury of irrational, inhumane, and unhuman forces, their cats dynamically tear through the canvas with claws out and fangs bared in an all-out assault on an unfortunate human or some symbol of civilization. Instead, Slevogt's cats and Menzel's bears flip the power dynamic on its head to lock the animal in a place of passivity where the prison-like structure reframes our attention on deprivation and vulnerability.

The cages in these artworks implicitly pose the question of suffering, such that Bentham had with his famous query or John Berger's images of "absolutely

---

26 See Pascal Eitler, "The 'Origin' of Emotions – Sensitive Humans, Sensitive Animals," in *Emotional Lexicons*, 91–117, here 94–98.

marginalized" animals later would in critiquing the conditions of the zoo. The all-too-human eyes of Menzel's bears leave no doubt to the ethical obligations contained in this query; their visages confront the viewer with the face of Levinas's Other, the face not unlike our own which, wholly separate and compellingly similar at once, calls us into moral accountability without expecting the same regard in return.[27] Like the assumptions of language underlying Levinas's theory of alterity, Menzel would likely draw criticism from Derrida for his humanist reliance on anthropomorphist strategies to elicit affective response by speaking through their eyes, so to say. Without soliciting the viewer so insistently, invasively, or obviously, Slevogt's zoo cats prompt the line of inquiry analogous to Derrida's thought experiment with his housecat: What if we were the ones powerless and naked behind bars, forcibly exposed and on exhibit for the world to see? What if the leopards and panthers occupied the privileged position of power outside the cage? As painted by Slevogt, the cats in their eternal inscrutability offer no indication of ethics or action, only the assuredness of their shared finitude with humans as living beings vulnerable to extinguishment.

Slevogt's desire for viewers to consider the perspective of the cats from inside the cage is more overtly stated in his other zoo cat paintings from the same year, *Schreitende Löwen im Käfig* (Caged lions pacing) and *Tiger im Zoo* (Zoo tiger).

Enclosing the viewer within the zoo cage, the artist transforms us, the observers, into the observed. Still, we do not become the cats, nor do the cats, normally observed, become the observers. Contrary to anthropomorphic fantasies of Expressionist Franz Marc who sought to "animalize" his audience, we do not presume to see and feel the world through the eyes of Slevogt's cats. Rather, we stare out at gawking human zoo-goers from within our own art-spectating human bodies which the artist strategically situates behind the big cats pacing the space of the cage between us and the bars. While the cage no longer forces our distance and reinforces our separateness, Slevogt effects our alienation from the cats by denying us their attention or even their front sides. They are unknowable and unreadable, the difference between them and us as abyssal as Derrida theorizes. We lurk in the background ignored by the impassive cats, not privy to their faces, but appreciative of their feline nature.

---

27 Berger, 24. As Berger writes, in zoos, animals are reduced to "the living monument to their own disappearance" in the face of human moral "indifference" (26). Berger's implicit call for morally obligated intervention resonates even more strongly a few lines later when comparing zoos with other "sites of enforced marginalisation – ghettos, shanty towns, prisons, madhouses, concentration camps [. . .]."

Figure 2: Slevogt, *Schreitende Löwen im Käfig*, 1901. Niedersächsisches Landesmuseum, Hannover, made available under the Creative Commons Zero Public Domain Designation.

Watching their skulking, sinewy bodies move about the cage that imprisons us as well, we imagine the restless energy and eternal monotony of zoo life conveyed by the agitated Impressionist strokes. The brighter palette and looser brushwork arrest the transient effects of sunlight and movement of trees, but only for the world beyond the cage. On our side of the bars, heavier shadows and thicker strokes darken the concrete confines which never change as the seasons and crowds cycle by. Indeed, Slevogt wields Impressionism against the cats, reproducing the constant energy of light with swift, spritely strokes only to accentuate the dreary tedium of cage life, an ennui also afflicting his leopards and panthers. These painted visions of the world behind and beyond bars are undeniably products of human perception, what the Impressionist modality explicitly thematizes in its effort to record raw visual data collected from the human retina on canvas. With Slevogt preserving our Otherness from the cats through stylistic choices and distancing devices, we look with our human eyes and feel whatever human emotions the cats' caged perspective arouses, all from within our human bodies. Though projecting ourselves into the cats' experience, neither we nor the artist purport to project our human feelings, thoughts, or vision onto the animal and claim it to be theirs.

In this regard, Slevogt maneuvers within an anthropocentric paradigm, but he does not solicit audience engagement through anthropomorphic overtures or use the cage to manipulate emotions through sentimentalizing gestures. This crucial distinction is made clear by comparison with the popular Berlin-based artist Paul Meyerheim, who executed more artworks containing caged cats than Slevogt, only with remarkably divergent effects and affect. Spanning the latter nineteenth century and the early twentieth, Meyerheim's paintings of captive circus and zoo cats bear the imprint of the social and scientific developments in their juxtaposition of gentleness and ferocity. Scenes like *Fütterung der Löwenjungen* (Feeding the lion cubs, ca. 1880s/1890s) and *Eifersüchtige Löwin* (Jealous lioness, 1885) exude the confidence that human intellect and technology could tenuously bring feline savagery under control while also creating a space for emotional connection. The two compositionally similar works feature a female lion tamer in the shallow foreground before a long cage of lions alternatively snarling and sleeping, depending on their gender. Whereas the cubs cuddle like human babies and the male lions nap and allow the trainer to pet them like house cats, the lionesses' silent snarls communicate stereotypically feminine human sentiments of motherly protectiveness and jealous love.

The ambivalence of Meyerheim's circus scenes is virtually absent in his zoo paintings where, rather than incite fear, the exotic beast becomes a vessel for *Gefühle*. To convey the cat's emotional depth, he transforms the eternally Othered cat into an essentially humanized being with human features, gender stereotypes, and familial patterns. *Löwenpaar im Berliner Zoo* (Lion pair in the Berlin zoo, 1901) and *Löwen im Käfig* (Caged lions, 1904) place us inside the zoo cages, but to promote the emotional attachment and anthropomorphic assumptions discouraged by Slevogt's caged cats. Though Meyerheim's crowds also materialize as harried hints of color blurring into undifferentiated background noise, the somber-toned solidity of the lions, whom we always face, is rendered in careful detail, permitting us to read their faces as physiognomic documents of human emotions. With furrowed brows and wilted jaws, the lions grimace with a sadness and unease reminiscent of Menzel's bears, while the lionesses look either anxious or apathetic. Staged intimate moments of loving couples and caring parents build familiar constellations of bourgeois familial life. His realistically rendered lions face us like Levinas's Other, asking the audience to discover interspecies equivalencies and see the inner human hidden within. Effacing the differences between viewer and animal, Meyerheim shows through behavior and facial expression the animal's capacity for *Gefühle*. Though these superficial similarities could prompt deeper reflection, the artist's anthropomorphized animal portraiture does not encourage us to contemplate our feelings, merely to feel them.

Unlike Meyerheim's lions, the aloof feline demeanor of Slevogt's zoo cats betrays no predilection for human sociability or social models, working instead to maintain a degree of distance that could facilitate critical reflection. Although his cages reinforce the essential human-animal divide and his cats thwart anthropomorphizing overtures, Slevogt does not deny the creatures emotional depth. Rather, in respecting the cat's identity as cat, he places different demands on the spectator for penetrating the distancing devices so that we believe in the potential for feline emotion without believing to know it or share at such. This type of emotional engagement paradoxically asks us to be in the cat's perspective albeit still separated as human; to imagine its being and feeling but with a self-conscious anthropocentrism that acknowledges its Other-beingness without expecting reciprocal response. Where Slevogt's artwork illustrates such a model, contemporaneously appearing poetic portrayals of zoo cats exemplify how it might be articulated with words and consequently distinguished from competing anthropomorphic forms.

The subjunctive jump: Feeling into Rilke's panther

"Does anyone know cats?" Rainer Maria Rilke poses this question in 1920 to preface his preface to *Mitsou*, a book of cat drawings.[28] The answer is clearly no. As opposed to the obsequious dog, Rilke writes, "[c]ats are just that: cats. And their world is utterly, through and through, a cat's world. You think they look at us? Has anyone ever truly known whether or not they deign to register on one instant on the sunken surface of their retina our trifling forms?"[29] Resonating with the radical alterity perceived by Derrida and perceptible in Slevogt's artwork, Rilke's observations on the unbridgeable distance between the self-contained cat and the human also constitute the core of his own creative work

28 Rainer Maria Rilke, preface to *Mitsou: Forty Images*, by Balthus, trans. Richard Miller (New York: Metropolitan Museum of Art, 1994), 9–13 (9). See too Kári Driscoll, "'Il n'y a pas de chats': Feline Absence and/as the Space of Zoopoetics," in *Texts, Animals, Environments: Zoopoetics and Ecopoetics*, eds. Frederike Middelhoff, Sebastian Schönbeck, Roland Bogards, and Catrin Gersdorf (Freiburg i. Br.: Rombach, 2019), 159–174.
29 Rilke, preface, 9.

involving a caged zoo cat. Published as part of the *Neue Gedichte* (1907), his 1903 poem "Der Panther" ("The Panther") comprises one of the relatively few lyric depictions of cats in cages. In poeticizing the panther, Rilke chose an animal with a literary lineage of Otherness as recorded in fables, myths, Biblical tales, and even other poems.[30] However, his account diverges from its predecessors in its avoidance of mythological, heraldic, and symbolic tropes. The poet moreover does not wield the panther as a didactic instrument or scientific object, nor does he set it in Orientalized or romanticized landscapes. Like Slevogt's two panthers, Rilke's cat lives right where the poet first encountered it in 1902: in its cage at the Jardin des Plantes, the Parisian public zoo where the poem begins.

> The bars which pass and strike across his gaze
> have stunned his sight: the eyes have lost their hold.
> To him it seems there are a thousand bars,
> and nothing else. No world.
>
> And pacing out that mean, constricted ground,
> so quiet, supple, powerful, his stride
> is like a ritual dance performed around
> the centre where his baffled will survives.
>
> The silent shutter of his eye sometimes
> slides open to admit some thing outside;
> an image runs through each expectant limb
> and penetrates his heart, and dies.[31]

Positioned outside the zoo cage watching the eponymous animal within, the reader enacts a progressive penetration of the panther as the poem's three stanzas move from cage, then to feline exterior, and finally to feline interior. The first stanza confronts us with the panther's gaze, a "Blick" weary from seeing the seemingly endless bars surrounding its limited living space. The long, umlauted vowels (*Vorübergehen der Stäbe, müd, gäbe*) cause the poem to slow and stretch into the eternal tedium of zoo life. For the panther, the world outside the

---

30 Unglaub, *Panther*, 68. After the lion, the panther was considered the most exotic animal.
31 The English-language translation along with subsequent citations stem from Rainer Maria Rilke, "The Panther," trans. Stephen Cohn, in *Neue Gedichte/New Poems* (Evanston, IL: Northwestern UP, 1998), 61. Rainer Maria Rilke, "Der Panther," in *Werke in drei Bänden*, vol. 1, *Gedicht-Zyklen* (Frankfurt a. M.: Insel, 1966), 261: "Sein Blick ist vom Vorübergehen der Stäbe/ so müd geworden, daß er nichts mehr hält./Ihm ist, als ob es tausend Stäbe gäbe/und hinter tausend Stäben keine Welt./Der weiche Gang geschmeidig starker Schritte,/der sich im allerkleinsten Kreise dreht,/ist wie ein Tanz von Kraft um eine Mitte,/in der betäubt ein großer Wille steht./Nur manchmal schiebt der Vorhang der Pupille/sich lautlos auf –. Dann geht ein Bild hinein,/geht durch der Glieder angespannte Stille –/und hört im Herzen auf zu sein."

zoo ceases to exist. Although the panther presumably faces us, we do not see a face nor its eye, only an abstruse gaze. Likewise, the second stanza thematizes its lithesome walk without detailing components of its physique. We apprehend its attributes from a well-preserved distance, even as these next four lines step into the space of the cage between the bars, no longer visible, and the cat. Trudging along in a metric rhythm of abab/cdcd/efef, its energy is constrained into ever-smaller circles to the point of numbness.

The final stanza brings readers near enough not only to identify its panther parts, but to enter the aperture exposed when the "Vorhang der Pupille" ("shutter of his eye") draws up at the first hyphen before falling shut again with the second. In the space between dashes, we accompany the actively advancing "Bild" into the passive panther to reach its inner essence, the heart which has simply ceased to be. That the animal relinquishes its *Dasein* is announced by the poem's final "sein" (*to be*) whose replication of the poem's initial "Sein" (*Its*, referencing the panther) carries us back to the start and collapses the entire poem into the panther's being (Sein = sein). Emotionally and spiritually dead inside, the panther nonetheless lives on physically to repeat the unending cycle of its existence behind bars. Returning to the beginning also situates us back outside the cage, beholding the creature at a remove. In this way, Rilke keeps the reader in check cycling through a perpetual dance of feeling into the panther only to find ourselves held at a bystander's distance.

Comparable poetic maneuvers are conducted by Kurt Tucholsky, whose 1918 "Im Käfig" (In the cage) takes readers into the inner thoughts of a tiger which, despite having opportunity to escape, is too depleted to act on its desires.

Behind the thick bars of my ideals
I stride from one wall to the other wall.
Out there go the nannies, generals,
Mrs. Widow-of-the-Leather-Merchant with Mr. Amant . . .
At times one looks over here. With empty stares:
Ah so! a tiger – yes, the poor animal . . .
Then they say "send auntie something too
in parchment paper."
I would so like be out. I stretch and elongate myself –
they have it so good, with their grand time! [. . .]
The tiger yawns. He would so love to come out . . .
Yet the bars of his cage hold fast.
And should the guard himself leave the door open:
you still don't go.[32]

32 Kurt Tucholsky, *Gesammelte Werke*, Band 1 (Rowohlt: Reinbek bei Hamburg, 1975) 301: "Hinter den dicken Stäben meiner Ideale/lauf ich von einer Wand zur andern Wand./Da

Tucholsky also dances between inner and outer, yet while also jumping more overtly between animal and human. As in Slevogt's tiger painting, we peer out from behind the cage, only from within the cat's body. Assuming its passive perspective, we consider the cage's impenetrably thick bars, walk from wall to wall, and listen to the middle-class crowds dutifully marvel at the tiger with empty stares before returning to unrelated conversations. In the third stanza, the lyrical voice of the poem even speaks in first person, using human language to express the tiger's wish for freedom (*Ich möcht so gern hinaus*). What might appear as the shared "auto" of autobiographical agency is quickly quashed in the fourth stanza, when the reader is abruptly dislocated to third-person omniscience to observe the animal yawning. Though detached from the tiger, we briefly project ourselves into its thoughts to imagine its sentiments (*Er käm so gern geloffen*). The third-person pronoun signifies that we again occupy our human bodies.

Rilke's "Der Panther" and Tucholsky's "Im Käfig" institute our physical and emotional remoteness from their respective cats, yet each offers inroads into a hypothetical inner emotional life. Hypothetical is truly the operative word, as the subjunctive verb forms announce. Neither Rilke's panther nor Tucholsky's tiger purport to be anything other than their cat-selves, but the poems suggest that the reader could span the interspecies divide with a subjunctive jump *into* the feline's psychology and skin. Signaling the occurrence of this jump, the subjunctive mood (*gäbe, möcht[e], käm[e]*) preserves our distance from the cat, because it marks the distinction between our projected human feelings and the animal feelings fundamentally unknowable to man. In this way, we "feel our way into" the cat via an empathetic experience of *Einfühlung* so that we may reflectively imagine how the caged life would be as cat without declaring the conjectured *Gefühle* as truth or certainty.[33] We think and feel *as if* we were the animal Other without disregarding the abyss lying between its essential unknowability and our human experience.

This understanding of *Einfühlung* contrasts with classical models, such as developed by Robert Vischer and Theodor Lipps for late-nineteenth century

---

draußen gehen Kindermädchen, Generale,/Frau Lederhändlerswitwe mit dem Herrn Amant . . . /Manchmal sieht einer her. Mit leeren Blicken:/Ah so! ein Tiger – ja, das arme Tier . . . /Dann sprechen sie von 'Tantchen auch was schicken/in Pergamentpapier'./Ich möcht so gern hinaus. Ich streck und dehn mich –/die habens gut, mit ihrer großen Zeit! [. . .]/Der Tiger gähnt. Er käm so gern geloffen . . . /Doch seines Käfigs Stäbe halten dicht./Und ließ der Wärter selbst die Türe offen:/Man geht ja nicht." The English translation is my own.

33 Unglaub offers comprehensive treatment of Rilke's panther and cultural history of the panther motif in art and literature (*Panther*).

aesthetics.[34] Relying on perceived visual parallels and anthropomorphizing tendencies, their foundational conceptualizations allowed for spectators to feel into inanimate objects or animate Others by ascribing human characteristics and behaviors to them. Whether conceiving a mutual moment of exchange (Vischer) or collapsing boundaries between subject and object (Lipps), their theorizations more closely resemble the unreflective emotional relationships promoted by Meyerheim's anthropomorphized lions. Rather than asking us to feel into the feline psyche from a critical distance, the artist's interest in asking us to see and feel our commonalities *with* the lions would seem to call forth the concept of *Mitgefühl* in all its linguistic transparency. We are meant to "feel with" them because we do and can share in their feelings.

Supportive of this reading is Richard Dehmel's poem "Ein Tierbändiger" (An animal tamer, 1908).[35] Arranging a scene between boy and caged tiger, the verses unfold from the child's perspective; the narration does not oblige the human deep reflection to be simpatico with the animal. The first stanza interweaves the equivocating verbs *werden* ("to become") and *sein* ("to be") to level the distinction between boy and tiger. From the boy's perspective, animals would happily be human (*würden gerne Menschen sein*) and extends his hand in friendship. Despite the cat's apparent wildness (*so wie?*), it can be taught human faculties and tamed into a purring, yawning housecat. All you need is love (*man braucht sie blos zu lieben*), because their feelings are ours (*das fühlen sie ganz wie wir*). Just as Meyerheim relied on anthropomorphic readings of the face, central to Dehmel's sympathetic interaction are the eyes, for it is through deep eye contact that the tiger and the boy understand, trust, and "feel with" each other. Contrary to the bottomless gaze of Derrida's cat or curtained "Blick" of Rilke's panther, the eyes of Dehmel's lion appeal to the boy with non-subjunctive assertions of human sadness.

Such less-reflective displays of *Mitgefühl* leave us more vulnerable to the dangers of humanizing the cat. In losing sight of its catness and "seeing" instead a person, we fall into the humanist trap of binary human/non-human categories. Conversely, the model for *Einfühlung* derived from Slevogt's cats and comparable to Rilke's panther would allow us to posit their cats as beings with

---

34 Compare to Theodor Lipps, "Empathy, Inner Imitation, and Sense Feelings," trans. Melvin Rader and Max schertel, in A *Modern Book of Esthetics*, ed. Melvin Rader (New York: Holt, 1979), 371–378; and Robert Vischer, "On the Optical Sense of Form: A Contribution to Aesthetics," trans. Nicholas Walker, in *Empathy, Form, and Space: Problems in German Aesthetics, 1873–1893*, eds. Harry Francis Mallgrave and Eleftherios Ikonomou (Santa Monica: Getty, 1994), 90–123.
35 Reproduced from Unglaub, *Panther und Ashanti*, 60–61.

Gefühle and even empathize with them while still maintaining enough distance through reflective thought so as not to violate its integrity as cat. Emergent from these pictorial and poetic displays of cats in cages is an emotional interaction grounded in the cognitive activity of perspective-taking where the crucial subjunctive jump calls on the audience to respond *as if* the animal Other *could* suffer and feel. Making this jump implies the theoretical existence of emotional depth that furnishes a locus for our thoughts and feelings to land. In effect, we take a leap of faith into the body of the Other to imagine our human emotional experience from their perspective without claiming to know it as our own. Like the caged cats, the animal (or any other Other) need not prove through human characteristics its deservedness to live. Its passive existence and potential for suffering is enough to feel ethically obligated to value its rights to exist – not as beholden to arbitrary categories of humanness or with respect to human features and behaviors, but as another being who could be so unknowable and dissimilar as only to share our human finitude and perhaps a posthumanist world.

Bibliography

Adamson, Peter, ed. *Animals: A History* (Oxford: Oxford UP, 2018).

Ames, Eric. *Carl Hagenbeck's Empire of Entertainments* (Seattle: U of Washington Press, 2008).

Artinger, Kai. *Von der Tierbude zum Turm der blauen Pferde: Die künstlerische Wahrnehmung der wilden Tiere im Zeitalter der zoologischen Gärten* (Berlin: Reimer, 1995).

Atterton, Peter, and Tamra Wright, eds. *Face to Face with Animals: Levinas and the Animal Question* (Albany: SUNY Press, 2019).

Baranzke, Heike. "Die Würde der Tiere. Zu den theologischen Wurzeln und dem ethischen Ort eines Topos der modernen Tierethik," in *Topos Tier. Neue Gestaltungen des Tier-Mensch-Verhältnisses*. Eds. Annette Bühler-Dietrich and Michael Weingarten (Bielefeld: transcript, 2016), 41–64.

Beiser, Frederick C. *German Idealism: The Struggle against Subjectivism, 1781–1801* (Cambridge, MA: Harvard UP, 2008).

Bentham, Jeremy. *An Introduction to the Principles of Morals and Legislation* (Oxford: Oxford UP, 1996).

Berger, Anne Emmanuelle, and Marta Segarra, eds. *Demenageries: Thinking (of) Animals after Derrida* (Amsterdam: Rodopi, 2011).

Berger, John. *About Looking* (New York: Pantheon Books, 1980).

Boddice, Rob. *The History of Emotions* (Manchester: Manchester UP, 2018).

Brown, Jane K. *Goethe's Allegories of Identity* (Philadelphia: U of Pennsylvania Press, 2014).

Calarco, Matthew. *Zoographies: The Question of the Animal from Heidegger to Derrida* (New York: Columbia UP, 2008).

Campe, Rüdiger, and Julia Weber. "Rethinking Emotion: Moving beyond Interiority," in
*Rethinking Emotion: Interiority and Exteriority in Premodern, Modern and Contemporary
Thought*. Eds. Rüdiger Campe and Julia Weber (Berlin: De Gruyter, 2014), 1–18.

Chrulew, Matthew, and Dinesh Wadiwel, eds. *Foucault and Animals* (Leiden: Brill, 2016).

Derrida, Jacques. *The Animal That Therefore I Am*. Trans. David Willis (New York: Fordham UP,
2008).

Derrida, Jacques. *The Beast & The Sovereign*, Vols. 1 &2. Trans. Geoff Bennington (Chicago: U
of Chicago Press, 2010).

Derrida, Jacques. "'Eating Well,' or The Calculation of the Subject: An Interview with Jacques
Derrida," in *Who Comes after the Subject?* (New York: Routledge, 1991), 96–119.

Derrida, Jacques. *Of Spirit: Heidegger and the Question*. Trans. Geoff Bennington and Rachel
Bowlby (Chicago: U of Chicago Press, 1991).

Driscoll, Kári. "'Il n'y a pas de chats': Feline Absence and/as the Space of Zoopoetics," in
Texts, Animals, Environments: Zoopoetics and Ecopoetics. Eds. Frederike Middelhoff,
Sebastian Schönbeck, Roland Bogards, and Catrin Gersdorf (Freiburg i.Br.: Rombach,
2019), 159–174.

Eisenman, Stephen. *The Abu Ghraib Effect* (London: Reaktion Books, 2007).

Eitler, Pascal. "Der 'Ursprung' der Gefühle: Reizbare Menschen und reizbare Tiere," in
Gefühlswissen: Eine lexikalische Spurensuche in der Moderne. Eds. Ute Frevert et al.
(Frankfurt a.M.: Campus, 2009), 93–119.

Eitler, Pascal. "The 'Origin' of Emotions – Sensitive Humans, Sensitive Animals," in *Emotional
Lexicons: Continuity and Change in the Vocabulary of Feeling 1700–2000*. Eds. Ute Frevert
et al. (Oxford: Oxford UP, 2014), 91–117.

Eitler, Pascal. "'Weil sie fühlen, was wir fühlen.' Menschen, Tiere und die Genealogie der
Emotionen im 19. Jahrhundert," in *Historische Anthropologie* 19, no. 2 (2011): 211–228.

Fellenz, Marc R. *The Moral Menagerie: Philosophy and Animal Rights* (Urbana: U of Illinois
Press, 2007).

Ferry, Luc. *The New Ecological Order*. Trans. Carol Volk (Chicago: U of Chicago Press, 1995).

Foucault, Michel. *Discipline and Punish: The Birth of the Prison* (New York: Vintage, 1995).

Frevert, Ute, et al., eds. *Emotional Lexicons: Continuity and Change in the Vocabulary of
Feeling 1700–2000* (Oxford: Oxford UP, 2014).

Haraway, Donna. *The Companion Species Manifesto: Dogs, People, and Significant Otherness*
(Chicago: Prickly Paradigm, 2003).

Haraway, Donna. "A Cyborg Manifesto: Science, Technology, and Socialist-Feminism in the
Late Twentieth Century," in *Simians, Cyborgs, and Women: The Reinvention of Nature*
(New York: Routledge, 1984), 149–181.

Hayles, N. Katherine. *How We Became Posthuman: Virtual Bodies in Cybernetics, Literature,
and Informatics* (Chicago: U of Chicago Press, 1999).

Heise, Ursula. "The Android and the Animal," *PMLA* 124, no. 2 (2009): 503–510.

Heise, Ursula. "From Extinction to Electronics: Dead Frogs, Live Dinosaurs, and Electric Sheep"
in *Zoontologies: The Question of the Animal* (Minneapolis: U of Minnesota Press, 2003),
59–81.

Hoage, Robert J., and William A. Deiss, eds. *New Worlds, New Animals: From Menagerie to
Zoological Park in the Nineteenth Century* (Baltimore: Johns Hopkins UP, 1996).

Jahr, Christoph. *Lager vor Auschwitz: Gewalt und Integration im 20. Jahrhunderts* (Berlin:
Metropol, 2013).

Kete, Kathleen. *The Beast in the Boudoir: Petkeeping in Nineteenth-Century Paris* (Berkeley: UC Press, 1994).

Klothmann, Nastasja. *Gefühlswelten im Zoo: Eine Emotionsgeschichte 1900–1945* (Bielefeld: transcript, 2015).

Krell, David Farrell. *Derrida and Our Animal Others: Derrida's Final Seminar, the Beast and the Sovereign* (Bloomington: Indiana UP, 2013).

Levinas, Emmanuel. *Totality and Infinity: An Essay on Exteriority*. Trans. Alphonso Lingis (Pittsburgh: Duquesne UP, 1969).

Lipps, Theodor. "Empathy, Inner Imitation, and Sense Feelings." Trans. Melvin Rader and Max Schertel, in *A Modern Book of Esthetics*. Ed. Melvin Rader (New York: Holt, 1979), 371–378.

Painter, Corinne Michelle. *Phenomenology and the Non-human Animal: At the Limits of Experience* (Dordrecht: Springer, 2007).

Pernau, Margit. "Zivilität und Barbarei – Gefühle als Differenzkriterien" in *Gefühlswissen: Eine lexikalische Spurensuche in der Moderne*. Eds. Ute Frevert et al. (Frankfurt a.M.: Campus, 2009), 233–262.

Plamper, Jan. *The History of Emotions: An Introduction* (Oxford: Oxford UP, 2015).

Regan, Tom. *The Case for Animal Rights* (Berkeley: UC Press, 1983).

Rilke, Rainer Maria. "Der Panther," in *Werke in drei Bänden*, vol. 1, *Gedicht-Zyklen* (Frankfurt a. M.: Insel, 1966), 261.

Rilke, Rainer Maria. "The Panther," trans. Stephen Cohn, in *Neue Gedichte/New Poems* (Evanston, IL: Northwestern UP, 1998), 61.

Rilke, Rainer Maria. Preface to *Mitsou: Forty Images*, by Balthus. Trans. Richard Miller (New York: Metropolitan Museum of Art, 1994), 9–13.

Rohman, Carrie. *Stalking the Subject: Modernism and the Animal* (New York: Columbia UP, 2009).

Rothfels, Nigel. *Savages and Beasts: The Birth of the Modern Zoo* (Baltimore: Johns Hopkins UP, 2002).

Seigel, Jerrold. *The Idea of the Self: Thought and Experience in Western Europe since the Seventeenth Century* (Cambridge: Cambridge UP, 2005).

Singer, Peter. *Animal Liberation: A New Ethics for Our Treatment of Animals* (New York: Avon, 1975).

Spickernagel, Ellen. *Der Fortgang der Tiere: Darstellungen in Menagerien und in der Kunst des 17.–19. Jahrhunderts* (Cologne: Böhlau, 2010).

Steiner, Gary. *Animals and the Limits of Postmodernism* (New York: Columbia UP, 2013).

Still, Judith. *Derrida and Other Animals: The Boundaries of the Human* (Edinburgh: Edinburgh UP, 2015).

Taylor, Charles. *Sources of the Self* (Cambridge: Cambridge UP, 1989).

Tucholsky, Kurt. *Gesammelte Werke*, Band 1 (Rowohlt: Reinbek bei Hamburg, 1975).

Unglaub, Erich. *Panther und Aschanti: Rilke-Gedichte in kulturwissenschaftlicher Sicht* (Frankfurt a. M.: Lang, 2005).

Vischer, Robert. "On the Optical Sense of Form: A Contribution to Aesthetics." Trans. Nicholas Walker, in *Empathy, Form, and Space: Problems in German Aesthetics, 1873–1893*. Eds. Harry Francis Mallgrave and Eleftherios Ikonomou (Santa Monica: Getty, 1994), 90–123.

Weingarten, Michael. "Das Tier in mir. Eine problematische anthropologische Fiktion des Liberalismus," in *Topos Tier. Neue Gestaltungen des Tier-Mensch-Verhältnisses*. Eds. Annette Bühler-Dietrich and Michael Weingarten (Bielefeld: transcript, 2016), 87–102.

Wirtz, Patrick. "Zoo City: Bourgeois Values and Scientific Culture in the Industrial Landscape," in *Journal of Urban Design* 2, no. 1 (1997): 61–82.

Wolfe, Cary. *Animal Rites: American Culture, the Discourse of Species, and Posthumanist Theory* (Chicago: U of Chicago Press, 2003).

Wolfe, Cary. "Human, All Too Human: 'Animal Studies' and the Humanities," *PMLA* 124, no. 2 (2009): 564–575.

Wolfe, Cary. *What is Posthumanism?* (Minneapolis: U of Minnesota Press, 2010).

Wolfe, Cary, ed. *Zoontologies: The Question of the Animal* (Minneapolis: U of Minnesota Press, 2003).

Holly Yanacek
Benevolent Bots

Human-Robot Friendship and Empathy in German Children's Literature

Should children have robot friends? If children form emotional bonds with artificial life forms, what are the implications for their social development and
human relationships? Child/robot friendship is a contested issue, as evident in
recent news articles and scholarly publications.[1] There are already examples of
social robots on the market for the home, such as Anki's Vector and Zoetic AI's
Kiki, both of which can display emotions and interpret and respond to human
voices and facial expressions. Social robots like these are designed primarily to
provide entertainment and companionship. While Japan currently leads the
world in social robotics research and development, the German Federal Government's 2018 Artificial Intelligence Strategy indicates that Germany seeks to be a
top competitor in AI research and robotics, which suggests a continued interest
in developing and implementing not only industrial robots, but also social robots for various purposes.[2] Social robots have already been studied for their potential to help preschool children ages 4–6 learn a second language[3] and serve
as personal care robots for the elderly in assisted living facilities.[4] Since children and the elderly are the demographics most likely to use social robots in
the future, ethical questions about the use of social robots with these groups in
particular have been raised.[5] Over the past decade, a number of German children's books featuring social robots have been published, a trend that mirrors

---

1 See, e.g., Dan Jolin, "Would you want a robot to be your child's best friend?" *The Guardian*,
11 September 2017, https://www.theguardian.com/technology/2017/sep/10/should-robot-be-
your-childs-best-friend; Olivera Stajić, "Roboter im Kindergarten – Freund oder Feind?" *Der
Standard*, 19 November 2019, https://www.derstandard.at/ story/2000111099279/roboter-im-
kindergarten-freund-oder-feind; and Alexis M. Elder, *Friendship, Robots, and Social Media:
False Friends and Second Selves* (New York: Routledge, 2018).
2 Die Bundesregierung, *Strategie Künstliche Intelligenz der Bundesregierung*, November 2018,
https://www.ki-strategie-deutschland.de.
3 Project L2TOR, "L2TOR – Second Language Tutoring Using Social Robots," *L2TOR*, http://
www.l2tor.eu/.
4 Nele Rößler, "Soziale Pflege-Roboter setzen sich nur langsam durch," *Deutschlandfunk*,
18 February 2019, https://www.deutschlandfunk.de/zukunft-der-pflege-soziale-pflege-roboter-
setzen-sich-nur.724.de.html?dram:article_id=441372.
5 Elder, *Friendship, Robots, and Social Media*, 80–82.

https://doi.org/10.1515/9783110753677-010

the rise of personal social robots for home and therapeutic uses. Do these examples of recent German children's stories about social robots prime young readers to embrace technology and befriend robots, or is there something else at stake?

This chapter examines the depiction of social robots and child/robot friendship in German children's fiction, including *Schlupp vom grünen Stern* (Schlupp from the green star, 1974), *Orbis Abenteuer: Ein kleiner Roboter büxt aus* (Orbi's adventures: a little robot runs away, 2011), *Roboter Sam, der beste Freund der Welt* (Robot Sam, the best friend in the world, 2017), and *Roki: Mein Freund mit Herz und Schraube* (Roki: my friend with heart and bolt, 2018).[6] Social robots, which interact with humans by displaying and responding to emotions, have been developed since the 1990s, concurrent with the emotional or affective turn in academic disciplines. As robotics technologies continue to advance and robots become more social, it is possible that children will have robot friends in the future. These German chapter books for children, then, depict a near-future reality in which humans live with robots and form emotional bonds with them. The attribution of emotions to artificial life and the "sympathy of humans for nonhuman cyborgs" are already contemporary phenomena with precedents in science fiction literature for adults, as Kathleen Woodward has argued.[7] Yet some warn of the possible dangers of humans empathizing too much with robots. Inspired by Woodward's concept, "prosthetic emotions,"[8] my analysis focuses on the feelings of emotional attachment that the child protagonists develop for their robot friends and considers the extent to which these social robots serve as positive identification figures for child readers. Although the robots depicted in these books are cute machines that bear little resemblance to the human characters, these chapter books blur the boundary between humans and machines by attributing emotions or a "soul" to the robot characters. Taken together, these books imagine a world in which humans and robots can peacefully coexist and even form meaningful friendships that do not threaten human relationships. My analysis demonstrates that the greatest aim of these chapter books is to teach children love and respect for all life forms, both human and non-human, organic and artificial.

One of the first German children's books to feature a sentient robot character is Ellis Kaut's *Schlupp vom grünen Stern* (1974), which was later adapted as a

---

6 Translations of all passages cited from the original German texts are mine.

7 Kathleen Woodward, *Statistical Panic: Cultural Politics and Poetics of the Emotions* (Durham, NC: Duke UP, 2009), 142.

8 Woodward, *Statistical Panic*, 140.

German television series by the Augsburger Puppenkiste marionette theater.[9] Only five years earlier in 1969, a phase of reforms began in the Federal Republic of Germany (FRG) that led to the democratization of the educational system and initiated general processes of modernization.[10] At this time of educational reforms, German children's and youth literature was revalued and recognized for its important role in the education and socialization of young people.[11] A changing concept of childhood in the 1970s called for books that developed critical thinking and dealt with the same socially relevant topics found in fiction for adults.[12] The German company KUKA developed the first robot-operated welding transfer line in 1971 and Famulus, the world's first industrial robot with six electrical motor-driven axes, in 1973, thus strengthening Germany's reputation for excellence in building machines.[13] Since that time, robots have become even more advanced and humanlike, with the ability to display "emotions" and respond to human voices and facial expressions. It is perhaps not surprising, then, that sentient robots and child/robot friendship are featured in children's literature published in a society and at a period of time characterized by the rapid development of social robotics and other technologies.

Previous scholarship on robots or machines in children's fiction has been limited, with most scholarly essays focusing on twentieth- and twenty-first-century examples of Anglo-American children's literature and film. Kerry Mallan's essay on the interplay between technoscience and children's fiction shows how social and cultural shifts ushered in by new technologies have impacted narratives, including depictions of relationships between the organic and inorganic.[14] In a chapter of her book on children's literature and the posthuman, Zoe Jaques examines how robotic protagonists in children's fiction "predict, obscure or subvert the posthuman possibilities encoded in cybernetic organisms for child audiences."[15] This essay aims to extend the limited scholarship on robots in children's and youth fiction not only by examining

---

9 *Schlupp vom grünen Stern*, dir. Sepp Strubel, writ. Ellis Kaut and Sepp Strubel (Das Erste, 1986).

10 Isa Schikorsky, *Schnellkurs Kinder- und Jugendliteratur* (Cologne: DuMont, 2003), 152.

11 Schikorsky, *Kinder- und Jugendliteratur*, 153.

12 Schikorsky, *Kinder- und Jugendliteratur*, 153.

13 KUKA Aktiengesellschaft Germany, "The History of KUKA," *KUKA*, https://www.kuka.com/en-us/about-kuka/history.

14 Kerry Mallan, "All That Matters: Technoscience, Critical Theory, and Children's Fiction," in *Contemporary Children's Literature and Film: Engaging with Theory*, eds. Kerry Mallan and Clare Bradford (New York: Palgrave Macmillan, 2011), 148.

15 Zoe Jaques, *Children's Literature and the Posthuman: Animal, Environment, Cyborg* (New York: Routledge, 2015), 180.

social robots in German chapter books but also by calling attention to the affective relationships between humans and robots and inviting readings from an emotion studies perspective. But first, how does children's fiction with robot characters differ from adult fiction, such as some of the examples studied in the other chapters of this volume?

As we have already seen in the introduction to this volume, in the chapters on E. T. A. Hoffmann's "Die Automate" ("The Automata," 1814), and Thea von Harbou's *Metropolis* (1925), automata and robots in fiction for adults commonly elicit the affective responses of attraction and aversion and represent warnings about the potential dangers of technology. By contrast, the examples of German children's fiction surveyed for this chapter feature overwhelmingly benevolent bots. In the 1960s, H. Joseph Schwarcz made a similar observation about American children's fiction: only benevolent animation appears in children's literature, and American children's books about robots published in the 1960s treat robots as equal to humans.[16] However, for Schwarcz, who argued that early children's books featuring benevolent machine animation communicated to children the repressed anxieties of adults, such stories would supposedly damage children by encouraging them to identify with animated machines rather than develop relationships with humans.[17] While in the 1960s Schwarcz may have viewed stories about benevolent machines as a threat to humanism and anthropocentrism, in the early twenty-first century, humanity's entanglement with the non-human is becoming increasingly obvious as posthuman discourses invite us to question the category of the human.

In the examples of German children's fiction considered in this chapter, the non-human characters are not merely benevolent bots – they become the friends and companions of the human child protagonists in the stories. These robots are helpful and non-threatening, modeling for both the child characters and child readers good behavior based on a strong sense of honesty and justice. In each of these German-language chapter books, a robot befriends a child (a boy around the age of 9–14 in most cases) who is either an orphan or lives with only one parent. In addition to alleviating the child protagonists' loneliness and boredom, the robot characters typically assist their human friends in some prosocial way, e.g., by helping them adjust to a new school or make friends with other children. The child protagonists and sometimes other human characters empathize with and develop feelings of attachment to their robot companions.

---

16 H. Joseph Schwarcz, "Machine Animism in Modern Children's Literature," *The Library Quarterly: Information, Community, Policy* 37, no. 1 (1967): 94.
17 Schwarcz, "Machine Animism," 94–95.

In these German children's books, feelings of attachment, empathy, and friendship between humans and robots are not taken for granted; instead, they are treated with critical reflection. Questions about robot sentience and the possibility of human/robot friendship are raised directly by the human characters themselves.

As noted in the introduction to this volume, the idea of humans developing feelings of attachment to machines like automata or robots is not new, but rather can be traced at least as far back as to the literary imagination of post-Enlightenment writers like E. T. A. Hoffmann. In fiction, representations of affective relationships between humans and humanlike machines have proliferated in books, film, and television since the mid-twentieth century, but even more so over the past decade. Researchers also continue to collect evidence that humans feel for robots in real life, for example in reports that soldiers feel distraught when a battlefield robot companion is destroyed in the line of duty[18] and in studies that measure empathetic concern for social robots like Ugobe's robotic dinosaur Pleo.[19] Drawing on Donna Haraway's *The Companion Species Manifesto* – in which Haraway emphasizes the coevolution of all species as a process that fosters "acts of love like caring about and for other, concatenated, emergent worlds"[20] – Kathleen Woodward develops the term "prosthetic emotions" to describe feelings of attachment (specifically, sympathy and love) to the non-human world, especially to the emerging lifeform that includes robots.[21] Her analysis of late twentieth-century Anglo-American science fiction reveals a cultural desire that "new and imagined technologies will help repair our own insufficiencies – here impoverished emotional resources in relation to others" and that these stories highlight "the importance of respect for material culture, for the world of our own making."[22] Following Woodward, I focus on these "prosthetic emotions" or feelings of attachment to robots that characterize depictions of child/robot friendship in German children's fiction. Although most of these German children's books do not dwell on the human emotional insufficiencies that Woodward identifies in Anglo-American science fiction for adults, the fictional robots in these texts serve as supplements for human

---

18 Julie Carpenter, *Culture and Human-Robot Interaction in Militarized Spaces: A War Story* (New York: Routledge, 2016), 103–105.
19 Astrid Marieke Rosenthal-von der Pütten et al., "An Experimental Study on Emotional Reactions Towards a Robot," *International Journal of Social Robotics* 5 (2013): 1.
20 Donna Haraway, *The Companion Species Manifesto: Dogs, People, and Significant Otherness* (Chicago: Prickly Paradigm Press, 2003), 61.
21 Woodward, *Statistical Panic*, 136.
22 Woodward, *Statistical Panic*, 155.

relationships and help meet the social and emotional needs of orphans or children in busy single-parent households. These fictional robots are distinguished by their capacity for emotion, which grants them a kind of human status. By modeling positive social relationships between children and their robot friends, these texts take a proactive approach in teaching children love, respect, and sympathy for all life forms, both human and non-human, organic and artificial.

These chapter books, which are recommended for children ages 7 and up, could appeal to young readers of any gender; however, it is significant that in each story the main protagonist who befriends the robot character is a white male child. All four of the German chapter books also gender the robot friends masculine – the German pronoun "er" (he) rather than "es" (it) or "sie" (she) is used to refer to the robot in each story. Consequently, while these stories could be interpreted as socializing young readers in general to love and respect all life forms, they address boys in particular. With their male child protagonists and many amusing illustrations of the robot characters, these books might aim first and foremost to cultivate in boys an interest in reading. These chapter books also could be interpreted as responding to the worldwide "boy crisis"[23] – described as crisis of mental health, physical health, education, fathering, and purpose – and encouraging boys to value emotions and the reciprocal care upon which the child/robot friendships in these texts are based. And yet, the fact that women and girls are somewhat marginalized in these texts and that the child protagonists are all white males reflects a narrow societal view of who gets to own and benefit from robots and other machines. This also suggests that these texts fall somewhat short of the inclusive, feminist ethics of care that they seem to promote.

In each of these German chapter books, the robots' cute, toy-like appearance facilitates feelings of emotional attachment and friendship. Descriptive words such as "Minibot"[24] and "klein"[25] (little, small) emphasize the smallness of the robots in these texts, thereby putting the robots on the same level as the child characters. Because they look like toy machines rather than poor imitations of humans, these robots also fall outside the uncanny valley[26] and therefore do not

---

23 Warren Farrell and John Gray, *The Boy Crisis: Why Our Boys Are Struggling and What We Can Do About It* (Dallas: BenBella Books, 2018).

24 Angelika Niestrath and Andreas Hüging, *Roki: Mein Freund mit Herz und Schraube* (Munich: cbj Kinder- und Jugendbuchverlag, 2018), 29.

25 See, for example, the subtitle of Thomas Christos, *Orbis Abenteuer: Ein kleiner Roboter büxt aus* (Frankfurt a. M.: Fischer Verlag, 2011).

26 Masahiro Mori, "The Uncanny Valley," trans. Karl F. MacDorman and Norri Kageki, *IEEE Spectrum*, 12 June 2012, https://spectrum.ieee.org/automaton/robotics/humanoids/the-uncanny-valley.

appear threatening. Recent science fiction television series and films from *Westworld* (2016–) to *Humans* (2015–2018) to *Life Like* (2019) comment on the difficulty of distinguishing between humans and androids when robots are designed to imitate humans closely in appearance, speech, and movement. By contrast, in these chapter books there is little danger of confusion between the human children and the robots. Despite the robot characters' appearance as toy-like machines, the emotional qualities of these robots make friendship, or at least the appearance of friendship, possible and in some cases allow the child protagonists to forget that the robot is not a human child.

The popular German children's book *Schlupp vom grünen Stern* (Schlupp from the green star, 1974) is an important forerunner of German children's fiction about social robots that has been published in the last ten years. Despite its popularity and adaptation for German television, *Schlupp* is left out of most histories of German-language children's and youth literature,[27] perhaps due to its relationship to science fiction, a genre that still tends to be stigmatized. While the robot Schlupp's ability to feel and possession of a soul result from an error in the robot production machine on planet Balda 7–3, the German chapter books that have appeared since the year 2010 feature somewhat more realistic depictions of social robots that display emotions and develop friendships with the child protagonists. Nonetheless, *Schlupp* comments on similar issues and, significantly, it does so decades before current developments in social robotics.

The robot in *Schlupp* is the 31 millionth of his kind and looks just like all of the other working robots on the green star Balda 7–3; however, it soon becomes clear that this one robot is unique. Like all of the other robots on Balda 7–3, this special robot bears the name "Schlupp," the onomatopoetic name that mimics the noise made when a new robot emerges from the production machine. All of the robots on the green star are designed to work efficiently and without interruption for Balda's human inhabitants, whom the narrator describes as "especially green."[28] Yet a production error causes this particular Schlupp to act differently than the other robots – he yawns, completes some tasks slowly, and hates other tasks. Schlupp also requires affection and physical touch; he occasionally stops carrying out tasks and only resumes his work after being petted as positive reinforcement. The third-person omniscient narrator describes and interprets Schlupp's sounds, light colors, and movements as signs of pleasurable

27 See, for example, Schikorsky, *Kinder- und Jugendliteratur*; Günter Lange, ed., *Kinder- und Jugendliteratur der Gegenwart: Ein Handbuch* (Baltmannsweiler: Schneider Verlag Hohengehren, 2011); and Reiner Wild, ed., *Geschichte der deutschen Kinder- und Jugendliteratur* (Stuttgart: J. B. Metzler, 2008).
28 Ellis Kaut, *Schlupp vom grünen Stern* (Munich: Lentz Verlag, 1985), 8.

and aversive states like joy and fear, respectively. Thus, unlike the other robots on the green star, Schlupp is sentient and has needs, desires, and emotions.

Contrasting attitudes toward Schlupp's behavior are represented by characters on Balda 7–3: by the inspector, Mr. Rrracks, and the other green men on the one hand and by the scientist and design engineer, Mr. Ritschwumm, on the other. At a deeper level, these two different attitudes toward Schlupp reflect conflicting views of humanity, and Mr. Rrracks and Mr. Ritschwumm's disagreement sets the rest of the narrative events in motion. Mr. Rrracks and the other men reject the human past on earth as barbaric and criticize humans for their constant wars, pollution, and primitive technology that is 3,456 years behind technology on Balda 7–3.[29] They enforce the prohibition of laughter, which is associated with stupidity, as well as the prohibition of feelings in general on the green star.[30] Worrying that chaos could ensue if all other robots need to be petted in order to continue to work, Mr. Rrracks calls for Schlupp to be destroyed by launching him into space. For Mr. Rrracks and the other green men, Schlupp's emotional needs and possession of a soul pose a threat to the cool rationality and efficiency of production that characterize life and work on Balda 7–3. The emotional regime on the green star resembles the West German postwar emotional regime, which, according to Frank Biess, persisted until the 1960s and was "characterized by a deep suspicion toward the open expression of strong emotions and resisted their injection in politics and public."[31] The narrator's distance from the worldview and emotional regime on Balda 7–3 implies a critique of the narrative of technological development in which "progress" is typically defined in terms of efficiency and rationality to the exclusion of emotions, empathetic understanding, and care work.[32]

By contrast, a positive view of humanity and emotions is held by Mr. Ritschwumm, who fondly remembers human life as it was on earth over 230 years ago.[33] Mr. Ritschwumm pets Schlupp compassionately, laughs, and suggests that the inhabitants of the green star can learn something from this sentient

29 Kaut, *Schlupp*, 55–56.
30 Kaut, *Schlupp*, 10.
31 Frank Biess, "Feelings in the Aftermath: Toward a History of Postwar Emotions," in *Histories of the Aftermath: The Legacies of the Second World War in Europe*, eds. Frank Biess and Robert G. Moeller (New York: Berghahn Books, 2010), 30–48, here 43.
32 See Kathleen Woodward, "Prosthetic Emotions," in *Emotion in Postmodernism*, eds. Gerhard Hoffmann and Alfred Hornung (Heidelberg: Universitätsverlag C. Winter, 1997), 97, for a discussion of the dominant view of technological development as "an increasingly elaborated regime of tools and machines, or prostheses, that extend and amplify the capabilities of the human."
33 Kaut, *Schlupp*, 10.

robot with a soul. During his trip to retrieve Schlupp from earth, Mr. Ritsch-wumm witnesses the emotional bond between Schlupp and a fourteen-year-old orphaned boy, Beni, and is moved to tears. In spite of laws against it, Mr. Ritschwumm is moved emotionally by humanity and dreams of the inclusion of touch and emotion back in society on Balda 7–3.[34] In general, the robots pro-duced on the green star represent the view of progress in technological develop-ment as an increase in productivity and efficiency, but Schlupp, who stands for emotions, introduces what Kathleen Woodward identifies as a second, parallel narrative of technological development, "one that does not privilege cool ratio-nality but rather empathetic understanding."[35]

In *Schlupp*, the narrator and Mr. Ritschwumm espouse humanist values and mourn the loss on Balda 7–3 of many qualities that are often considered central to what it means to be human, including emotion and physical affection. This children's book extends humanity to non-humans, in this case to the sentient robot Schlupp, and it imagines emotional bonds and friendship between hu-mans and non-humans as possible. Not only does Beni develop a kind of friend-ship with Schlupp and treat him with care and compassion, but he also seems to forget that Schlupp is a robot, calling him "the best human in the world"[36] at the end of the story. Indeed, the non-human figure Schlupp embodies the "human" qualities that had been suppressed in the technocrat- and male-dominated, post-emotion society on the green star for well over two centuries. In this way, *Schlupp* comments on West German social movements of the 1960s and early 1970s, including anti-technocracy and the women's move-ment, casting doubt on the vision that scientific and technological progress should be the main goals for a modern society. Through the book's positive valuation of emotions, *Schlupp* also reflects what has been interpreted as a "more permissive emotional culture"[37] that emerged in West Germany in the 1960s. According to Dolores L. Augustine, as a result of this greater accep-tance of emotions in public life beginning in the 1960s, "emotions forced elites to confront scientific and technological problems in new ways and to allow the public to participate in debates and negotiations."[38]

Compared to the more recent German children's fiction about social robots, child/robot friendship is less central to the narrative events and didactic

---

34 Kaut, *Schlupp*, 69.

35 Woodward, "Prosthetic Emotions," 97.

36 Kaut, *Schlupp*, 161.

37 Biess, "Feelings in the Aftermath," 37.

38 Dolores L. Augustine, *Taking on Technocracy: Nuclear Power in Germany, 1945 to the Pres-ent* (New York: Berghahn Books, 2018), 6.

message in *Schlupp*. Nonetheless, the affective bond of friendship between Beni and Schlupp still plays important roles in the story. For Beni, the friendship with Schlupp eases his loneliness and provides a substitute emotional connection that was missing in his life after the death of his parents. Although Beni's brief friendship with Schlupp does not seem to facilitate prosthetic emotions that connect him to other humans, it does influence his decision to pursue technical training and build robots in the future.[39] More significantly, Schlupp's capacity to feel and his friendship with Beni deeply move Mr. Ritschwumm and highlights what the post-emotion society on Balda 7–3 lacks. *Schlupp vom grünen Stern* concludes not with the introduction of emotion and touch on Balda 7–3, but with an open ending that indicates Mr. Ritschwumm's compassion for humans on earth and desire to travel to the planet again.

Child/robot friendship is more central to Thomas Christos's German chapter book *Orbis Abenteuer: Ein kleiner Roboter büxt aus* (Orbi's adventures: a little robot runs away, 2011), but, as in *Schlupp*, many aspects of the story are based more on fantasy than on actual recent developments in social robotics. Orbi is a super-intelligent robot designed to steer a spaceship on his own and explore other planets over a period of many years. The prologue states that since humans have families at home or flowers to water and since a return to Earth was not planned, "only a robot could be considered for this trip."[40] However, Orbi never leaves Earth because he becomes sentient and escapes the lab just in time. Orbi's ability to feel derives not from programming but from a powerful lightning strike and power outage that blow one of his important fuses. The fact that both Schlupp's and Orbi's capacity to feel results from accidents (i.e., a production error in the case of the former and a natural phenomenon in the case of the latter), reveals a cultural assumption that robots lack emotions and autonomy and are not intentionally programmed with these capacities. Instead of accomplishing a scientific mission in outer space, Orbi becomes sentient and fulfills a social and emotional mission on earth by helping children in need.

Orbis Abenteuer anthropomorphizes its robot protagonist through the attribution of emotions, yet the story does not attempt to erase differences between humans and machines. After Orbi becomes sentient, the first emotion that he expresses is sadness. He considers it cruel that he will be sent to outer space and that the spaceship will never fly back to earth. The narrator reports: "It was very sad, and if the inventors had looked closely, they would have noticed that

---

39 Kaut, *Schlupp*, 172–173.
40 Christos, *Orbis Abenteuer*, 7.

a tear rolled down his metal cheek."[41] When Orbi successfully escapes the lab, the narrator describes the robot's feelings of relief: "Orbi was so relieved that a screw fell from his heart."[42] In these passages, the depictions of Orbi's sadness and relief resemble the treatment of his emotions in the rest of the book – Orbi is anthropomorphized; however, at the same time certain details like Orbi's visual appearance and construction from metal parts remind readers that he is not a human but a robot with a supercomputer "brain." The story attributes to Orbi a range of other complex emotions from anticipation to joy to love, and these emotions are commonly indicated by descriptions of flashing lights in Orbi's eyes, nose, and ears. All of these examples highlight the importance of the body, in this case the mechanical body of the robot, for emotional practices and invite us to "rethink the ways in which bodies and things give rise to and shape emotions."[43] Even though the book's text and images remind readers that Orbi is a machine, the robot's ability to feel and express emotions facilitates friendship across the human-machine boundary with the two child protagonists, Linus and Frederike.

Orbis Abenteuer addresses potential anxieties about child/robot friendships by imagining a situation in which a robot helps strengthen human relationships. The main child protagonist in the story is a nine-year-old boy named Linus, who just moved to a new city with his mother and is the new kid at his school. Linus finds Orbi one day on his way home from school, and the narrator reports that, after seeing that Orbi needs help charging his battery, Linus "immediately had compassion for the little robot."[44] Linus likes Orbi and is happy to have met "someone who did not laugh at him or make him angry,"[45] unlike the students who pick on him at school. Orbi enjoys making himself useful and helps Linus clean his room, do homework, and solve problems. After only a few days together, Linus cannot imagine life without Orbi, and the little robot becomes his best friend. Yet Orbi also plays an important role as mediator between Linus and his female classmate, Frederike, who also befriends the robot later in the story. Orbi tells the truth and helps Linus overcome his initial dislike of Frederike, which allows them to communicate, overcome their gender differences, and build a friendship. Thus, *Orbis Abenteuer* depicts a sentient robot

---

41 Christos, *Orbis Abenteuer*, 12.
42 Christos, *Orbis Abenteuer*, 16.
43 Derek Hillard, Heikki Lempa, and Russell Spinney, "Introduction," in *Feelings Materialized: Emotions, Bodies, and Things in Germany, 1500–1950*, eds. Derek Hillard, Heikki Lempa, and Russell Spinney (New York: Berghahn Books, 2020), 1–21, here 2.
44 Christos, *Orbis Abenteuer*, 26.
45 Christos, *Orbis Abenteuer*, 28.

that neither isolates the human characters nor threatens to take the place of human relationships. This children's book attributes emotions to the robot character and shows that human/robot friendship is possible, but, more significantly, it depicts a robot that fosters connection and friendship between humans.

Like Schlupp and other benevolent bots in children's fiction, Orbi also possesses a strong sense of robot ethics. The narrator calls Orbi "super smart" and "super honest" and notes that "for Orbi, justice was above all else."[46] With his honesty and sense of justice, Orbi serves as a positive identification figure who helps children in need, especially those who feel like outsiders. For example, Orbi helps Linus defend himself from members of a moped gang who try to bully him after school, and Orbi is happy when justice is served. Later in the story, Linus and Frederike work together to save their best friend Orbi after he is stolen by two burglars and almost destroyed in a scrap metal press in a junkyard. Newspapers report that Orbi had been stolen and then destroyed in the scrap metal press, thus the inventors in the lab no longer try to search for Orbi to send him to space. At the end of the story, Orbi departs from his two friends but promises to return after helping other children in need.[47] Even though this chapter book does not allow readers to forget that Orbi is not human, Orbi is depicted as a good role model and best friend. The little robot serves as an exemplar of ethical, prosocial behavior for both the child characters in the story and child readers.

Compared to *Schlupp* and *Orbis Abenteuer*, Frauke Nahrgang's *Roboter Sam, der beste Freund der Welt* (Robot Sam, the best friend in the world, 2017) is more detailed and accurate in terms of its depiction of contemporary robotic technologies. The robot character Sam is a "Smart Acting Machine" (S.A.M.) created by Robert Justus, an inventor and father of Jakob, the story's child protagonist.[48] At first, Sam does not seem to have a true purpose, unlike other robots produced in the robot factory. The narrator distinguishes between the hitherto unsuccessful type of "Smart Acting Machine" robots developed by Robert Justus and the "useful robots" developed by Dr. Zimperling that complete different automated tasks (e.g., vacuuming, mowing lawns, assembly line production) and earn a lot of money for the company.[49] Many of these "useful" robots in the factory are part of the production line and have "no head or body. Each

---

46 Christos, *Orbis Abenteuer*, 32 and 43.
47 Christos, *Orbis Abenteuer*, 116.
48 Frauke Nahrgang, *Roboter Sam, der beste Freund der Welt* (Ravensburg: Ravensburger Buchverlag, 2017), 9.
49 Nahrgang, *Roboter Sam*, 14.

consisted of only one arm to which a tool was attached."[50] After Sam is nearly destroyed by the robotic arms of the production line for an excavator machine, Robert Justus regrets building Smart Acting Machines and nearly gives up: "No matter how hard I try, nothing works with my invention. Sam is useless."[51] Yet by the end of the story it becomes clear that Sam's purpose is to be a friend, much like some of "useless" social robots marketed as companions today.

At the center of this children's book is the development of the child/robot friendship between Jakob and Sam. Jakob contradicts his father's assertion that Sam is "useless" and proclaims: "Sam is useful. In fact, he's good for many things. He is my friend."[52] The desire for friendship is depicted as mutual, and the friendship with Sam occupies Jakob, who has been sad and wishing for a friend ever since his mother died. However, Robert Justus claims that it is not possible for Sam to be Jakob's friend: "Robots are machines, nothing more, and a machine cannot be a friend."[53] Jakob protests and again calls Sam his friend, but direct interior monologue is used to show how, as a result of Robert Justus's explanation, Sam questions the possibility of human/robot friendship and blames himself, explaining away the warm sensation of friendship whenever he sees or thinks about Jakob as a "technical malfunction."[54] By comparison with *Schlupp* and *Orbis Abenteuer*, *Roboter Sam* meditates much more directly on questions about the possibility of human/robot friendship. Sam helps unite a lost child named Nina with her mother, and Sam is happy because Nina calls him a friend, and he finally realizes his value as a companion. Shortly thereafter, Dr. Zimperling attempts to sabotage Robert Justus's work by stealing Sam and taking him apart, but Nina reports the crime and rescues the robot with the help of her mother, Jakob, and Robert Justus. The question of the possibility of child/robot friendship is addressed again in the book's final chapters. Jakob calls Sam his "best friend ever" and direct interior monologue reveals "the most important information" in Sam's supercomputer brain: "I was Jakob's friend and he was mine. We were friends and it doesn't matter that one of us was a human and the other a robot."[55] In *Roboter Sam*, the assumed superior knowledge of the "rational," human, adult male scientist is destabilized, making room for non-human forms of wisdom and the wisdom of children. Robert Justus did not know that a robot could be a friend, for example, but he changes his

---

50 Nahrgang, *Roboter Sam*, 56–57.
51 Nahrgang, *Roboter Sam*, 61.
52 Nahrgang, *Roboter Sam*, 62.
53 Nahrgang, *Roboter Sam*, 62.
54 Nahrgang, *Roboter Sam*, 65.
55 Nahrgang, *Roboter Sam*, 125.

view in the story's final chapters. He continues to develop more Smart Acting Machines to meet the new high demand for social robots that can assist with the supervision of children in kindergarten, help care for dogs in a kennel, and act as playmates for children at home.[56] Thus, much like in *Schlupp*, the sentient social robot in *Roboter Sam* not only teaches children skills and facilitates friendship, but also rehumanizes the figure of the adult male scientist.

Roboter Sam inspires empathetic understanding for its non-human protagonist through two techniques: first, by drawing comparisons between the physical, mental, and emotional qualities of humans and the robot, and second, by de-centering the human and narrating the entire story from the perspective of the robot character. The chapter book attributes emotions to Sam; however, there is less anthropomorphism and more attention to the robot's ability to express and respond to emotions as an aspect of his programming. While *Roboter Sam* neither attributes all emotions to the little robot nor erases the distinction between human and non-human, it does humanize Sam by drawing parallels between humans and robots. For example, Jakob has a father and Sam has an inventor, and, for robots, inventors are "something similar to fathers for humans."[57] Humans also need sleep to recharge and Sam requires electricity to charge his battery. "Thoughts" come directly from Sam's hard drive, sensors and cables enable him to "feel," and an "emotion scanner" allows Sam to translate and respond to human emotions and gestures.[58] Like Jakob, Sam also needs affection, seeks friendship, and feels tired, alone, jealous, bored, or afraid at different points in the story. The aforementioned emotions are apparently programmed, but Sam could not cry even if he wanted to because "unfortunately tears are not programmable" for robots.[59] All of Sam's thoughts, feelings, and experiences described in the text are narrated from the first-person perspective of the little robot after the fact. For example, when the Director of the robot factory first inspects Robert Justus's work, Sam reports, "Unease ran through all my cables" and later recounts "[. . .] my whole electronic inner life was thrown off balance" when he witnesses Dr. Zimperling in an embarrassing situation.[60] This narrative style invites child readers to imagine what it is like to be a robot like Sam with a supercomputer brain and makes possible empathetic understanding and respect for the non-human perspective and for artificial beings created in our image.

---

56 Nahrgang, *Roboter Sam*, 116–117.
57 Nahrgang, *Roboter Sam*, 13.
58 Nahrgang, *Roboter Sam*, 11, 30.
59 Nahrgang, *Roboter Sam*, 116.
60 Nahrgang, *Roboter Sam*, 19 and 41.

Out of all of the German chapter books included in this essay, *Roboter Sam* is most closely related to early twenty-first-century developments in social robotics. For instance, Smart Acting Machines like Sam become desirable for use in the home, childcare facilities, businesses, and media and advertising, similar to how social robots are being tested in different settings today. Yet the literary text focuses on the *possibility* rather than the *ethics* of child/robot friendship and of the use of social robots in different spheres of life. In other words, concerns about the potential of social robots to replace workers or human interaction are not addressed directly, which is perhaps unsurprising, as children's fiction tends to feature benevolent bots and suppress such adult anxieties. Like other fictional benevolent bots, Sam helps children in need and brings humans together – the robot poses no threat to human relationships. Even if some of these anxieties and concerns do surface for adult readers, the overall message at the end of *Roboter Sam* is that social robots like Sam, far from being useless, can help meet the social and emotional needs of humans, including the need for friendship. The book's technological optimism could also suggest a possible shift in comfort with social robots and technology in general across generations. After all, children of Generation Alpha will be the first ones to grow up using AI and interacting with robots.[61]

Finally, the last German children's book under consideration here, Angelika Niestrath and Andreas Hüging's *Roki: Mein Freund mit Herz und Schraube* (Roki: my friend with heart and bolt, 2018), engages with questions related to the development of social robots today, but, compared to the other chapter books, *Roki* blurs the boundaries between human and robot to a greater extent. The story's robot character, Roki, is a self-learning autonomous robot developed by a scientist named Adam. Adam rents space for his lab from Valerie, the mother of the story's child protagonist, Paul, and develops his robot there. The narrator draws parallels between Roki and humans; for example, the robot has an electric computer "brain," which Adam says is not that different from a human brain.[62] Like humans, Roki also gets bored and has a thirst for knowledge, and he learns and saves new information in his "Rokipedia memory."[63] Particularly the name that Adam gives his autonomous robot also suggests a blurring of the human/robot boundary – "Roki" combines the first two letters of the German words "Roboter"

61 IEEE, "Generation AI 2018: Second Annual Study of Millennial Parents of Generation Alpha Kids," *IEEE Transmitter*, 10 July 2018, https://transmitter.ieee.org/generation-ai-2018-second-annual-study-of-millennial-parents-of-generation-alpha-kids/.
62 Niestrath and Hüging, *Roki*, 84.
63 Niestrath and Hüging, *Roki*, 83.

and "Kind" and stands for "half robot and half child."[64] Roki is programmed with something like what is known as deep learning in robotics today because he learns through his own methods and experiences. Roki's deep learning processes resemble the learning and development of human children. However, one primary difference is that Roki learns much faster than a human child – a child learns to walk over months, while Roki learns in a matter of hours.[65] Roki's comparison with a human child occurs throughout the story and further blurs the human/robot boundary.

Like the social robots in the other German children's books, the "highly sensitive machine" Roki displays and responds to emotions.[66] As in *Roboter Sam*, however, *Roki* makes frequent references to these emotions as a result of the robot's programming and AI learning. Boredom is an important emotion in the text – feelings of boredom drive Roki to escape on more than one occasion. The more autonomous Roki becomes, the more he needs to learn and experience new things in the world to fill his Rokipedia memory and alleviate his boredom. References to Roki's laughter also appear in the text and humanize the little robot. Although Adam did not program Roki to laugh, the robot learns to laugh on his own via machine learning. Roki's ability to learn new skills like laughing makes Adam realize that the robot is more similar to a child than he had thought.[67]

In *Roki*, the robot's similarity to a human child accelerates his friendship with Paul. As in the other German chapter books, *Roki* reflects upon the possibility of child/robot friendship. The story, which features a third-person narrator, does this primarily through indirect interior monologue and character focalization through the child protagonist, Paul:

> Paul kept forgetting that Roki wasn't actually human at all – more like a talking computer on two legs. That made him a bit pensive: Could you be friends with a computer? Paul would have loved to have Roki as a friend. He was so exciting and funny. When the little robot laughed, everyone had to laugh along – even Valerie! And if someone could make you laugh, Paul decided that he could be a friend too. "My friend Roki," he said to himself. "Sounds good!"[68]

It is significant that Paul continues to forget that Roki is not human, especially because the child protagonists in the other three chapter books do not experience

64 Niestrath and Hüging, *Roki*, 35.
65 Niestrath and Hüging, *Roki*, 29.
66 Niestrath and Hüging, *Roki*, 74.
67 Niestrath and Hüging, *Roki*, 38.
68 Niestrath and Hüging, *Roki*, 65–66.

this in the same way with their robot friends. The reason for this forgetting seems related to a common objection to social robot friends, namely, "enchantment,"[69] or the idea that robots evoke our emotions and responses as if they were real humans. As evident in the above passage, the friendship between Paul and Roki has an affective basis. Roki not only inspires feelings of excitement and makes Paul laugh, but the little robot also evokes empathy and care in Paul. Paul *knows* that Roki is a smart machine, but it does not *feel* that way, and Paul and Roki think alike in many ways.[70] Indeed, in *Roki*, the child protagonist identifies with the non-human perspective of the robot better than the robot's creator himself. Paul understands Roki's behaviors and needs because they are similar to his own, while Paul thinks that Adam does not understand Roki or children particularly well.[71]

Roki depicts Paul's empathetic understanding and care for his robot friend, and, through the narration of Paul's thoughts and feelings, the narrator likewise invites child readers to imagine what it is like to be a robot. When Roki wanders off and gets lost after a visit to the zoo, Paul worries and starts to imagine what Roki feels: "Paul had to take a deep breath again. The worry about Roki weighed on his mind. Does the little robot also have such feelings? Did he even know what fear was? What did he feel when he laughed? And how is he feeling right now in this moment?"[72] Here, Paul empathizes with his robot friend and contemplates what Roki feels and experiences. While the robot character in *Roboter Sam* narrates from his first-person perspective, the third-person narrator in *Roki* does not have access to the robot character's private thoughts, emotions, or "inner life." One exception occurs in four short chapters, which are focalized through the character Roki.[73] In these chapters, readers follow Roki's search for a dog and attempt to free himself after he is stolen by two robot kidnappers. The effect of these techniques is that the text evokes narrative empathy for Roki and invites child readers to follow Paul's example and imagine what it is like to be a robot.

Like the other German chapter books discussed here, *Roki* features a benevolent bot and exemplifies technological optimism. Roki learns new skills and information quickly and completes various tasks, but, fitting in with current trends in social robotics, the robot mostly offers social interaction and

---

69 See Elder, *Friendship, Robots, and Social Media*, 122–123, for a discussion of the enchantment objection to robot friends.
70 Niestrath and Hüging, *Roki*, 145 and 69.
71 Niestrath and Hüging, *Roki*, 68–69.
72 Niestrath and Hüging, *Roki*, 144.
73 See Niestrath and Hüging, *Roki*, 130–142.

companionship. This story depicts an equal friendship between a child and a robot and highlights generational differences in the ability of adults and children to understand and relate to social robots, which seems to suggest that, like Paul, children will grow up alongside social robots and have robot friends in the near future. Just as Paul engages in perspective taking and imagines what Roki feels and what it is like to be a robot, social robots could help teach children social skills and empathetic understanding, for both humans and nonhumans. For the most part, then, *Roki* exemplifies technological optimism about social robots, albeit with one caution: social robots and other examples of powerful AI need monitoring. The chapter book concludes on a humorous note that again draws the comparison between the robot Roki and a human child – Adam creates a kind of baby monitor called a "Rokifon" so that he can keep track of Roki when the little robot attempts to wander off. While a child eventually outgrows a baby monitor, Adam notes that for Roki, "The bigger he gets, the more you have to keep an eye on him."[74] On the one hand, this statement applies to Roki's tendency to get bored, wander off to learn new things, and surprise his creator with his ability to quickly learn skills that are not programmed; however, on the other hand, the statement has broader significance, emphasizing the need to monitor and consider the ethical implications of social robots and other powerful new AI technologies.

What, then, is at stake in German children's fiction about social robots? Taken together, these depictions of child/robot friendship emphasize similarities between humans, especially children, and robots, while at the same time acknowledging features like bodies and minds vs. materials and programming that distinguish humans from humanlike machines. In each case, the fictional robot's ability to show and respond to emotions makes friendship with the child protagonists possible. This attention to emotion in these robot stories corresponds to the recent developments in robotics and affective computing of emotional AI technologies that read and respond to human emotions. The question of what these robots experience and feel is taken up in each text, and this idea, together with the robots' emotional responses, inspire the children's empathetic understanding and care for their robot friends. Thus, the benevolent bots in these chapter books are not the only positive role models for child readers. While these fictional robots help children in need and stand for values like honesty and justice, the child and adult characters who treat both their fellow humans and these sentient machines with compassion and respect also serve as positive identification figures.

---

74 Niestrath and Hüging, *Roki*, 165.

Despite the overwhelmingly positive portrayal of social robots and child/robot friendship in these chapter books, a number of possible objections to companion robots may arise, even if the texts do not address these directly. Overall, perhaps because these texts were written for young readers, they focus mostly on the question of the possibility of having a robot friend and very little on the potential dangers or ethical implications of robot companions. *Roki* stands out as an exception to this, as it ends with a message about the importance of monitoring powerful AI technologies like social robots. In each of the texts, though, the robots do things that are not programmed or that their inventors did not intend for them to do, especially as the robots become more autonomous. Aside from the need for monitoring, another potential pitfall and objection to social robot companions is that humans may grow to trust robots too much. Trust, though important for friendships between humans, could become a problem, especially for children and vulnerable groups, if robot companions negatively impact one's judgement or create psychological dependencies.[75] In addition, the "enchantment objection" to robot friends emphasizes that robots may engage human social and emotional responses, but reciprocal care between human and machine does not actually exist.[76] Moreover, even though these chapter books depict benevolent bots that do not threaten human relationships but rather help children in need and bring people together, this way of imagining child/robot friendship tends to oversimplify issues, especially because it is not yet fully known how children's attachment to social robots may affect their development and relationships with other humans. This is currently a burning question given how much time children have spent at home and isolated from each other during the COVID-19 pandemic. On the one hand, during a deadly global pandemic social robot companions may represent a safe alternative to contact with other humans and promise to help children overcome isolation, loneliness, and stress. Socially assistive robots may also help address the perceived loss of social skills and guide children toward long-term goals for social behavior. On the other hand, the ethical consequences of using robots for emotional support remain to be seen. In addition, unequal access to social robots and other new technologies will worsen the digital divide and therefore social and economic inequality. In spite of the possible objections to robot friends for children, these texts imagine as possible not only peaceful coexistence with these sentient nonhuman others but also empathetic understanding, care, and friendship.

---

75 See Elder, *Friendship, Robots, and Social Media*, 122–125.
76 See Elder, *Friendship, Robots, and Social Media*, 122–125.

These German chapter books humanize the little robots through the attribution of emotions, and this capacity for feeling enables the friendship between the human children and their robot companions to develop. These texts narrate many different feelings from sadness to boredom to happiness, but the "prosthetic emotions" (e.g., sympathy and love) that connect the human characters to these artificial life forms are the transformative, boundary-breaking emotions in these stories. *Schlupp, Orbis Abenteuer, Roboter Sam*, and *Roki* communicate the importance of love, respect, and care for all life forms, both real and artificial. They imply not merely that the old Kantian argument – that humans should treat non-human animals well because to do otherwise would be demeaning to ourselves – should be extended to robots and other artificial life forms.[77] Instead, these texts imagine a near-future reality in which humans are even more emotionally connected to the non-human world than they are today and in which respect and care for emerging life forms are cultivated because they are valuable in their own right.

Bibliography

Augustine, Dolores L. *Taking on Technocracy: Nuclear Power in Germany, 1945 to the Present* (New York: Berghahn Books, 2018).

Biess, Frank. "Feelings in the Aftermath: Toward a History of Postwar Emotions," in *Histories of the Aftermath: The Legacies of the Second World War in Europe*. Eds. Frank Biess and Robert G. Moeller (New York: Berghahn Books, 2010), 30–48.

Die Bundesregierung. *Strategie Künstliche Intelligenz der Bundesregierung*, November 2018. Accessed 20 June 2020. https://www.ki-strategie-deutschland.de.

Carpenter, Julie. *Culture and Human-Robot Interaction in Militarized Spaces: A War Story* (New York: Routledge, 2016).

Christos, Thomas. *Orbis Abenteuer: Ein kleiner Roboter büxt aus* (Frankfurt a. M.: S. Fischer Verlag, 2014).

Elder, Alexis M. *Friendship, Robots, and Social Media: False Friends and Second Selves* (New York: Routledge, 2018).

Farrell, Warren, and John Gray. *The Boy Crisis: Why Our Boys Are Struggling and What We Can Do About It* (Dallas: BenBella Books, 2018).

Haraway, Donna. *The Companion Species Manifesto: Dogs, People, and Significant Otherness* (Chicago: Prickly Paradigm Press, 2003).

---

[77] "Any action whereby we may torment animals, or let them suffer distress, or otherwise treat them without love, is demeaning to ourselves." Immanuel Kant, *Lectures on Ethics*, eds. Peter Heath and J. B. Schneewind, trans. Peter Heath (Cambridge: Cambridge UP, 1997), 434.

Hillard, Derek, Heikki Lempa, and Russell Spinney, "Introduction." *Feelings Materialized: Emotions, Bodies, and Things in Germany, 1500–1950.* Eds. Derek Hillard, Heikki Lempa, and Russell Spinney (New York: Berghahn Books, 2020), 1–21.

IEEE. "Generation AI 2018: Second Annual Study of Millennial Parents of Generation Alpha Kids." *IEEE Transmitter*, 10 July 2018. Accessed 14 July 2020. https://transmitter.ieee. org/generation-ai-2018-second-annual-study-of-millennial-parents-of-generation-alpha- kids/.

Jaques, Zoe. *Children's Literature and the Posthuman: Animal, Environment, Cyborg* (New York: Routledge, 2015).

Jolin, Dan. "Would you want a robot to be your child's best friend?" *The Guardian*, September 11, 2017. Accessed 10 July 2020. https://www.theguardian.com/technology/ 2017/sep/10/should-robot-be-your-childs-best-friend.

Kant, Immanuel. *Lectures on Ethics.* Eds. Peter Heath and J. B. Schneewind. Trans. Peter Heath (Cambridge: Cambridge UP, 1997).

Kaut, Ellis. *Schlupp vom grünen Stern* (Munich: Lentz Verlag, 1985).

KUKA Aktiengesellschaft Germany. "The History of KUKA." *KUKA*. Accessed 24 June 2020. https://www.kuka.com/en-us/about-kuka/history.

Lange, Günter, ed. *Kinder- und Jugendliteratur der Gegenwart: Ein Handbuch* (Baltmannsweiler: Schneider Verlag Hohengehren, 2011).

Mallan, Kerry. "All That Matters: Technoscience, Critical Theory, and Children's Fiction," in *Contemporary Children's Literature and Film: Engaging with Theory.* Eds. Kerry Mallan and Clare Bradford (New York: Palgrave Macmillan, 2011), 147–167.

Mori, Masahiro. "The Uncanny Valley," trans. Karl F. MacDorman and Norri Kageki, *IEEE Spectrum*, 12 June 2012. Accessed 10 June 2020. https://spectrum.ieee.org/automaton/ robotics/humanoids/the-uncanny-valley.

Nahrgang, Frauke. *Roboter Sam, der beste Freund der Welt* (Ravensburg: Ravensburger Buchverlag, 2017).

Niestrath, Angelika, and Andreas Hüging. *Roki: Mein Freund mit Herz und Schraube* (Munich: cbj Kinder- und Jugendbuchverlag, 2018).

Project L2TOR. "L2TOR – Second Language Tutoring Using Social Robots." *L2TOR*. Accessed 12 June 2020. http://www.l2tor.eu/.

Rößler, Nele. "Soziale Pflege-Roboter setzen sich nur langsam durch." *Deutschlandfunk*, 18 February 2019. Accessed 20 June 2020. https://www.deutschlandfunk.de/zukunft-der- pflege-soziale-pflege-roboter-setzen-sich-nur.724.de.html?dram:article_id=441372.

Rosenthal-von der Pütten, Astrid Marieke, Nicole C. Krämer, Laura Hoffmann, Sabrina Sobieraj, and Sabrina C. Eimler. "An Experimental Study on Emotional Reactions Towards a Robot," *International Journal of Social Robotics* 5 (2013): 17–34.

Schikorsky, Isa. *Schnellkurs Kinder- und Jugendliteratur* (Cologne: DuMont, 2003).

Schlupp vom grünen Stern. Dir. Sepp Strubel. Writ. Ellis Kaut and Sepp Strubel (Das Erste, 1986).

Schwarcz, H. Joseph. "Machine Animism in Modern Children's Literature," in *The Library Quarterly: Information, Community, Policy* 37, no. 1 (1967): 78–95. https://doi.org/ 10.1086/619504.

Stajić, Olivera. "Roboter im Kindergarten – Freund oder Feind?" *Der Standard*, 19 November 2019. Accessed 12 June 2020. https://www.derstandard.at/story/ 2000111099279/roboter-im-kindergarten-freund-oder-feind.

Wild, Reiner, ed. *Geschichte der deutschen Kinder- und Jugendliteratur* (Stuttgart: J. B. Metzler, 2008).

Woodward, Kathleen. "Prosthetic Emotions," in *Emotion in Postmodernism*. Eds. Gerhard Hoffmann and Alfred Hornung (Heidelberg: Universitätsverlag C. Winter, 1997), 95–107.

Woodward, Kathleen. *Statistical Panic: Cultural Politics and Poetics of the Emotions* (Durham, NC: Duke UP, 2009).

Notes on Contributors

Derek Hillard is Professor of German at Kansas State University. His primary research concerns German modernism. In particular he has investigated the languages of emotion and pain, the representation of violence and sacrifice, and discourses of the mind. He is the author of *Poetry as Individuality: The Discourse of Observation in Paul Celan* (2010) and co-editor of *Feelings Materialized: Emotions, Bodies, and Things in Germany 1500–1950* (2020). He has also published recently on Paul Celan, Alfred Döblin, Ernst Jünger, and Rainer Maria Rilke.

Sarah L. Leonard is Associate Professor of History at Simmons University. She specializes in German cultural history. Her book *Fragile Minds and Vulnerable Souls: The Matter of Obscenity in Nineteenth-Century Germany* was published in 2015 by University of Pennsylvania Press. She is currently working on two projects: the first on the role of German Jews in early photography; the second on early photography and the history of emotions.

Brett Martz is Associate Professor of German at Longwood University. He has been program coordinator for Modern Languages since 2012. He co-edited the volume, *Robert Musil's Intellectual Affinities* (2017) and is currently translating Norbert Christian Wolff's *Kakanien als Gesellschaftskonstruktion: Robert Musils Sozioanalyse des 20. Jahrhunderts.*

Madalina Meirosu teaches German Studies and Gender & Sexuality Studies at Swarthmore College, having received her Ph.D. in Comparative Literature from the University of Massachusetts, Amherst. She specializes in comparative approaches to nineteenth-century political and social thought in German literature. She teaches a wide range of courses on artificial humans, nature and ecology, migration, gender, literature and medicine, and disability studies. She has published on migration, gendered experience, and embodied experiences of suffering. She has also written about translation theory and is a published translator herself. Her current research project explores the political undertones of nineteenth-century literature featuring artificial humanoids.

Andrea Meyertholen is Assistant Professor of German Studies at the University of Kansas. Her interests connect German literature and culture with art history and visual culture, with particular focus on literature and painting from the nineteenth to early twentieth centuries, museum and tourism studies, and fairy tales as represented through and in relation to different media. She has published and presented on a range of topics, including Goethe's poetry and science, animals and zoos in art, fairy tales and gender, Socialist aesthetics, and Expressionist art. Her articles have appeared in *German Quarterly*, *German Studies Review*, and *Seminar: A Journal of German Studies*. Her book *The Myth of Abstraction: The Hidden Origins of Abstract Art in German Literature* was published by Camden House in 2021.

Claudia Mueller-Greene studied History, English, Philosophy, and German at the University of Heidelberg and is currently writing her doctoral thesis on "Literature and Memory: Günter Grass's *The Tin Drum* and Salman Rushdie's *Midnight's Children*." She lives in West Lafayette, Indiana, and is a visiting scholar in the Department of German and Russian at Purdue University. Her main research interests are narratology, theories of memory, and comparative literature.

https://doi.org/10.1515/9783110753677-011

Interdisciplinary approaches provide the basis for her recent publications which discuss problems of meta-autobiographical texts, liminality, emotional memory, and aesthetic obstinacy.

Jared Poley is Professor of History at Georgia State University. He is the author of *Decolonization in Germany: Weimar Narratives of Colonial Loss and Foreign Occupation* (2005) and *The Devil's Riches: A Modern History of Greed* (2016). He is co-editor of the volumes *Religious Conversion in Early Modern Germany* (2012); *Kinship, Community, and Self* (2015); *Migrations in the German Lands* (2016); and *Money in the German Speaking Lands* (2017).

Erika Quinn is Professor of History at Eureka College. Her research interests lie in Central European cultural history, focusing on subjectivity and the history of emotions. Her book, *Franz Liszt: A Story of Central European Subjectivity*, was published by Brill in 2014. She has also published articles on twentieth-century war widowhood in the *Journal of First World War Studies*, the *Women in German Yearbook*, and elsewhere. She is currently at work on a microhistory of World War Two based on a woman's diary.

Holly Yanacek is Assistant Professor of German at James Madison University. Her research focuses on emotion, narration, gender, ethics, and the non-human in 19th- to 21st-century German literature and culture. She is currently finishing a book manuscript on emotion in *fin-de-siècle* German literature provisionally titled "Rethinking Feeling." Her previous research has been supported by grants from Fulbright, the German Historical Institute, and the German Academic Exchange Service (DAAD), and she has recently published articles in *German Life and Letters*, *Monatshefte*, *Colloquia Germanica*, and *Novel: A Forum on Fiction*. Yanacek co-edited (with Colin MacCabe) the collaborative book *Keywords for Today: A 21st Century Vocabulary*, which was published by Oxford University Press in 2018.

Selected Bibliography

Aaltola, Elisa. *Varieties of Empathy: Moral Psychology and Animal Ethics* (London: Rowman & Littlefield, 2018).

Acampora, Ralph R. *Corporal Compassion: Animal Ethics and Philosophy of Body* (Pittsburgh: U of Pittsburgh Press, 2006).

Adamson, Peter, ed. *Animals: A History* (Oxford: Oxford UP, 2018).

Agamben, Giorgio. *The Open: Man and Animal.* Trans. Kevin Attell (Stanford: Stanford UP, 2004).

Ahmed, Sara. *The Cultural Politics of Emotion* (London: Routledge, 2014).

Berger, John. "Why Look at Animals?" in *About Looking* (New York: Vintage Books, 1991), 3–28.

Biro, Matthew. *The Dada Cyborg: Visions of the New Human in Weimar Berlin* (Minneapolis: U of Minnesota Press, 2009).

Boddice, Rob. *The History of Emotions* (Manchester: Manchester UP, 2018).

Braidotti, Rosi. "Animals, Anomalies, and Inorganic Others," *PMLA* 124, no. 2 (2009): 526–532.

Braidotti, Rosi. *The Posthuman* (Cambridge: Polity, 2013).

Braidotti, Rosi, and Maria Hlavajova, eds. *Posthuman Glossary* (London: Bloomsbury Academic, 2018).

Breithaupt, Fritz. *The Dark Sides of Empathy.* Trans. Andrew Hamilton (Ithaca, NY: Cornell UP, 2019).

Bühler-Dietrich, Annette, and Michael Weingarten, eds. *Topos Tier. Neue Gestaltungen des Tier-Mensch-Verhältnisses* (Bielefeld: transcript, 2016).

Burt, Jonathan. "John Berger's 'Why Look at Animals?': A Close Reading," *Worldviews* 9, no. 2 (2005): 203–218.

Calarco, Matthew. *Zoographies: The Question of the Animal from Heidegger to Derrida* (New York: Columbia UP, 2008).

Campe, Rüdiger, and Julia Weber, eds. *Rethinking Emotion: Interiority and Exteriority in Premodern, Modern and Contemporary Thought* (Berlin: De Gruyter, 2014).

Carpenter, Julie. *Culture and Human-Robot Interaction in Militarized Spaces: A War Story* (New York: Routledge, 2016).

Curtis, Robin, and Gertrud Koch, eds. *Einfühlung: Zur Geschichte und Gegenwart eines ästhetischen Konzepts* (Munich: Fink Verlag), 2009.

Darling, Kate. *The New Breed: What Our History of Animals Reveals about Our History with Robots* (New York: Henry Holt and Company, 2021).

Darwin, Charles. *The Expression of the Emotions in Man and Animals* (London: J. Murray, 1872).

Daston, Lorraine, and Gregg Mitman, eds. *Thinking with Animals: New Perspectives on Anthropomorphism* (New York: Columbia UP, 2005).

Derrida, Jacques. *The Animal That Therefore I Am.* Trans. David Willis (New York: Fordham UP, 2008).

de Waal, Frans. *Mama's Last Hug: Animal Emotions and What They Tell Us about Ourselves* (New York: W. W. Norton, 2019).

Eitler, Pascal. "'Weil sie fühlen, was wir fühlen.' Menschen, Tiere und die Genealogie der Emotionen im 19. Jahrhundert," *Historische Anthropologie* 19, no. 2 (2011): 211–228.

Elder, Alexis M. *Friendship, Robots, and Social Media: False Friends and Second Selves* (New York: Routledge, 2018).

https://doi.org/10.1515/9783110753677-012

Fernandez, Luke, and Susan J. Matt. *Bored, Lonely, Angry, Stupid: Changing Feelings about Technology, from the Telegraph to Twitter* (Cambridge, MA: Harvard UP, 2019).

Freud, Sigmund. "The 'Uncanny," in *The Standard Edition of the Complete Psychological Works of Sigmund Freud,* vol. XVII (1917–1919). Trans. James Strachey (London: Hogarth Press, 1955), 218–252.

Frevert, Ute, et al., eds. *Emotional Lexicons: Continuity and Change in the Vocabulary of Feeling 1700–2000* (Oxford: Oxford UP, 2014).

Frevert, Ute. *Vergängliche Gefühle* (Göttingen: Wallstein, 2013).

Gammerl, Benno. "Emotional Styles – Concepts and Challenges," *Rethinking History* 15, no. 2 (June 2012): 161–175.

Gruen, Lori, ed. *Critical Terms for Animal Studies* (Chicago: U of Chicago Press, 2018).

Gruen, Lori. *Entangled Empathy: An Alternative Ethic for Our Relationships with Animals* (New York: Lantern Books, 2015).

Grusin, Richard, ed. *The Nonhuman Turn* (Minneapolis: U of Minnesota Press, 2015).

Haraway, Donna. *The Companion Species Manifesto: Dogs, People, and Significant Otherness* (Chicago: Prickly Paradigm, 2003).

Haraway, Donna. "A Cyborg Manifesto: Science, Technology, and Socialist-Feminism in the Late Twentieth Century," in *Simians, Cyborgs, and Women: The Reinvention of Nature* (New York: Routledge, 1984), 149–181.

Haraway, Donna. *When Species Meet* (Minneapolis: U of Minnesota Press, 2008).

Hayles, N. Katherine. *How We Became Posthuman: Virtual Bodies in Cybernetics, Literature, and Informatics* (Chicago: U of Chicago Press, 1999).

Heise, Ursula. "The Android and the Animal," *PMLA* 124, no. 2 (2009): 503–510.

Herman, David. *Narratology beyond the Human: Storytelling and Animal Life* (Oxford: Oxford UP, 2018).

Hillard, Derek, Heikki Lempa, and Russell Spinney, eds. *Feelings Materialized: Emotions, Bodies, and Things in Germany, 1500–1950* (New York: Berghahn Books, 2020).

Hirt, Katherine. *When Machines Play Chopin: Musical Spirit and Automation in Nineteenth-Century German Literature* (Berlin: De Gruyter, 2010).

Hoage, Robert J., and William A. Deiss, eds. *New Worlds, New Animals: From Menagerie to Zoological Park in the Nineteenth Century* (Baltimore: Johns Hopkins UP, 1996).

Jaques, Zoe. *Children's Literature and the Posthuman: Animal, Environment, Cyborg* (New York: Routledge, 2015).

Kakoudaki, Despina. *Anatomy of a Robot: Literature, Cinema, and the Cultural Work of Artificial People* (New Brunswick, NJ: Rutgers UP, 2014).

Kang, Minsoo. *Sublime Dreams of Living Machines: The Automaton in the European Imagination* (Cambridge, MA: Harvard UP, 2011).

Klothmann, Nastasja. *Gefühlswelten im Zoo: Eine Emotionsgeschichte 1900–1945* (Bielefeld: transcript, 2015).

Koppenfels, Martin von, and Cornelia Zumbusch, eds. *Handbuch Literatur & Emotionen* (Berlin: De Gruyter, 2018).

Kuzniar, Alice. *Melancholia's Dog: Reflections on Our Animal Kinship* (Chicago: U of Chicago Press, 2005).

Maran, Timo, Dario Martinelli, and Aleksei Turovski, eds. *Readings in Zoosemiotics* (Berlin: De Gruyter, 2011).

Matt, Susan J., and Peter N. Stearns. *Doing Emotions History* (Champaign: U of Illinois Press, 2013).

Mazis, Glen A. *Humans, Animals, Machines: Blurring Boundaries* (Albany: SUNY Press, 2008).

Menely, Tobias. *The Animal Claim: Sensibility and the Creaturely Voice* (Chicago: U of Chicago Press, 2015).

Merrell, Floyd. *Sensing Corporeally: Toward a Posthuman Understanding* (Toronto: U of Toronto Press, 2016).

Middelhoff, Frederike, Sebastian Schönbeck, Roland Bogards, and Catrin Gersdorf, eds. *Texts, Animals, Environments: Zoopoetics and Ecopoetics* (Freiburg i.Br.: Rombach, 2019).

Mori, Masahiro. "The Uncanny Valley." Trans. Karl F. MacDorman and Norri Kageki, *IEEE Spectrum*, 12 June 2012. https://spectrum.ieee.org/automaton/robotics/humanoids/the-uncanny-valley.

Nussbaum, Martha. *Political Emotions: Why Love Matters for Justice* (Cambridge, MA: Harvard UP, 2013).

Oliver, Kelly. *Animal Lessons: How They Teach Us to Be Human* (New York: Columbia UP, 2009).

Plamper, Jan. *The History of Emotions: An Introduction* (Oxford: Oxford UP, 2017).

Rhee, Jennifer. *The Robotic Imaginary: The Human and the Price of Dehumanized Labor* (Minnneapolis: U of Minnesota Press).

Rohman, Carrie. *Stalking the Subject: Modernism and the Animal* (New York: Columbia UP, 2009).

Rothfels, Nigel, ed. *Representing Animals* (Bloomington: Indiana UP, 2002).

Ryan, Derek. *Animal Theory: A Critical Introduction* (Edinburgh: Edinburgh UP, 2015).

Sheehan, James J., and Morton Sosna, eds. *The Boundaries of Humanity: Humans, Animals, Machines* (Berkeley: UC Press, 1991).

Simons, John. *Animal Rights and the Politics of Literary Representation* (New York: Palgrave, 2002).

Singer, Peter. *Animal Liberation: A New Ethics for Our Treatment of Animals* (New York: Avon, 1975).

Spickernagel, Ellen. *Der Fortgang der Tiere: Darstellungen in Menagerien und in der Kunst des 17.–19. Jahrhunderts* (Cologne: Böhlau, 2010).

Steiner, Gary. *Animals and the Limits of Postmodernism* (New York: Columbia UP, 2013).

Telotte, J. P. *Robot Ecology and the Science Fiction Film* (New York: Routledge, 2016).

Uexküll, Jakob von. *A Foray into the Worlds of Animals and Humans: With A Theory of Meaning*. Trans. Joseph D. O'Neil (Minneapolis: U of Minnesota Press, 2010).

Ullrich, Jessica, and Friedrich Weltzien, eds. *Tierstudien 3: Tierliebe* (Berlin: Neofelis Verlag, 2013).

Weil, Kari. *Thinking Animals: Why Animal Studies Now?* (New York: Columbia UP, 2012).

Willis, Martin. *Mesmerists, Monsters, and Machines: Science Fiction and the Cultures of Science in the Nineteenth Century* (Kent, OH: Kent State UP, 2005).

Wittig, Frank. *Maschinenmenschen: Zur Geschichte eines literarischen Motivs im Kontext von Philosophie, Naturwissenschaft und Technik* (Würzburg: Königshausen & Neumann, 1997).

Wolfe, Cary. *What is Posthumanism?* (Minneapolis: U of Minnesota Press, 2010).

Wolfe, Cary, ed. *Zoontologies: The Question of the Animal* (Minneapolis: U of Minnesota Press, 2003).

Woodward, Kathleen. *Statistical Panic: Cultural Politics and Poetics of the Emotions* (Durham, NC: Duke UP, 2009).

Yonck, Richard. *The Heart of the Machine: Our Future in a World of Artificial Emotional Intelligence* (New York: Arcade Publishing, 2017).

Index

https://doi.org/10.1515/9783110753677-013

www.ingramcontent.com/pod-product-compliance
Lightning Source LLC
Chambersburg PA
CBHW050647270326
41927CB00012B/2907